Dedication

Warman's® Bottles Field Guide, 2nd Edition, is dedicated to all my fellow bottle collectors who "keep having fun with the hobby of bottle collecting." Keep turning that dirt over and dig deeper.

Photo Credits

Acknowledgments

Rodney Baer: Thank you for your contribution of photographs of perfume bottles and your overall support of the project.

Charles and Julie Blake: Thank you for your contribution of the great photographs and background information and pricing on cobalt blue medicine bottles.

Penny Dolnick: Thank you for writing the great introduction article for the perfume and cologne chapter along with pricing input and background information.

Jim Hagenbuch (Antique Bottle & Glass Collector & Glass Works Auctions): Thank you for the great assortment of photographs, pricing input, and overall support of the project.

Bud Hastin (Avon Collector's Encyclopedia): Thanks for the great photographs and your help with the Avon collectibles pricing.

Norm Heckler (Heckler Auctions): Thank you for your contribution of photographs and your support of the project.

Fred Holabird: Thanks for your great friendship and continued help with understanding Nevada bottles.

David Graci: Thanks for your contribution of photographs and background information on soda and beer bottle closures.

Bob Kay: Thanks for your contribution of pricing input on miniature bottles and your support of the project.

Gary and Vickie Lewis: Thanks for your contribution of photographs of ACL soda bottles and your overall support of the project.

Randall Monsen: Thank you for your contribution of photographs of perfume bottles and your overall support of the project.

Jacque Pace Polak: A special thank you to my wife for your continued patience and invaluable moral support.

Steve Ritter (Steve Ritter Auctioneering): Thanks for your help in obtaining the ACL soda bottle photographs and your help with the pricing.

David Spaid: Thanks for your help with understanding the world of miniature bottles and your support of the project.

Rick Sweeney: Thanks for your help with the pricing of applied color label soda bottles.

John Tutton: Thank you for your contribution of photographs of milk bottles and your overall support of the project.

Violin Bottle Collectors Association and Members: Thanks for all of your help with the contribution of photographs and an overall understanding of violin bottles. A special thank you to Bob Linden, Frank Bartlett, Samia Koudsi, and Bob Moore for their time and effort in providing photographs, pricing data, and resource information.

Jeff Wichman (American Bottle Auctions): Thanks for your great assortment of Western bottle photographs and overall support of the project.

Contents

Introduction

Welcome again to the fun hobby of antique bottle collecting with the second edition of *Warman's® Bottles Field Guide*. In order to make the second edition the best informative reference and pricing guide available, I have provided the beginner and veteran collector with a broader range of detailed information and data. In response to numerous requests from collectors, I have included four new chapters: Fire Grenades, Patriotic Bottles, Perfume & Cologne Bottles, and Target Balls. Plus, another exciting addition to this edition is 300 new photographs in stunning color.

Interest in bottle collecting continues to grow, with new bottle clubs forming throughout the United States and Europe. More collectors are spending their free time digging through old dumps, foraging through old ghost towns, digging out old outhouses (that's right), exploring abandoned mine shafts, and searching their favorite bottle and antique shows, swap meets, flea markets, and garage sales.

In addition, the Internet has greatly

expanded, with many new auction sites offering collectors numerous opportunities and resources to buy and sell bottles without even leaving the house. Many bottle clubs now have Web sites providing even more information for the collector. Having more resources available is always a very good thing for the hobby.

Most collectors, however, still look beyond the type and value of a bottle to its origin and history. I find that researching the history of bottles has at times proved to be more interesting than finding the bottle itself. I enjoy both pursuits for their close ties to the rich history of the United States and the early methods of merchandising.

My goal has always been to enhance the hobby of bottle collecting for both the beginner and expert collectors, and experience the excitement of antique bottle collecting, especially the thrill of making a special find. I hope the second edition of *Warman's® Bottles Field Guide* continues to bring an increased understanding and enjoyment of the hobby of bottle collecting.

For a more in-depth study of bottle collecting, I recommend you read my full-length book, *Antique Trader®*

Bottles Identification and Price Guide, 5th Edition. With 51 categories of bottles containing thousands of price listings, the fifth edition covers far more pricing and reference information than can be included in this second edition of the field guide.

The fifth edition contains a number of chapters not included in this field guide, such as twenty-nine more categories of bottles and a number of chapters to aid more extensive research, such as Bottles: History and Origin (which also explains the various ways antique glass bottle were made), Digging for Bottles, Bottle Clubs and Dealers, Auction Companies, Museums and Research Resources, and a much more extensive bibliography.

If you would like to provide feedback regarding this second edition or would just like to talk bottles, I can be contacted by e-mail at bottleking@earthlink.net or on my Web site, www.bottlebible.com. Good bottle hunting and have fun with the hobby of bottle collecting!

What's Happening in the World of Bottle Collecting

What's happening with bottle collecting? Everything! Antique bottle collecting continues to gain more popularity and has brought an overall greater awareness to a wide spectrum of antique collectors.

Can you handle 184 proof whiskey? The Bruichladdich distillery off the Scotland's west coast, founded in 1881, is reviving a 17th-century recipe "purely for fun" said managing director Mark Reynier. The recipe, known in Gaelic as usquebaugh-baul translates to "perilous water of life." But you'll have to wait a while if you're brave enough to try a drink. The whiskey will be aged in oak barrels for ten years before it's ready for release.

While I'm on the subject of old whiskey, George Washington's

still is back in business again after a 200-year hiatus. On March 30, 2007, George Washington's Mount Vernon estate officially opened a $2.1 million reconstruction of Washington's original distillery on the exact site where it was located in 1799. Mount Vernon officials said the distillery is the only one in the nation, and possibly the world, that authentically demonstrates 18th century distilling techniques. The whiskey will be made only on special occasions and will be available for purchase at the estate. But be ready for a kick when you take a drink. Washington did not age his whiskey as distillers do today, so Mount Vernon director James Rees compares it to "white lightning."

If a 200-year still isn't old enough for you, how about digging out a 400-year-old well at historic Jamestown in Virginia. In July 2006, a team of 12 archeologists began digging and, among many artifacts, found an intact ceramic bottle called a Bartmann jug, or a "bearded man" made in Germany and dating back to 1590. The English landed in Jamestown in 1607, which was the first permanent British settlement in America. It was also the site of the first attempt to manufacture glass in America, which was a failure.

Coca-Cola is at it again with another new drink called Coca-Cola Blak. In simple terms, it's Coke with coffee. Coke spokesman Scott Williamson said, "People are looking for different things to drink at different times of the day, so it's incumbent on us to innovate." The new drink is actually a flurry of a group of new products being introduced to the consumer; a new chocolate coffee drink in partnership with Godiva, Coke Zero (reformulated Diet Coke), Coke C2 (a middle-ground between diet and regular Coke, Diet Coke with Splenda, and a number of varieties flavored with lemon and lime.

Can your budget handle $17,000 for a target ball? That's exactly what happened on July 5, 2006, during an auction held by American Bottle Auctions in San Francisco, California. The item, a rare Bogardus glass target ball, was part of the Alex Kerr (Kerr Glass Company) collection. This specific auction included 10 balls that ended up going for a total of $45,000, a new world record. What are target balls? They are approximately 3-inch round spheres of many colors and design manufactured in the mid-1870s that were tossed in the air by a special mechanical thrower for marksmen to shoot. In this same auction, one of the "throwers" from 1870 sold for $3,520.

So you think $17,000 is a lot? On November 17, 2006, Rago Auctions achieved a world-record price of $216,000 for a 1939 Lalique perfume bottle known as Tresor de la Mer (Treasure from the Sea). The oyster-shell-form box and pearl-form bottle were designed specifically for a 1939 Lalique exhibit at Saks Fifth Avenue in New York. Overall, the auction netted a total of $1.2 million for the entire collection of Lalique and other collectors' perfume bottles.

Ready for another digging story? Recently while the Los Angeles Metropolitan Transportation Authority was building an extension of the

Gold Line commuter rail, it discovered an 1885 Chinese cemetery. Historians believe the site may be that of a lost potter's field that became obscured by development after the 1920s. During excavation many medicine and opium bottles were found along with numerous other artifacts.

Bottle collecting has hit the Travel Channel. On February 6, 2007, and February 10, 2007, the show aired a half-hour segment of the series *Cash & Treasures* devoted entirely to bottle collecting. The focus of the segment was the 2006 Bottle Show in Saratoga, New York; the Saratoga National Bottle Museum; and a bottle dig conducted by Museum trustees Fran Hughes and Roy Topka with his son Mike. There was also film shot in other out-of-state locations. The digging portion of the show gave the audience an opportunity to share the excitement of finding the treasures along with an understanding and respect for the artifact as well as respect for private property. As you can see, the discoveries and news events of bottle collecting continue to include all aspects of antique collecting, which increases the interest and fun in the antique bottle collecting hobby.

The Beginning Collector

The first thing to understand about antique bottle collecting is that there aren't set rules. Your finances, spare time, storage space, and preferences will influence your approach. As a collector, you need to think about whether to specialize and focus on a specific type of bottle or group of bottles or become a maverick collector who acquires everything. The majority of bottle collectors that I have known, including me, took the maverick approach as new collectors. We grabbed everything in sight, ending up with bottles of every type, shape, and color.

Now after 30 years of collecting, I recommend that beginners only do a small amount of maverick collecting and focus on a specific group of bottles. Taking the general approach gave me a broader background of knowledge about bottles and glass, but specializing provides the following distinct advantages:

• More time for organization, study, and research

- The ability to become an authority in a particular area
- The opportunity to trade with other specialists who may have duplicate or unwanted bottles
- The ability to negotiate a better deal by spotting underpriced bottles

Specialized collectors will still be tempted by bottles that don't quite fit into their collection, so they will cheat a little and give in to the maverick urge. This occasional cheating sometimes results in a smaller side collection, or turns the collector back to being a maverick. Remember, there are no set rules except to have fun.

Starting a Collection

What does it cost to start a collection and how do you know the value of a bottle? The beginner can do well with just a few pointers. Let's start with buying bottles, instead of digging for bottles. This is a quicker approach for the new bottle collector.

What Should I Pay?

Over the years, I've developed a quick method of buying bottles by grouping them into three categories:

Low End or Common Bottles

These bottles have noticeable wear and are never embossed. The labels are typically missing or not visible. In most cases, the labels are completely gone. The bottles are dirty and not easily cleaned. They have some scrapes but are free of chips. These bottles are usually clear.

Average Grade/Common Bottles

These bottles show some wear and labels may be visible but are usually faded. They are generally clear in color or aqua and free of scrapes or chips. Some of these bottles may have minimal embossing, but not likely.

High End and Unique Bottles

These bottles can be empty or partially or completely full, and have the original stoppers and labels or embossing. Bottles can be clear but are usually green, teal blue, yellow, or yellow green with no chips or scrapes and very little wear. If it has been stored in a box, the bottle is most likely in good or excellent condition. Also, the box must be in very good condition.

Price ranges will be discussed briefly since there is a "Determining Bottle Values" section. Usually, low-end bottles can be found for $1 to $5, average from $5 to $20, and high end from $20 to $100, although some high-end bottles sell for $1, 000 or more. Any bottles above $100 should be closely examined by an experienced and knowledgeable collector.

As a general rule, I try not to spend more than $2 per bottle for low-end bottles and $5 to $7 for average. It's easier to stick to this guideline when you've done your homework, but sometimes you just get lucky. As an example, during a number of bottle and antique shows, I have found sellers who had grab bags full of bottles for $2 a bag. I never pass up a bargain like this because of the lure of potential treasures. After one show, I discovered a total of nine bottles, some purple, all earlier than 1900 in great shape, with embossing, for a total cost of 22 cents per bottle. What could be better than that? Well, I found a Tonopah, Nevada, medicine valued at $100.

In the high-end category, deals are usually made after some good old horse trading and bartering. But, hey, that's part of the fun. Always let the seller know that you are a new collector with a limited budget. It really helps. I have never run across a bottle seller who wouldn't work with a new collector to try to give the best deal on a limited budget.

Is It Old or New?

Collectors should also know the difference between old and new bottles. Quite often, new collectors assume that any old bottle is an antique, and if a bottle isn't old it isn't collectible. With bottle collecting, that isn't necessarily the case. In the antique world, an antique is defined as an article more than 100 years old, but a number of bottles listed in this book that are less than 100 years old are just as valuable, and perhaps more, than those that by definition are antiques.

The number and variety of old and antique bottles is greater than the new collectible items in today's market. On the other hand, the Jim Beams, Ezra Brooks, Avons, recent Coke bottles, figurals, and miniature soda and liquor bottles manufactured more recently are very desirable and collectible and are manufactured for that purpose. If you decide you want to collect new bottles, the best time to buy is when the first issue comes out on the market. When the first issues are gone, the collector market is the only available source, which limits availability and drives up prices considerably.

For all collectors, books, references guides, magazines, and other similar literature are readily available at libraries, in bookstores, and on the Internet.

Beware Reproductions and Repairs

I want to emphasize the importance of being aware of reproductions and repaired bottles. Always check bottles, jars, and pottery carefully to make sure that there have been no repairs or special treatments. It's best to hold the item up to the light or take it outside with the dealer to look for cracks, nicks, or dings. Also, look for scratches that may have occurred during cleaning. Also check the closures. Having the proper closure can make a big difference in the value of a bottle, so it's important to make sure the closure fits securely, and the metal lid is stamped with the correct patent dates or lettering. If you need help, ask an experienced collector, and if you have any doubt about a bottle's authenticity, request that the dealer provide a money-back guarantee.

Now, check out those antique and bottle shows, flea markets, swap meets, garage sales, and antique shops. Pick up those bottles, ask plenty of questions, and you will be surprised by how much you'll learn and how much fun you'll have.

Bottle Basics

New bottle collectors need to learn certain facts such as age identification, grading, labeling, glass imperfections, and peculiarities.

Age

The common methods of determining age are mold seams, lips/tops, stoppers/closures, and color variations.

Mold Seams

Prior to 1900, bottle manufacturing was done by either a blowpipe (free blown) to 1860 or with a mold to 1900. The mouth or lip was formed last and applied to the bottle after completion (applied lip). The applied lip can be identified by the mold seam that runs from the base up to the neck, and near the end of the lip. For machine-made bottles, the lip is formed first and the mold seam runs over the lip. The closer the seam extends to the top of the bottle, the more recent the bottle.

On bottles manufactured before 1860, the mold seams end low on the neck or at the shoulder. Between 1860 and 1880, the mold seam stops right below the mouth and makes it easy to detect where the lip was separately formed. Around 1880, the closed mold was utilized, in which the neck and lip were mechanically shaped, and the glass was severed from the blowpipe with the ridge being evened off by hand sanding or filing. This mold seam usually ends within one-quarter inch from the top of the bottle. After 1900, the seam extends clear to the top.

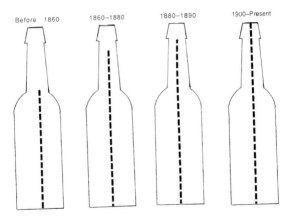

Identifying Bottle Age by Mold Seams

Before 1860: *Seams extend to just over the shoulders.*
1860-1880: *Seams go most of the way up the neck of the bottle.*
1880-1890: *Seams continue through the top but not through or over the lip.*
1900-present: *Seams extend the full length of the bottle and over the lip.*

Above are just four examples of the myriad types of lips and tops created on antique bottles.

Lips and Tops

One of the best ways to identify bottles manufactured prior to 1840 is by the presence of a "sheared lip." This type of lip was formed by cutting or snipping the glass free of the blowpipe with a pair of shears that left the lip with a stovepipe look.

Around 1840, bottle manufacturers began to apply a glass ring around the sheared lip forming a "laid-on-ring" lip. Between 1840 and 1880, numerous variations of lips or tops were produced using a variety of tools.

After 1880, manufacturers started to pool their processing information, resulting in more evenly finished and uniform tops. As a general rule, the more uneven and crude the lip or top, the older the bottle.

Closures/Stoppers

The Romans used small stones rolled in tar as stoppers, and for many centuries there was little advancement. For most of the 15th and 16th centuries, the closure consisted of a sized cloth tied down with heavy thread or string. The stopper beneath the cover was made of wax or bombase (cotton wadding). Cotton wool was also dipped in wax and used as a stopper along with coverings of parchment, paper, or leather. Corks and glass stoppers were used in great numbers, with the cork sometimes being tied or wired down for effervescent liquids. When the "close mold" came into existence, the shape of the lip was more accurately controlled, making it possible to invent capping devices.

On July 23, 1872, British inventor Hiram Codd invented a bottle made with a groove inside the neck and was granted Patent No. 129,652. A glass marble was inserted and then a ring of cork or rubber was fitted into the groove.

Glass stoppers, 1850-1900.

When an effervescing liquid was used, the pressure of the gas forced the marble to the top of the neck, sealing the bottle. A second patent, Patent No. 138,230, issued April 29, 1873, contained the interior lug, ball holding element. Interestingly, many young boys broke these bottles to get the marble.

From 1879 to the early 1900s, the Hutchinson stopper became a common bottle closure after Patent No. 213,992 was issued on April 8, 1879. Hutchinson's concept used a heavy wire loop to control a rubber gasket that stayed inside the neck of the bottle. After filling the bottle, the gasket was pulled up against the shoulders and was kept in place by the carbonation. The Hutchinson stopper was easily adaptable to a number of other bottle types. Until the invention of the crown cap in 1892, the lightning stopper was the best closure for beer bottles. The lightning stopper was a porcelain or rubber plug anchored to the outside of the bottle by a permanently attached wire. The wire formed a bar that controlled the opening and closing of the bottle.

Hiram Codd interior ball stopper, Patent #129,652, July 23, 1872. Carbonation pushed the glass ball to the top of the neck, forming a tight seal.

Charles G. Hutchinson stopper, Patent #213,992, April 8, (year uncertain). A wire loop was pulled upward to seat a rubber gasket in the neck of the bottle. Carbonation helped keep it in place.

The lightning stopper, designed to hold carbonated beverages, was eventually replaced by the crown cap.

William Painter crown cap, Patent #468,226, Feb. 2, 1892.

In 1892, William Painter patented the crown cap, which consisted of metal and a cork gasket crimped over the mouth of the bottle. This cap revolutionized the soft drink and beer bottling industry. By 1915, all major bottlers had switched to the crown-type cap. Finally, in 1902, threads were manufactured on the outside of the lip to enable a threaded cap to be screwed onto the mouth of the bottle. This wasn't a new idea. Early glass blowers produced bottles with inside and outside screw caps long before the bottle-making machines. Early methods of production were so complex, however, that screw-topped bottles produced before the 1800s were considered specialty bottles. They were expensive to replace and today are considered rare and quite collectible. The conventional screw-top bottle did not become common until after 1924, when the glass industry standardized the threads.

In 1875, some glass manufacturers introduced an

Dumfries Ale (English). The bottle's inside threads were sealed with a rubber stopper. This device was unpopular because the rubber interacted with the contents, distorting its color and taste.

inside screw-neck whiskey bottle using a rubber stopper. This invention wasn't popular because the alcohol interacted with the rubber, which discolored the whiskey and made it bitter.

The following list is a portion of the brands of embossed whiskeys that featured the inside threaded neck and the approximate dates of manufacture:

Whiskey Company	Date of Circulation
Adolph Harris	1907-1912
Chevalier Castle	1907-1910
Crown (squatty)	1905-1912
Crown (pint)	1896-1899
Donnelly Rye	1910-1917
Old Gilt Edge	1907-1912
Roth (aqua)	1903-1911
Roth (amber sq.)	1898-1909
Roth (amber fluted shoulder)	1903-1911
Roth (amber qt.)	1903-1911
Rusconi-Fisher	1902-1915
Taussig (clear)	1915-1918

Glass Color

Another effective method of determining age is the color of the glass. Producing colored and clear glass were major challenges for all glass manufacturers. Prior to 1840, intentionally colored or colorless glass was reserved for fancy figured flasks and vessels. Bottle color was essentially considered unimportant until 1880, when food preservation packers began to demand clear glass for food products. Because most glass produced prior to this time was green, glass manufacturers began using manganese to bleach out the green tinge created by the iron content. Only then did clear bottles become common.

Iron slag was used up to 1860 and produced a dark olive green or olive amber glass that has become known as black glass and was used for wine and beverage bottles that needed protection from light. Colors natural to bottle glass are brown, amber, olive green, and aqua.

Blue, green, and purple were produced by metallic oxides added to the glass batch. Cobalt was added for blue glass, sulfur for yellow and green, manganese and nickel for purple, nickel for brown, copper or gold for red, and tin or zinc for milk-colored glass (for apothecary vials, druggist bottles, and pocket bottles).

The Hocking Glass Company discovered a process for making a brilliant red glass described as copper-ruby. The color was achieved by adding copper oxide to a glass batch as it was cooling and then immediately reheating the batch before use. Since these bright colors were expensive to produce, they are very rare and sought after by most collectors. Many bottle collectors think purple is the most appealing color appeal and therefore is prized above others. The iron contained in sand caused glass to take on color between green and blue. Glass manufacturers used manganese that counteracted the aqua to produce clear glass. When exposed to ultraviolet light from the sun, the manganese in the glass oxidizes and turns the glass to purple. The longer the glass is exposed to the sunlight, the deeper the purple color. Glass with manganese content was most common in bottles produced between 1880 and 1914. Because Germany was the main producer of manganese, the supply ceased at the beginning of World War I. By 1916, the glass making industry began to use selenium as a neutralizing agent. Glass produced between 1914 and 1930 is most likely to change to an amber or straw color.

Imperfections

Imperfections and blemishes also provide clues to how old a bottle is and often add to the charm and value of an individual piece. Blemishes usually show up as bubbles or "seeds" in the glass. In the process of making glass, air bubbles form and rise to the surface where they pop. As the fining out (elimination process) became more advanced around 1920, these bubbles or seeds were eliminated.

Another peculiarity of the antique bottle is the uneven thickness of the glass. Often one side of the base has a one-inch thick side that slants off to paper thinness on the opposite edge. This imperfection was eliminated with the introduction of the Owens bottle-making machine in 1903.

In addition, the various marks of stress and strain, sunken sides, twisted necks, and whittle marks (usually at the neck, where the wood mold made impressions in the glass) also give clues to indicate that a bottle was produced before 1900.

Labeling and Embossing

While embossing and labeling were a common practice in the rest of the world for a number of centuries, American bottle manufacturers did not adopt the inscription process until 1869. The inscriptions included information about the contents, manufacturer, distributor, slogans, or other messages advertising the product.

Manufacturers produced raised lettering using a plate mold, sometimes called a slug plate, fitted inside the casting mold. This plate created a sunken area and has

Log Cabin bottle with paper label.

resulted in these bottles being of a special value to collectors. Irregularities such as a misspelled name add to the value of the bottle as will any name embossed with hand etching or other method of crude grinding. These bottles are very old, collectible, and valuable.

Inscription and embossing customs came to an end with the introduction of paper labels and the production of machine-made bottles beginning in 1903. In 1933, with the repeal of prohibition, the distilling of whiskey and other spirits was resumed under new strict government regulations. One of the major regulations was that the following statement was required to be embossed on all bottles containing alcohol: "Federal Law Forbids Sale or Re-Use of this Bottle." This regulation was in effect until 1964 and is an excellent method of dating spirit bottles from 1933 to 1964.

Vermont Springs soda bottle with embossing (molded raised letters).

Determining Bottle Values

Collectors and dealers typically use rarity, age, condition, and color to determine bottle values. These factors are consistent with the criteria I have used over the years.

Supply and Demand

As with any product, when demand increases and supply decreases, prices increase.

Condition

Mint: An empty or full bottle (preferably full) with a label or embossing. The bottle must be clean and have good color, with no chips, scrapes, or wear. If the bottle comes in a box, the box must be in perfect condition too.

Extra Fine: An empty or full bottle with slight wear on the label or embossing. The bottle must be clean with clear color, and no chips or scrapes. There is usually no box, or the box is not in very good condition.

Very Good: The bottle shows some wear, and the label is usually missing or not very visible. Most likely there is no embossing and no box.

Good: The bottle shows additional wear and label is completely absent. The color is usually faded and the bottle is dirty and has some scrapes and minor chips. Most likely there is no box.

Fair or Average: The bottle shows considerable wear, the label is missing, and embossing is damaged.

Rarity

Unique: A bottle is considered to be unique if only one is known to exist. These bottles are the most valuable and expensive.

Extremely Rare: Only 5 to 10 known specimens.

Very Rare: Only 10 to 20 known specimens.

Rare: Only 20 to 40 known specimens.

Very Scarce: No more than 50 bottles in existence.

Scarce: No more that 100 bottles in existence.

Common: Common bottles, such as clear 1880 to 1900 medicine bottles, are abundant, easy to acquire, usually very inexpensive, and great bottles for the beginning collector.

Historic Appeal, Significance, and Geography

For example: territorial bottles (bottles made in regions that had not yet been admitted to the Union) vs. bottles made in states admitted to the Union.

Embossing Labeling and Design

Bottles without embossing are common and have little dollar value to many collectors. Exceptions are bottles handblown before 1840, which usually don't have embossing.

Embossing describes the name of the contents, manufacturer, state, city, dates, trademarks, and other valuable information. Embossed images and trademarks can also increase the value of the bottle.

Labeling found intact with all the specific information about the bottle also increases the value of the bottle.

Age

While age can play an important role in the value of a bottle, there's not always a direct correlation. As stated in The Beginning Collector chapter, the history, rarity, and use of a bottle can be more important that age to a collector.

Color

Low Price: clear, aqua, amber

Average Price: milk glass, green, black, basic olive green

High Price: teal blue, cobalt blue, purple (amethyst), yellow, yellow green, puce

Unique Features

The following characteristics can also significantly affect value: pontil marks, whittle marks, glass imperfections (thickness and bubbles), slug plates, and crudely applied tops or lips.

Even with the above guidelines, it's important to consult more detailed references, especially concerning rare and valuable bottles. See the bibliography and the Web site listing at the back of this book. Remember, never miss a chance to ask other collectors and dealers for advice and assistance.

The crooked lip of this ink bottle is typical of imperfections that occurred before automatic bottle-making machines created more uniformity.

Bottle Sources

Collectible bottles can be found in a variety of places and sometimes where you would least expect them. Excluding digging, the following sources are good potential hiding places for all types of bottles.

The Internet

In the 30 years that I've been collecting, I've never seen anything impact the hobby of bottle collecting as much as the Internet. Go to the Internet, type in the words "antique bottle collecting," and you'll be amazed at the amount of data instantly at your fingertips. Numerous Web sites throughout the United States, Canada, Europe, and Asia provide information about clubs, dealers, antique publications, and auction companies. These sites have opened up the entire world and are convenient and inexpensive resources for collectors and dealers.

Flea Markets, Swap Meets, Thrift Stores, Garage Sales & Salvage Stores

For the beginner collector, these sources will likely be the most fun (next to digging) and yield the most bottles at the best prices. As a rule, the majority of bottles found at these sources will fall into the common or common-but-above-average category.

Flea Markets, Swap Meets, and Thrift Stores: Target those areas where household goods are being sold. It's a good bet they will have at least some bottles.

Garage Sales: Focus on the older areas of town, since the items will often be older, more collectible, and more likely to fall into a rare or scarce category.

Salvage Stores or Salvage Yards: These are great places to search for bottles because these businesses buy from companies that salvage old houses, apartments, and businesses. A New York company discovered an untouched illegal prohibition-era distillery complete with bottles, unused labels, and equipment. What a find!

Local Bottle Clubs and Collectors

By joining a local bottle club or working with other collectors, you will find more ways to add your collection, gather information, and do more digging. Members usually have quantities of unwanted or duplicate bottles, which they will sell very reasonably, trade, or sometimes even give away, especially to an enthusiastic new collector.

Bottle Shows

Bottle shows not only expose new collectors to bottles of every type, but provide the opportunity to talk with experts in specialized fields. In addition, there are publications relating to all aspects of the hobby. There is always something new to learn and share and, of course, bottles to buy or trade. Look under the tables at these shows, since great bargains may be lurking where you least expect them.

Auctions

Auction houses are a great source of bottles and glassware. When evaluating auction houses, try to find one that specializes in antiques and estate buyouts. They usually publish catalogs with bottle descriptions, conditions, and photographs, which can also be used as a reference source. I recommend, however, that you first visit an auction to learn how the process works before you decide to participate. When buying, be sure of the color and condition of the bottle, and terms of the sale. These guidelines also apply to all Internet auctions. Use caution and follow these general rules:

Buying at Auctions
• Purchase the catalog and review all of the items in the auction. Before a live auction, a preview is usually held to inspect the items.
• After reviewing the catalog and making your choice, phone or mail

your bid. A 10 percent to 20 percent buyer's premium is
usually added to the sale price.

- Callbacks allow bidders to increase the previous high bid
  on certain items.
- The winning bidder receives an invoice in the mail. After
  payment clears, the item will be shipped.
- Most auction houses have a return policy, as well as a
  refund policy, for items that differ from the description in
  the catalog.

Selling at Auctions

- Evaluate the auction venue before consigning any
  merchandise. Make sure the auction venue is legitimate
  and has not had any problems with payments or quality of
  products.
- Package the item with plenty of bubble pack, insure it,
  and mail the package by certified mail, signed receipt
  requested.
- Allow 30 days to receive payment and be aware that most
  firms charge 15 percent commission fee on the sales
  price.

Estate Sales

An estate sale can be a great source for bottles if the home
is in a very old neighborhood or section of the city that has

historical significance. These sales are a lot of fun, especially when the people running the sale let you look over and handle the items to be able to make careful selections. Prices are usually good and are always negotiable.

Knife and Gun Shows

Bottles at knife and gun shows? Quite a few gun and knife enthusiasts are also great fans of the West and keep an eye open for related artifacts. Every knife and gun show I've attended has had at least 10 dealers with bottles on their tables (or under the tables) for sale. And the prices were about right, since they were more interested in selling their knives and guns than the bottles. Plus, these dealers will often provide information on where they made their finds, which you can put to good use later.

Retail Antique Dealers

This group includes dealers who sell bottles at or near full market prices. Buying from a dealer has advantages and disadvantages. Dealers usually have a large selection and will provide helpful information and details about the bottles, and it's a safe bet that the bottles for sale are authentic.

It can be very expensive to build a collection this way. However, these shops are a good place to browse and learn.

General Antique and Specialty Shops

The primary difference between general and retail antique shops is that general shops usually have lower prices and a more limited selection than retail shops. This is partly because merchants in general shops are not as well informed about bottles and may overlook critical characteristics. Knowledgeable collectors can find great opportunities to acquire quality underpriced bottles at a general shop.

Bottle Handling

While selling bottles and listening to buyers at various shows, I am inevitably asked questions about cleaning, handling, and storing bottles. Some collectors believe that cleaning a bottle diminishes its collectible value and desirability. Leaving a bottle in its natural state, as it was found, can be special. Others prefer to remove as much dirt and residue as possible. The choice rests with the owner. The following information will provide some help with how to clean, store, and take care of those special finds.

Bottle Cleaning

First, never attempt to clean your new find in the field. In the excitement of the moment, it's easy to break the bottle or otherwise damage the embossing. With the exception of soda and ale bottles, glass bottles manufactured before 1875 usually have very thin walls. Even bottles with thicker walls should be handled very carefully.

The first step is to remove as much loose dirt, sand, or other particles as possible with a small hand brush or a soft-bristled toothbrush followed by a quick warm water rinse. Then, using a warm water solution and bleach (stir the mixture first), soak the bottles for a number of days (depending upon the amount of caked-on dirt). This should remove most of the excess grime. Also, adding some vinegar to warm water will add an extra sparkle to the glass. Other experienced collectors use cleaning mixtures such as straight ammonia, kerosene, Lime-A-Way, Mr. Clean, and chlorine borax bleach. Do not use mixtures that are not recommended for cleaning glass, never mix cleaners, and do not clean with acids of any type. Mixing cleaners has been known to release toxic gasses and poisonous vapors and fumes.

After soaking, the bottles may be cleaned with a bottle brush, steel wool, an old toothbrush, any semi-stiff brush, Q-tips, or used dental picks. At this point, you may want to soak the bottles again in lukewarm water to remove any traces of cleaning materials. Either let the bottles air-dry or dry them with a soft towel. If the bottle has a paper label, the work will be more painstaking since soaking is not a cleaning option. I've used a Q-tip to clean and dry the residue around the paper label.

Never clean your bottles in a dishwasher. While the hot water and detergent may produce a very clean bottle, these older bottles were not designed to withstand the extreme heat of a dishwasher. As a result, the extreme heat, along with the shaking, could crack or even shatter the bottles. In addition, bottles with any type of painted label may also be subjected to severe damage.

A better option is to consult a specialist who will clean your rare bottles with special tumbling, or cleaning machines. These machines work on the same principle as a rock tumbler

with two parallel bars running horizontally acting as a "cradle" for the cleaning canisters. The key to the machine cleaning process is the two types of oxides that are used: polishing and cutting. The polishing oxides include aluminum, cerium, and tin, which remove stains and give the glass a crystal clean and polished appearance. The polishing oxides do not harm the embossing. The cutting oxides such as silicon carbide remove the etching and scratching. There are many individuals who are in the business of cleaning bottles with these machines, or you can also purchase the machines for personal use.

Bottle Display

Now that you have clean, beautiful bottles, display them to their best advantage. My advice is to arrange your bottles in a cabinet rather than on wall shelving or randomly around the house. While the last two options are more decorative, the bottles are more susceptible to damage. When choosing a cabinet, try to find one with glass sides that will provide more light and better viewing. As an added touch, a light fixture sets off a collection beautifully. If you still desire a wall shelving arrangement, make sure the shelf is approximately one inch wide, with a front lip for added protection. This can be accomplished with round molding. After the bottle is placed in its spot, draw an outline around the base of the bottle and then drill four 1/4-inch holes for pegs just outside the outline. These pegs will provide stability for the bottle. If you have picked up any other goodies from your digging, like coins or gambling chips, scatter them around the bottles for a little Western flavor.

Bottle Protection

Because of earthquakes, especially in northern and southern California, bottle collectors across the country have taken added steps to protect their valuable pieces.

Since most of us have our collections in some type of display cabinet, it's important to know how to best secure it. First, fasten the cabinet to the wall studs with brackets and bolts. If you are working with drywall and it's not possible to secure the cabinet to a stud, butterfly bolts will provide a tight hold. Always secure the cabinet at both the top and bottom for extra protection.

Next, lock or latch the cabinet doors. This will prevent the doors from flying open. If your cabinet has glass shelves, be sure to not overload them. In an earthquake, the glass shelving can break under the stress of excess weight.

Finally, it's important to secure the bottles to the shelves with materials such microcrystalline wax, beeswax, silicone adhesive, double-sided foam tape, adhesive-backed Velcro spots or strips. These materials are available at local home improvement centers and hardware stores. One of the newest and most commonly used adhesives is called Quake Hold. This substance, which is available in wax, putty, and gel, is similar to the wax product now used extensively by numerous museums to secure their artwork, sculptures, and various glass pieces. It is readily available to the general public at many home improvement stores and antique shops.

Bottle Storage

The best method for storing bottles you've chosen not to display is to place them in empty liquor boxes with cardboard dividers (which prevent bottles from knocking into each other). As added protection, wrap the individual bottles in paper prior to packing them in the boxes.

Recordkeeping

Last but not least, it's a good idea to keep records of your collection. Use index cards detailing where the bottle was found or purchased, including the dealer's name and price you paid. Assign a catalog number to each bottle, record it on the card, and then make an index. Many collectors keep records with the help of a photocopy machine. If the bottle has embossing or a label, put the bottle on the machine and make a copy of it. Another method is to make a pencil sketch by applying white paper to the bottle and rubbing over the embossing with a No. 2 pencil. Then, type all the pertinent information on the back of the image and put it in a binder. When it comes to trading and selling, excellent recordkeeping will prove to be invaluable.

Old Bottles (Pre-1900)

The bottles listed in this section have been categorized by physical type and/or by the original contents of the bottle. For most categories, the trade names can be found in alphabetical order if they exist. Note that in the case of certain early bottles such as flasks, a trade name does not appear on the bottle. These bottles have been listed by subject according to the embossing, label, or other identification found on them.

Since it is impossible to list every bottle available, I've provided a good cross section of bottles in various price ranges and categories, rather than listing only the rarest or most collectible pieces.

The pricing shown reflects the value of the particular bottle listed. Similar bottles could have higher or lower values than the bottles specifically listed in this book, but the listings provide an excellent starting point for determining a reasonable price range for the collector.

Barber Bottles

Starting in the mid-1860s and continuing to 1920, barbers in America used colorful decorated bottles filled with various tonics and colognes. The finish of these unique and colorful pieces originated when the newly formed Pure Food and Drug Act of 1906 restricted the use of alcohol-based ingredients in unlabeled or refillable containers.

Very early examples have rough pontil scars with numerous types of ornamentation such as fancy pressed designs, paintings, and labels under glass. The bottles were usually fitted with a cork, metal, or porcelain-type closure. Since the value of barber bottles is very dependent on the painted or enameled lettering or decoration, it is important to note that when determining the value of a barber bottle, any type of wear such as faded decoration or color, faded lettering, or chipping will lower the value of these bottles.

Bay Rum, milk glass with black and gold gilt decoration, 8-5/8", pontil-scarred base, rolled lip, American 1890-1925 . . . .**$155-200**

Barber Bottle, cobalt blue with white enamel floral decorations, 8", smooth base, tooled mouth, American 1885-1930 (scarce) **$85-100**

Barber Bottle, emerald with red and white enamel decorations, 7-3/4", pontil-scarred base, tooled lip, American 1885-1930 . . . .**$85-100**

Barber Bottle, yellow green with red and white enamel decorations, 7-3/4", pontil-scarred base, tooled lip, American 1885-1930 . . . .**$85-100**

Barber Bottle, deep purple amethyst with white and orange enamel floral decorations, 8", smooth base, ABM lip, American 1885-1930 . . . .**$95-125**

Barber Bottle, clear glass with ice blue flashing, white enamel floral decoration, 8", smooth base, ABM lip, American 1910-1930 . . . .**$90-140**

Barber Bottle with Hobnail Pattern, turquoise blue, 6-3/4", polished pontil, rolled lip, American 1885-1930 . . . .**$65-80**

Barber Bottle with Hobnail Pattern, fiery opalescent clear glass, 8-1/2", pontil-scarred, rolled lip, American 1895-1930 .**$110-150**

Barber Bottle With Hobnail Pattern, purple amethyst, 7-5/8", smooth base, rolled lip, American 1900-1925 . . . .**$120-150**

Barber Bottle with Rib Pattern, frosted lime green, multicolored enamel rose decoration, 8-1/2", pontil-scarred base, tooled lip, American 1885-1930 . . . .**$250-350**

Barber bottle, Adam S. Eberhard, American, 1885-1925, **$200-300.**

Barber bottle, Wm. F. Stolte, American, 1885-1925, **$450-550.**

Barber bottle, Art Nouveau, American, 1885-1925, **$250-350**.

Barber bottle, American, 1885-1925, **$140-200**.

Barber Bottle with Rib Pattern, deep emerald green with yellow, orange, and white enamel decoration, 7-1/8", pontil-scarred base, tooled mouth, American 1885-1925 . . . .**$110-150**

Barber Bottle with Rib Pattern, deep cobalt blue with silver and yellow enamel floral decoration, 8-1/4", pontil-scarred base, tooled lip, American 1885-1930 . . . .**$90-120**

Barber Bottle – Mary Gregory Style Tennis Player, deep cobalt blue with white enamel decoration, 8-1/8", pontil-scarred base, rolled lip, American 1885-1930 . . . .**$225-300**

Barber bottle, American, 1885-1925, **$100-150.**

Barber bottle, American, 1885-1925, **$100-150.**

Barber Bottle – Mary Gregory Cameo – Coinspot Pattern, light lime green, 8", pontil-scarred base, rolled lip, American 1885-1926 . . . . **$300-375**

Barber Bottle – Mary Gregory – Girl with Butterfly Net Decorations, medium grass green with white enamel, 8-1/8", pontil-scarred base, tooled mouth, American 1885-1925 . . . . **$175-275**

Barber Bottle – Art Nouveau Decoration, dark amethyst with yellow and gold, 8-1/4", pontil-scarred base, rolled lip, American 1890-1925 . . . . **$360-450**

Barber Bottle – Art Nouveau Decoration, frosted lime green, rib pattern with multicolored style floral decorations, 8-1/4", pontil-scarred base, rolled lip, American 1890-1925 . . . . **$285-375**

Barber Bottle – Rib Pattern, deep purple amethyst, bell pattern form with white, orange, and gold enamel, 6-7/8", pontil-scarred base, tooled lip, American 18901-1910 (rare) **$550-700**

Colyptoline Auxilliator for the Hair, opalescent milk glass with black, orange, and blue lettering, 7-3/8", pontil-scarred base, tooled lip, American 1890-1925, (rare) **$650-800**

Hair Oil – Koken St. Louis (on base), milk glass with multicolored enamel rose decoration, 9", smooth base, tooled mouth, American 1890-1925 . . . . **$385-475**

Hair Tonic, mint green milk glass with multicolored enamel floral decoration, 9-1/4", pontil-scarred base, rolled lip, American 1890-1925 (rare in this color) **$750-1,200**

Hair Tonic – Flying Swallow (on label), milk glass with multicolored enamel decoration, 9", smooth base, rolled lip, American 1890-1925 . . . . **$325-400**

Barber bottle, American, 1885-1925, **$150-250.**

Barber bottle, label-under-glass, "Violet," American, 1885-1910, **$150-200.**

Barber bottle, "Witch Hazel," American, 1885-1926, $150-250.

Barber bottle, "Bay Rum," American, 1885-1925, $130-160.

Barber bottle, "Toilet Water," American, 1885-1925, **$150-250.**

Barber bottle, "Shampoo," American, **$250-350.**

Jack Schieles Violet, milk glass with multicolored enamel floral and clover decorations, 8", smooth base, tooled lip, American 1885-1930 . . . . **$65-80**

Kdx – Koken Companies – St. Louis, Mo., black glass, 8-1/8", smooth base, tooled lip, crown pour stopper, American 1895-1930 . . . . **$120-140**

Koken Barbers – Supply Co – St. Louis – K – U.S.A (on base) Toilet Water (on front), milk glass with multicolored floral decoration, 7-7/8", smooth base, tooled mouth, American 1885-1925 . . . . **$185-250**

Labeled Barber Bottle – Arista Antiseptic Face Tonic Arista M'f'g' Co – Limited Detroit, Mich, clear glass with red, black, and white pyro label, 7-1/4", smooth base, tooled mouth, American 1890-1925 . . . . **$195-275**

Labeled Barber Bottle – Levigated Barber Soap, Central Soap Co – Canton, O – Patented May 25th – 1875 (on base), clear glass with black, pink, and gold label, 5-1/2", smooth base, ground lip, American 1875-1910 (rare) **$450-600**

Labeled Barber Bottle – Retona A Tonique For The Hair – F.E. Baker & Co. – Lewiston, ME, clear glass with white, blue, yellow, and gold label, 8-1/4", smooth base, tooled lip, American 1890-1925 . . . . **$250-350**

Mini-Barber Bottle, opaque milk glass with multicolored enamel decorations, 5", smooth base, rolled lip, American 1995-1925 . . . . **$135-175**

N. Wapler – N.Y, cobalt blue, 7-1/4", smooth base, rolled lip, American 1885-1930 . . . . **$55-75**

PDQ (monogram) – Quinine Tonic – N. Wapler (on base), milk glass with red transfer, 7-1/2", smooth base, tooled mouth, American 1890-1925 . . . . **$160-200**

Personalized Barber Bottle – Geo. Eissler Tonic (peafowl sitting on a half moon), milk glass with multicolored enamel decoration, 8", smooth base, group lip, pewter screw stopper, American 1890-1925 (rare) **$425-700**

Personalized Barber Bottle – R.R. Hean – Tonic, milk glass with floral decoration, 8-7/8", smooth base, ground lip, original screw-off dispensing cap, American 1885-1925 . . . .**$350-450**

Sea Foam, mint green milk glass with multicolored enamel floral decorations, 9-1/4", pontil-scarred base, rolled lip, American 1890-1925 (rare in this color) **$750-1,200**

Shampoo (on front panel), milk glass with photograph of pretty woman, 10-1/4", smooth base, rolled lip, American 1885-1915 . . . .**$550-700**

T. Noonan & Co – Barber Supplies – Boston, Mass, cobalt blue, 7-5/8", smooth base, tooled mouth, American 1885-1930. **$55-75**

T. Noonan & Co – Barber Supplies – Boston, Mass, frosted green, 7-5/8", smooth base, tooled mouth, American 1885-1930 . . . .**$60-75**

Three Cherubs and Dog Head (on label), milk glass with labeled decoration, 7-1/2", pontil-scarred base, tooled lip, American 1885-1925 . . . .**$150-200**

Vegederma, deep purple amethyst with white enamel girl decoration, 8-1/8", pontil-scarred base, rolled lip, American 1885-1925 . . . .**$550-700**

Witch Hazel, milk glass with multicolored enamel poppy floral decoration, 9", pontil-scarred base, applied mouth, American 1890-1925 . . . .**$260-350**

Beer Bottles

Attempting to find an American beer bottle made before the mid-19th century is a difficult task. Up until that time, most of the bottles used for beer and spirits were imported. The majority of these imported bottles were black glass pontiled bottles made in three-piece molds and rarely embossed. There are four types of early beer bottles:

1. Porter, the most common, from 1820 to 1920
2. Ale from 1845 to 1850
3. Early lager from 1847 to 1850 (rare)
4. Late lager from 1850 to 1860

In spite of the large amounts of beer consumed in America before 1860, beer bottles were very rare and all have pontiled bases. Most of the beer manufactured during this time was distributed and dispensed from wooden barrels, or kegs, and sold to local taverns and private bottlers. Collectors often ask why the various breweries did not bottle the beer they manufactured. During the Civil

War, the federal government placed a special tax on all brewed beverages that was levied by the barrel. This taxing system prevented the brewery from making the beer and bottling the beer in the same building. Selling the beer to taverns and private bottlers was much simpler than erecting another building just for bottling. This entire process changed after 1890 when the federal government revised the law to allow breweries to bottle the beer straight from the beer lines. The chart below reflects the age and rarity of beer bottles.

Year	Rare	Scarce	Semi-Common	Common
1860-1870	X			
1870-1880		X		
1880-1890			X	
1890-1930				X

Embossed bottles marked "Ale" or "Porter" were manufactured between 1850 and 1860. In the late 1860s, the breweries began to emboss their bottles with names and promotional messages. This practice continued into the 20th century. It is interesting to note that Pennsylvania breweries made most of the beer bottles from the second half of the 19th century. By 1890, beer was readily available in bottles around most of the country.

The first bottles used for beer in the United States were made of pottery, not glass. Glass did not become widely used until after the Civil War (1865). A wholesaler for Adolphus Busch named C. Conrad sold the original Budweiser beer from 1877 to 1890.

The Budweiser name was a trademark of C. Conrad, but in 1891, it was sold to the Anheuser-Busch Brewing Association. Up until the 1870s, beer bottles were sealed with cork stoppers. Late in the 19th century, the lightning stopper was invented. It proved a convenient way of sealing and resealing blob top bottles. In 1891, corks were replaced with the crown cork closure invented by William Painter. This made use of a thin slice of cork within a tight-fitting metal cap. Once these were removed, they couldn't be used again.

Up until the 1930s, beer came in green glass bottles. After Prohibition, brown glass came into use, since it was thought to filter damaging sun rays and preserve freshness.

A. Palmtag & Co – Eureka Cal, medium amber, quart, smooth base, tooled top, American 1885-1900 . . . . **$35-60**

Alabama Brewing Co – San Francisco (with monogram), golden amber, 7-3/4", smooth base, tooled top, American 1880-1890 . . . . **$40-55**

B. & J. Oakland, medium light amber, 7-3/8", smooth base, tooled top, American 1880-1890 . . . . **$35-55**

Breckenfelder & Jochem – Oakland, Cal (with label), medium amber, 9-1/4", smooth base, tooled top with wire bail, American 1890-1910. . . . . **$45-55**

Buffalo Brewing & Co. – S.F. Agency (with monogram), medium amber, 7-1/2", smooth base, crown top, American 1900-1910 . . . . **$35-45**

C.C. Haley – & Co. – Celebrated – California – Pop Beer – Trade Mark – Patented – Oct. 29th 1872 – This Bottle – Is Never Sold, amber olive, 11-1/2", smooth base, applied mouth, American 1885-1895 . . . . **$55-75**

Cal. Bottling Co. – Export Beer, light amber, 6-7/8", smooth base, applied top, American 1880-1890 . . . . **$35-50**

Cascade Lager – S.F. Cal. (UB & MCO monogram), amber, quart, smooth base, crown top with porcelain and wire stopper, American 1907-1908 . . . . **$20-35**

City – Bottling Works – McKeesport PA – H & W, golden yellow amber, 11-1/2", smooth base, applied blob gravitating stopper type mouth, American 1875-1885 . . . . **$140-180**

*J.C. Coulter - Cor. 9th &
Market - McKeesport,
PA - A.G.W. - This Bottle
- Not To Be Sold, 1885-
1900, 9-5/8",* **$60-80.**

*City Brewery
(motif of hop) CB
- Titusville, PA, 1885-
1900, 9-5/8",* **$60-80.**

Bibbey & Ferguson - 101 & 103 - Maple St. - Glens Falls, N.Y. - This Bottle - Not To - Be Sold, Made By - Dean Foster & Co. - Boston (on base), 1880-1895, 9", **$140-180.**

E. Tousley - Cronk's Beer, 12-sided, 1855-1870, 10", **$1,500-2,500 (rare).**

City Brewery (motif of hop) CB – Titusville, PA, golden yellow amber, 9-5/8", smooth base, tooled mouth for gravitating stopper, American 1885-1900 . . . .**$65-80**

Continental Brewing Co – Philadelphia (embossed with Revolutionary soldier), aqua blue, pint, smooth base, applied top, American 1870-1880 . . . .**$35-60**

Dallas Brewery – Malt Wein – Dallas, Texas, medium amber, 8-1/4", smooth base, tooled mouth, American 1890-1900 . . . .**$90-140**

Dr. Cronk – R. McC, deep cobalt blue, 12-sided, 9-3/4", iron pontil, applied sloping collar mouth, American 1850-1865 . . . .**$2,500-3,500**

E. Tousley – Cronk's Beer, cobalt blue, 12-sided, 10", smooth base, applied sloping collar mouth, American 1850-1865 . . . .**$425-700**

Eagle – Bottling Works – Cincinnati, O, yellow olive, 11-1/2", smooth base, applied mouth, American 1885-1895 . . . . .**$55-70**

Enterprise Brewing Co – S.F. Cal., medium amber, quart, smooth base, tooled top, American 1880-1900 . . . .**$35-50**

Etna Brewery – Etna Mills, amber, 7-5/8", smooth base, tooled top, American 1880-1890 . . . .**$35-45**

Findlay Bottling Works – E. Bacher – Findlay, O, aqua, 11", smooth base, tooled mouth, American 1880 – 1910 . . . .**$65-90**

Foundersmith's – Beer, deep amber, 12-sided, 9-7/8", smooth base, applied sloping collar mouth, American 1855-1860 (very rare beer from the Fondersmith's Company of Cincinnati, Ohio) **$650-800**

Foundersmith's – Beer, deep amber, 12-sided, 10", red iron pontil, applied sloping collar mouth, American 1850-1860 (extremely rare beer from the Fondersmith's Company of Cincinnati, Ohio) **$725-900**

Fredicksburg Lager Beer – S.F. Bottling Company (with shield and monogram), light amber, 7-1/2", smooth base, tooled top, American 1880-1890 . . . . **$35-50**

Fredicksburg Lager Beer – San Francisco Cal – Adolph B. Lang (embossed eagle), medium amber, 11-5/8", smooth base, applied top, American 1890-1910 . . . . **$45-55**

G. Andrae – Port Huron – Mich, cobalt blue, 11-7/8", smooth base, applied sloping collar mouth, American 1875-1885 . . . . **$850-1,200**

G. H. Hausburg – Blue Island – Ill, yellow olive green, 8-3/8", smooth base, tooled mouth, American 1885-1900 . . . . **$90-120**

Gambrinus Stock Co (motif of Gambrinus) – Bottled Beer – Cincinnati, O, olive amber glass, 10-3/4", smooth base, applied mouth, American 1875-1885 (rare) **$825-1,000**

Gowdy's (star) – Medicated Beer – Manufactured – 10 Ormond Place – This Bottle – Not To Be Sold – Trade Mark – L & S – Registered July 24th 1890, deep bluish aqua, 10-1/2", smooth base, tooled mouth, American 1885-1895 . . . . **$50-75**

Grace Bros. Brewing Co. GBEC (monogram) – Santa Rosa, Ca – This Bottle Not To Be Sold, amber, 7-3/4", smooth base, tooled top, American 1890-1910 . . . . **$40-55**

Gambrinus Stock Co. (motif of Gambrinus) - Bottled Beer - Cincinnati, O, 1875-1885, 10-3/4", **$800-1,000.**

G. Andrae - Port Huron - Mich, 1875-1885, 11-7/8", **$800-1,200.**

H. Bro's – X.O., medium amber, 9", smooth base, applied sloping collar mouth, American 1875-1885 . . . .**$85-125**

H. Floto's – Lager Beer – Reading, PA, aqua, 7-1/2", smooth base, applied mouth, American 1875-1885 . . . .**$75-100**

H & K – Dayton, O, deep red amber, 9-1/2", smooth base, applied sloping collar mouth, American 1875-1885 . . . .**$85-125**

Haley's – California – Pop Beer – Pat. Oct. 29th 1872 – Manufactured By – McKee & Blehl – Philadelphia – This Bottle – Not To Be Sold, deep yellow amber, 10-3/4", smooth base, applied mouth, American 1875-1885 . . . .**$360-450**

Hansen & Kahler – Oakland, Cal. H & K (monogram) – This Bottle Not To Be Sold, light amber, quart, smooth base, tooled top, American 1890-1900 . . . .**$35-45**

J.C. Coulter – Cor. 9th & Market – McKeesport, PA – A.G.W. – This Bottle – Not To Be Sold, golden yellow amber, 9-5/8", smooth base, tooled mouth for gravitating stopper, American 1885-1900 . . . .**$65-85**

J. Gahm – 83 State St. – Boston – Mass – Milwaukee – JG (inside motif of mug) – Lager Beer, yellow olive, 9-7/8", smooth base, applied sloping blob top, American 1880-1890 . . . .**$160-200**

John Rapp & Son – S.F. Cal., light amethyst, 7-3/4", smooth base, crown top, American 1910-1920 . . . .**$35-45**

J. Schleenbaker – Bryan – Ohio – This – Bottle – Not To Be Sold, amber olive, 11-1/2", smooth base, applied mouth, American 1885-1895 . . . .**$55-75**

J. Gahm - 83 State St. - Boston (over peened-out letters) Mass - Milwaukee - JG (inside motif of mug) - Lager Beer, 1880-1890, 9-7/8", **$150-200.**

J. Voelker & Bro. - Cleveland. O - V Bro, 1875-1885, 10", **$400-600.**

John Stanton Brewing Co – Trade – JSBCO (monogram) – Mark – Troy, N.Y., bright yellow green, 9-1/2", smooth base, tooled mouth, American 1885-1900 . . . .**$110-150**

John Stanton Brewing Co – Trade – (monogram) – Mark – Troy, N.Y., medium lime green, 9-1/2", smooth base, tooled mouth (porcelain stopper marked John Stanton Brewing Co. Troy, N.Y.), American 1885-1900 . . . . **$100-150**

Joseph Beltz – Weiss Beer – Cor – Slater Ave – Outwait Ave – Cleveland Ohio – Weiss Beer, bluish aqua, 7-5/8", smooth base, applied mouth, American 1840-1875 . . . . **$110-150**

Joseph Schlitz's – Milwaukee – Lager Beer – Registered – J. Gahm – Trade (J.G. inside motif of mug) – Boston Mass, medium golden amber, 9-3/8", smooth base, tooled mouth, American 1885-1895 . . . . **$140-180**

Mirrasooul Bros – S.F., light amber, 7-5/8", smooth base, tooled top with wire bail, American 1890-1910. . . . .**$35-55**

Moerlein's Jug Lager Krug Bier (stoneware ginger beer), tan pottery with dark brown glaze on neck with black transfer, 8-3/4", smooth base, tooled mouth, American 1880-1900 . . . .**$50-80**

N. Cervelli – 615 Francisco St – S.F., medium amber, quart, smooth base, tooled top, American 1898-1906 . . . .**$40-80**

National Lager Beer – H. Rohrbacher Agt. – Stockton, Cal, golden amber, 7-7/8", smooth base, tooled top with wire bail, American 1880-1910 . . . .**$30-50**

North Star Bottling Works – San Francisco, Cal, medium amber, 7-7/8", smooth base, tooled top, American 1890-1900 . . . .**$30-60**

*John Stanton Brewing Co -
Trade - JSBCO (monogram)
Mark - Troy, N.Y., 1885-
1900, 9-1/2",* **$100-150.**

*P. Stumpf & Co - 1817 Main St
- Richmond VA - This Bottle
- Is Never - Sold, 1875-1885,
8-1/4",* **$250-350.**

*Joseph Schlitz's - Milwaukee - Lager Beer - Registered - J. Gahm - Trade (J.G. inside motif of mug) - Boston Mass, 1885-1895, 9-3/8", **$140-180**.*

*John Stanton Brewing Co - Trade - (monogram) Mark - Troy. N.Y., 1885-1895, 9-1/2", **$150-200**.*

*City - Bottling Works - McKeesport PA - H & W, 1875-1885, 11-1/2", **$140-180**.*

P. Stumpf & Co – 1817 Main St – Richmond VA – This Bottle – Is Never – Sold, golden yellow amber, 8-1/4", smooth base, applied mouth, American 1875-1885 (Peter Stumpf was the original distributor in Richmond, VA, for the Budweiser Brewing Company)....................................**$250-350**

Phillip Best Brewing Co – Old Milwaukee Lager Beer – Bottled By A.P. Fulmer, Lancaster, PA, olive amber, 9-3/4", smooth base, tooled mouth, American 1880-1900 ....**$50-70**

Ruhstaller's Gild Edge Lager Beer, medium amber, 11-1/2", smooth base, tooled top, American 1890-1910 (This beer was produced by Kenison & Co. in Auburn, CA) **$35-55**

Salinas Valley Bottling Co. – Salinas, Cal, medium amber, 7-5/8", smooth base, tooled top, American 1880-1890 ....**$35-50**

San Jose Bottling Com – San Jose Cal, medium amber, 7-1/2", smooth base, tooled top, American 1880-1890 ....**$30-50**

St. Louis Bottling Co. – McC.& B – Vallejo, Cal, amber, quart, smooth base, crown top, American 1900-1920 (rare) **$45-55**

Sunset Bottling Co – San Francisco (with monogram), light amber, 7-1/2", smooth base, tooled top, American 1880-1890 ....**$30-50**

Take & Veile – Lager Beer – Easton PA (in a slug plate), medium blue green, 7-1/4", smooth base, applied sloping double collar mouth, American 1850-1865 ....**$425-600**

Phillip Best Brewing Co., Old Milwaukee Lager Beer, Bottled By A.P. Fulmer, Lancaster, PA, 1880-1900, 9-3/4", $50-70.

Stoneware Ginger Beer, Moerlein's Jug Lager Krug Bier, 1880-1900, 8-3/4", $50-80.

Robert Portner - Brewing CO - Tivoli (inside diamond) - Alexandria VA - This Bottle - Not To - Be Sold, 1890-1910, 9", $75-100.

WM Pfeifer - Trade WP (Monogram) Mark - Chicago, 1890-1910, 9-1/2", $75-100.

Schroeder's - B.W.B. Co. - St. Louis Mo, 1890-1910, 9-1/2", ***$70-90.***

Wittemann Rost Brewing - Co - St. Louis, 1890-1910, 9-1/2", ***$70-90.***

Theodore Lutge & Co – This Bottle Not To Be Sold – San Jose Cal, sea foam green, quart, smooth base, applied top, American 1875-1890 . . . .**$60-100**

Thos. Downing Haford, Cal – Not To Be Sold, medium amber, 7-3/4", smooth base, crown top, American 1900-1910. . .**$30-40**

T.l. Neff's Sons – 105 Maujer St – Brooklyn, N.Y. – Trade (motif of case of bottles) Mark – Registered – 1895, deep bluish aqua, 10-1/2", smooth base, tooled mouth, American 1885-1895 . . . .**$50-75**

Ticoulet & Beshorman – Sac. Ca, medium amber, quart, smooth base, tooled top, American 1900-1910 . . . .**$30-40**

Wallabout Potter Co (stoneware beer), reddish brown pottery, 6", smooth base, tooled top, American 1870-1890 (rare). . .**$100-150**

Wunder Bottling – Works – E. Greenwald – Stockton Cal – Pacific Club Beer, Brewed By Wunder Brewing Co. – San Francisco, Cal, medium amber, 9-1/4", smooth base, tooled mouth (porcelain stopper marked D.W. McCarthy Stockton, Cal), American 1895-1910 . . . .**$70-90**

Bitters

Bitter bottles have long been one of the favorite bottles to collect. Because of their uniqueness, bitter bottles were saved in great numbers, giving today's collector some great opportunities to build a special and varied collection.

Bitters originated in England as a type of medicine made from roots or herbs named for their bitter taste. During the 18th century, bitters were added to water, ale, or spirits with the intent to cure all types of ailments. Because of the pretense that the mixtures had some medicinal value, bitters became popular in America since Colonists could import them from England without paying the liquor tax. While most bitters had low alcohol content, some brands were as high as 120 proof, higher than most hard liquor available at the time. As physicians became convinced bitters did have some type of healing value, the drink became socially acceptable. This promoted sales among people who normally weren't liquor drinkers and also provided a good excuse for a customer to have it at home (for medicinal purposes, of course).

The best-known physician who made his own bitters for patients was Dr. Jacob Hostetter. After his retirement in 1853, he gave his son David permission to manufacture it commercially. The Hostetter Bitters were known for colorful, dramatic, and extreme advertising. While Hostetter said it wouldn't cure everything, the list of ailments it claimed to alleviate with regular use covered most everything: indigestion, diarrhea, dysentery, chills and fever, liver ailments, and pains and weakness that came with old age (at that time, a euphemism for impotence). Despite these claims, David Hostetter died in 1888 from a kidney failure that should have been cured by his own formula.

One of the most sought-after bitter bottles is the Drakes Plantation Bitters. Drakes first appeared in 1860 and recorded a patent in 1862. The bottles are shaped like log cabins and can be found in a four-log and a six-log variant with colors in various shades of amber, yellow, citron, puce, green and black. Another interesting characteristic of the Drake bitters is the miscellaneous dots and marks including the "X" on the base of the bottles that are thought to be identification marks of the various glass houses that manufactured the bottles.

Most bitter bottles, over 1,000 types, were manufactured between 1860 and 1905. The more unusual shapes, called figurals, were in the likeness of cannons, drums, pigs, fish, and ears of corn. In addition, other shapes were made including round, square, rectangular, twelve-sided, barreled-shaped, gin-bottle shaped, and flask shaped. The embossed varieties are the oldest and most valuable.

The most common color was amber (pale golden yellow to dark amber brown), then aqua (light blue), and sometimes green or clear glass was used. The rarest and most collectible colors are dark blue, amethyst, milk glass, and puce (a purplish brown).

Amazon – Bitters – Peter McQuade – New York, medium amber, 9-3/8", smooth base, applied sloping collar mouth, American 1875-1885 (rare) **$285-375**

Applied Seal Bitters Bottle – HK (above motif of fish inside star on applied seal), deep olive green, 7-3/8", smooth base, applied mouth and seal, German 1880-1895 . . . .**$110-150**

Applied Seal Bitters Bottle – IWL (inside motif of star above fish), medium yellow olive amber, 6-7/8", smooth base, applied mouth and seal, German 1870-1900 . . . .**$140-170**

Big – Bill – Best – Bitters, medium amber, 12-1/8", smooth base, tooled mouth, American 1900-1910 . . . .**$90-120**

Bourbon Whiskey – Bitters, copper puce, 9-1/4", barrel, smooth base, applied mouth, American 1855-1870 . . . .**$200-275**

Brown's Catalina – Patd Sept 17th 72, medium golden amber, 10-5/8", smooth base, applied mouth, American 1865-1875 (extremely rare) **$550-700**

Brown's – Celebrated – Indian Herb Bitters – Patented – Feb. 11 – 1868, medium amber, 12-1/8", Indian queen, smooth base, group lip, American 1863-1870 . . . .**$560-700**

Bryant's – Stomach – Bitters, olive green, 12-1/2", 8-sided lady's leg, pontil-scarred base, applied sloping double collar mouth, American 1865-1875 . . . . **$3,600-4,500**

B.T. 1865 S.C. – Smiths – Druid Bitters, medium yellow amber, 9-1/2", barrel, smooth base, applied mouth, American 1855-1870 . . . . **$1,100-1,500**

Buhrer's – Gentian Bitters – S. Buhrer – Proprietor, yellow amber, 9", smooth base, applied sloping collar mouth, American 1870-1880 . . . .**$65-85**

Bell's Cocktail Bitters - Jas. M. Bell & Co. - New York, American, 1865-1800, **$500-700**.

Bourbon Whiskey Bitters, American, 1865-1975, **$374-475**.

Brown's Celebrated Indian Herb Bitters - Patented Feb 11, 1868, American, 1868-1875, **$500-700.**

California Fig & Herb – Bitters – California Fig Products Co – San Francisco, Cal, medium amber, 9-7/8", smooth base, tooled mouth, American 1890-1900 . . . . **$90-120**

Carl Mampe – Berlin (motif of elephant inside oval) – Carl Mampe, golden amber, 8", smooth base, tooled mouth, German 1890-1915 (scarce variant) **$140-180**

Carl Mampe Berlin (motif of elephant inside oval) – S.W. Halleschestrasse 17, olive green, 10", smooth base, applied sloping collar mouth, German 1880-1895 . . . . **$80-120**

Castilian Bitters, medium golden amber, 10", smooth base, applied mouth, American 1865-1875 (scarce figural cannon bitters) **$900-1,200**

Celebrated – Crown Bitters – F. Chevalier & Co – Sole Agents, medium amber, 8-7/8", smooth base, applied sloping collar mouth, American 1885-1895 (scarce California bitters) **$325-400**

Celebrated Nectar – Stomach Bitters – and Nerve Tonic – The – Nectar Bitter Co – Toledo, O, medium yellow green, 9-3/8", smooth base, tooled mouth, American 1890-1900 (rare) **$750-900**

C.H. Swains – Bourbon – Bitters, amber, 9-1/4", smooth base, applied mouth, American 1865-1875 . . . . **$285-375**

Clarke's – Vegetable – Sherry Wine – Bitters – Sharon Mass, bluish aqua, 14", smooth base, applied sloping collar mouth, American 1850-1865 . . . . **$550-700**

Dingen's – Napolean Cocktail Bitters – Dingen Brothers – Buffalo N.Y., medium olive green, 10-1/4", lady's leg drum, iron pontil, applied sloping collar mouth, American 1865-1875 (rare color and form) **$15,000-20,000**

The Great Tonic - Caldwell's Herb Bitters, American, 1865-1875, **$300-400.**

The Great Tonic - Dr. Caldwell's Herb Bitters, American, 1865-1875, **$250-350.**

Dr. C.W. Roback's – Stomach Bitters – Cincinnati, O, medium amber, 9-3/8", barrel, smooth base, applied sloping collar mouth, American 1860-1870 . . . . **$260-300**

Dr. Green's Polish Bitters, yellow amber, 10-7/8", iron pontil, applied mouth, American 1845-1860 (rare) **$450-600**

Dr. J. Hostetter's – Stomach Bitters, deep olive green, 9-1/2", smooth base, applied sloping collar mouth, American 1865-1875 . . . . **$285-375**

Dr. J. Hostetter's – Stomach Bitters, medium golden amber, 8-3/4", smooth base, applied sloping collar mouth, American 1875-1885 . . . . **$285-375**

Dr. MacKenzie's – Wild Cherry – Bitters – Chicago, clear glass, 8-3/8", smooth base, tooled mouth, American 1890-1900 . . . . **$180-275**

Dr. Shoule's – Hop – Bitters – 1872 (motif of hop berries and leaves), yellow olive, 10", semi-cabin, smooth base, applied sloping double collar mouth, American 1872-1880 . . . . **$225-300**

Dr. Shoule's – Hop – Bitters – 1872 (motif of hop berries and leaves), yellow olive green, 9-5/8", semi-cabin, smooth base, applied sloping double collar mouth, American 1872-1880 (rare) **$1,400-1,800**

Dr. Sperry's – Female – Strengthening – Bitters – Waterbury CT, deep bluish aqua, 9-1/8", smooth base, applied mouth, American 1880-1890 . . . . **$225-300**

Dr. Wood's – Sarsaparilla – & – Wild Cherry – Bitters, aqua, 8-3/4", open pontil, applied mouth, American 1845-1855 . . . . **$275-350**

The Royal Bitters - Geo. A. Clement - Niagara, Ont., Canadian, 1875-1885, **$400-600.**

St. Drakes 1860 Plantation X Bitters - Patented 1862, American, 1862-1875, **$250-350.**

Curtis & Perkins Wild Cherry Bitters, American, 1840-1860, **$75-100**.

John Moffat - Price $1.00 - Phoenix Bitters - New York, American, 1840-1860, **$75-100**.

*Dr. Flint's Quaker Bitters -
Providence, R.I., American,
1872-1880,* **$250-350.**

*Dr. A.S. Hopkins - Union
Stomach Bitters - Hartford,
Conn., American, 1870-1880,*
$1,200-1,600.

Edw Wilder's – Stomach Bitters (motif of five-story building) – Edw Wilder & Co – Wholesale Druggists – Louisville KY, clear glass semi-cabin, 10-3/4", smooth base, applied sloping double collar mouth, American 1880-1890 (rare variant) **$385-475**

E.S. Royer's – Excelsior Bitters, yellow amber, 9-1/2", smooth base, applied mouth, American 1870-1880 . . . . **$185-275**

Faith – Whitcomb's – Bitters – Faith Whitcomb's Agency – Boston Mass, U.S.A., aqua, 9-1/2", smooth base, applied double collar mouth, American 1880-1890 . . . . **$185-275**

Fulton M. McCrae – Yazoo Valley Bitters, medium amber, 8-3/4", smooth base, applied sloping collar mouth, American 1875-1885 . . . .**$225-300**

German Balsam Bitters – W.M. Watson & Co – Sole Agents For U.S., milk glass, 9", smooth base, applied sloping collar mouth, American 1879-1880 . . . .**$550-800**

Greeley's – Bourbon Whiskey – Bitters – Greeley's, bluish aqua, 9-3/8", barrel, smooth base, applied mouth, American 1855-1870 . . . . **$3,000-4,000**

Greeley's Bourbon – Bitters, smoky olive topaz, 9-3/8", barrel, smooth base, applied mouth, American 1855-1870 **$1,400-1,800**

Hall's Bitters – E.E. Hall New Haven – Established 1842, medium amber, 9-1/4", barrel, smooth base, applied mouth, American 1860-1870 . . . .**$350-400**

Hesperidina – Bagles – Un Barril, medium yellow amber, 9-5/8", barrel, smooth base (Rio De La Plaata – Brazil), smooth base, applied mouth, Brazil 1875-1895 . . . .**$120-140**

Germania Bitters, American, 1880-1895, **$1,500-2,000.**

Griel's Herb Bitters - Griel & Young - MF'TRS - Lancaster, PA U.S.A., American, 1890-1900, **$275-400.**

H.P. Herb – Wild – Cherry – Bitters – Reading – PA – Wild Cherry (motif of cherry tree) – Bitters – Bitters (on four roof panels), amber, 10-1/8", cabin, smooth base, tooled mouth, American 1885-1895 . . . .**$325-400**

Hunki Dori – Bitters – H.B. Matthews – Chicago, medium amber, 8-7/8", smooth base, applied sloping collar mouth, American 1875-1885 (scarce) **$185-275**

1834 – John Roots Bitters – 1834 – Buffalo, N.Y., medium blue green, 10-1/8", semi-cabin, smooth base, applied sloping collar mouth, American 1865-1875 . . . . **$1,300-1,800**

J.W. Hutchinson's – Tonic Bitters – Mobile Ala, deep olive green, 9", smooth base, applied sloping collar mouth, American 1865-1875 (one of only two known examples) . . . **$2,500-3,500**

J.W. Hutchinson's – Tonic Bitters – Mobile Ala, medium golden amber, 8-7/8", smooth base, applied sloping collar mouth, American 1865-1875 (one of only two known examples) **$3,500-4,500**

John Moffat – Phoenix – Bitters – New York – Price 1 Dollar, medium amber, 5-1/2", open pontil, rolled lip, American 1835-1845 . . . . **$1,000-1,500**

John Root's Bitters – Buffalo, N.Y. – 1834 – 1834, medium blue green, 10-1/4", semi-cabin, smooth base, applied mouth, American 1865-1875 . . . . **$2,500-3,000**

John Steele's – Niagara (star) Bitters – John Steele's Niagara (star) Bitters – 1864 (on roof), deep amber, semi-cabin, 9-7/8", smooth base, applied mouth, American 1865-1875 . . . .**$395-475**

Hart's Star Bitters -
Philadelphia PA, American,
1880-1890, **$400-600.**

Unembossed Barrel,
American, 1865-1875,
$2,500-4,000.

Karlsbader Sprudel Bitter – G (motif of fountain) – G – Karlsbader Sprudel Likor – Ges Gesch – Edmund – Weiss – Karlsbad, milk glass, 8-1/8", smooth base, tooled mouth, German 1880-1895 . . . . **$140-180**

Kelly's – Old Cabin – Bitters – Patented – 1863 – Kelly's – Old Cabin – Bitters – Patented – 1863, amber, 9-1/4", log cabin, smooth base, applied sloping collar mouth, American 1865-1875 . . . . **$1,600-2,000**

Kimball's – Jaundice – Bitters – Troy N.H., medium yellow amber, 7", iron pontil, applied sloping collar mouth, American 1840-1860 . . . . **$1,100-1,500**

Leopold Sahl's – Aromatic – Stomach Bitters – Pittsburgh, PA, medium amber, 10-1/4", smooth base, applied sloping collar mouth, American 1855-1870 . . . . **$2,500-3,500**

McConnon's – Stomach Bitters – McConnon & Company – Winona, Minn, medium reddish amber, 9-1/8", smooth base, tooled mouth, American 1880-1900 . . . . **$375-550**

McKeever's Army Bitters (cannon balls on drums), medium amber, 10-5/8", smooth base, applied sloping collar mouth, American 1865-1875 . . . . **$1,600-2,500**

Mishler's Herb Bitters – Tablespoon Graduation – Dr. S.B. Hartman & Co, yellow with copper tone, 8-3/4", smooth base (Stoeckel's Grad Pat Feb 6 66), applied sloping collar mouth, American 1866-1875 . . . . **$325-400**

National – Bitters, medium amber, 12-3/8", smooth base, applied collar mouth, American 1867-1875 . . . . **$385-475**

Patented – A863 – OK – Plantation – 1840, medium amber, 11", triangular shape, smooth base, applied mouth, American 1863-1870 (rare) **$2,500-3,500**

McKeever's Army Bitters, American, 1865-1875, **$2,000-3,000.**

Mexican Bitters - A.S.F.5 - 1866 - Henry C. Weaver - Lancaster, O. - A.S.F.5 - 1866, American, 1866-1868, **$1,800-2,750.**

Napoleon Bitters - 1866 - Dingens Brothers - Buffalo, N.Y., American, 1866-1875, **$2,000-3,000.**

New York Hop Bitters Company, American, 1870-1885, **$1,500-2,500.**

Old – Homestead – Wild Cherry – Bitters – Patent, medium amber, 9-3/4", cabin, smooth base, applied sloping collar mouth, American 1865-1875 . . . .**$140-180**

Old – Homestead – Wild Cherry – Bitters – Patent, golden yellow amber, 9-5/8", cabin, smooth base, applied sloping collar mouth, American 1865-1875 . . . .**$350-450**

Old Sachem – Bitters – and – Wigwam Tonic, deep strawberry puce, 9-3/8", barrel, smooth base, applied mouth, American 1855-1870 . . . .**$550-800**

Old Sachem – Bitters – and – Wigwam Tonic, bright yellow amber, 9-1/4", barrel, smooth base, applied mouth, American 1855-1870 . . . .**$150-200**

Orient Bitters – Wm. M. Leslie – N.Y., clear glass, 9-1/2", smooth base, tooled lip, American 1880-1895 (rare) **$185-275**

Prickly Ash – Bitters Co., medium amber, 9-7/8", smooth base, applied sloping collar mouth, American 1880-1890 . . .**$160-250**

Red Jacket – Bitters – Bennett Peters & Co., root beer amber, 9-3/4", smooth base, applied sloping collar mouth, American 1870-1880 . . . .**$250-300**

Reed's – Bitters – Reed's Bitters, medium golden yellow amber, 12-1/2" lady's leg, smooth base, applied mouth, American 1875-1885 . . . .**$325-400**

Rising Sun – Bitters – John C. Hurst – Philada, yellow with light amber and olive, 9-1/4", smooth base, applied mouth, American 1870-1880 . . . .**$310-400**

Rocky Mountain – Tonic Bitters – 1840 Try Me 1870, medium yellow amber, 9-3/4", smooth base, applied mouth, American 1870-1880 (rare) **$360-450**

Royal – Italian Bitters – Registered (motif of crown, shield and crossed flags) – Trade Mark – A.M.F. Gianelli – Genova, medium pink amethyst, 13-3/4", smooth base, applied mouth, Canadian 1875-1885 . . . .**$650-900**

Rush's – Bitters – A.H. Flanders, M.D. – New York, yellow with light amber, 9-1/4", smooth base, applied mouth, American 1875-1885 . . . .**$125-175**

Sanitarium – Bitters – Hi Hi Bitters Co. – Rock Island, Ill, bright lime green, 9-1/2", smooth base, tooled lip, American 1880-1890 . . . .**$260-350**

Shurtleff's – Bitters – Shurtleff's – Bitters, amber, 12-1/2", lady's leg, smooth base, applied mouth, American 1870-1880 (one of the rarest bitter bottles in the lady leg form) **$550-700**

S.O. Richardson – Bitters – South – Reading – Mass, aqua, 6-1/2", open pontil, flared out tooled lip, American 1845-1855 . . . .**$125-175**

Solomons' – Strengthening & – Invigoration Bitters – Savannah – Georgia, deep cobalt blue, 9-7/8", smooth base, applied sloping collar mouth, American 1870-1880 . . . . **$1,100-1,500**

St – Drakes – 1860 – Plantation – X – Bitters – Patented – 1862, deep purple amethyst, 10", smooth base, applied sloping collar mouth, American 1862-1875 . . . . **$1,400-1,800**

St – Drakes – 1860 – Plantation – X – Bitters – Patented – 1862, dark cherry puce, 10", 6-log cabin, smooth base, applied sloping collar mouth, American 1862-1875 . . . . . . **$1,400-1,800**

St. – Nicholas – Stomach – Bitters – Imported – By – Gentry – & Otis – N.Y., amber, 7-5/8", pontil-scarred base, wedge form, applied collar mouth, American 1865-1875 . . . .**$450-700**

Suffolk Bitters – Philbrook & Tucker – Boston, golden amber, 10", smooth base, applied double collar mouth, American 1865-1875 . . . .**$650-800**

The – Fish Bitters – W.H. Ware – Patented 1866, amber, 11-3/4", fish form, smooth base (W.H. Ware – Patent 1866) applied mouth, American 1866-1875 . . . .**$260-350**

Tyree's – Chamomile – Bitters, yellow amber, 6-5/8", smooth base, tooled lip, American 1880-1890. . . . .**$195-275**

Von Humboldt's – German Bitters – Dyspepsia & C. – Liver Complaint, bluish aqua, 7", pontil-scarred base, applied mouth, American 1845-1855 . . . .**$550-700**

Warner's – Safe – Bitters (motif of safe) – Rochester N.Y., yellow amber, 7-1/2", smooth base, applied mouth, American 1880-1895 . . . .**$650-800**

Wheeler's – Genuine – Bitters, aqua, 9-1/4", pontil-scarred base, applied mouth, American 1845-1855 (rare with pontil) **$450-600**

Winter's – Stomach Bitters, reddish amber, 9-5/8", smooth base, tooled lip, American 1880-1895. . . . .**$185-275**

W.R. Tyree's – Chamomile – Bitters – 1880, amber, 8-5/8", semi-cabin, smooth base, tooled mouth, American 1880-1890 (rare) **$850-1,200**

Sample Bitter Bottles

As discussed earlier, the history and beginning of bitter bottles began in the early 1800s, but sample bitters and other types of samples weren't introduced until the 1890s. What makes these sample bottles so unique is that they were produced to be identical to the normal size bottles. The sample bitter bottles depicted following are from the collection of Omer and Helen Sherwood, who began collecting sample bitters in the mid-1960s. Another unique part of the Sherwoods' collection is that along with the sample bitters, they also collected the matching full-size bitter bottles.

Augauer Bitters – Augauer Bitters Co – Chicago, medium emerald green, 4-1/4", smooth base, tooled mouth, American 1890-1910 . . . . **$285**

California – Fig & Herb – Bitters – California Fig Products Co – San Francisco, Cal, yellow amber, 4-1/2", smooth base, tooled lip, American 1885-1900 . . . . **$750**

Carl – Mampe (motif of elephant) – Berlin, medium amber, 2-1/4", smooth base, tooled mouth, 99% label, German 1900-1915 . . . . **$60**

Carmeliter – Stomach Bitters Co. – New York – SJ (monogram) Registered, medium amber, 4-7/8", smooth base, tooled mouth, original labels, foil neck seal, and contents, American 1890-1910 . . . . **$870**

Deimel Bros & Co – New York – U.S.A., milk glass, 4-1/8", case gin, smooth base, tooled mouth, American 1890-1900 . . . . . **$150**

Digestine – Bitters, yellowish amber, 3-1/2", smooth base, tooled lip, American 1890-1900 . . . .$1,300

Dr. Loew's Celebrated – Stomach Bitters – Nerve Tonic – The – Loew & Sons Co. – Cleveland, O, pale aqua, 3-7/8", smooth base, tooled mouth, American 1890-1910 . . . .$160

Eagle Angostura Bark Bitters, medium amber, 3-7/8", smooth base, tooled mouth, American 1895-1910 . . . .$450

Ferro Quina – Bitters – D.P. Rossi – Dogliani – Italia – S.F. Cal, yellow amber, 3-3/4", smooth base, tooled lip, American 1890-1910 . . . .$130

Dr. Loew's Celebrated Stomach Bitters - Nerve Tonic - The Loew & Sons Co. - Cleveland, O, American, 1890-1910, $300-400 (sample size 3-7/8").

Geo. Benz – & – Sons – Appetine – Bitters – St. Paul, Minn, amber, 3-1/2", smooth base (Pat – Nov. 23 – 1897), tooled lip, American 1897-1910 . . . . **$435**

Golden – Bitters – Geo. C. Hubbel & Co – Geo. C. Hubbel & Co., pale aqua, 3-5/8", semi-cabin, smooth base, inward rolled lip, American 1875-1885 . . . . **$285**

H. Kantorowicz – Co – Hamburg – Berlin – Osen – New York, milk glass, 4-1/8", case gin, smooth base, tooled mouth, American 1880-1890 . . . . **$130**

Holtzermann's Stomach Bitters – Piqua O, medium amber, 4-1/8", log cabin, smooth base, tooled mouth, original label, foil neck seal, and contents, American 1885-1900 . . . . **$860**

Hops – & – Malt – Bitters (on four roof panels) – Hops & Malt – Trade (sheaf of grain) Mark – Bitters, yellow amber, 3-5/8", semi-cabin, smooth base, tooled mouth, American 1885-1895 . . . . **$1,500**

Kennedys – East India – Bitters – Iler & Co – Omaha, Neb, clear glass, 4-1/8", smooth base, tooled mouth, American 1885-1895 . . . . **$110**

Morning (star) – Bitters – Inceptum 5869 – Patented – 5869, yellow amber, 5-1/8", smooth base, tooled mouth, American 1880-1890 (thought to be one of only two known examples) . . . **$1,400**

Pepsin Bitters – R.W. Davis Drug Co. – Chicago U.S.A., apple green, 4-1/2", smooth base, tooled top, American 1890-1910**$250**

Sarasina – Stomach Bitters, amber, 4", smooth base, tooled lip, American 1890-1910 . . . . **$325**

Schroeder's – Bitters – Louisville, KY, medium amber, 5-1/4", lady leg, smooth base, tooled lip, American 1880-1890. . . . . **$285**

Blown/Pattern-Molded Bottles

A pattern-molded bottle is one that is blown into a ribbed or pattern mold. This group includes globular and chestnut flasks. One of these, the Stiegel bottle, manufactured during the late 18th century, is considered very rare and valuable. The two types of Stiegel bottles manufactured at the Stiegel Glass Factory are the diamond daisy and hexagon designs.

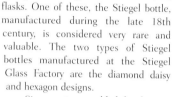

Since pattern-molded bottles are among the more valuable and rare pieces, collectors need to familiarize themselves with the types, sizes, colors, and the various manufacturers of these bottles.

Blown Decanter, medium lavender, 6", 15-vertical rib pattern, applied ring mouth, American 1840-1860 . . . .**$450-700**

Blown Three-Mold Toilet Water Bottle, cobalt blue, 5-1/4", pontil-scarred base, flared out mouth with inward folded rim, American 1815-1835 . . . .**$225-300**

Blown Three-Mold Toilet Water Bottle, cobalt blue, 6-1/8", pontil-scarred base, inward rolled lip, American 1815-1835 . . . .**$225-300**

Chestnut Flask, medium amber, 4-3/4", 24-vertical rib pattern, pontil-scarred base, tooled mouth, American 1820-1835 . . . .**$260-350**

Chestnut Flask, golden yellow amber, 5-1/2", 16-vertical rib pattern, pontil-scarred base, sheared lip, American 1820-1835 .**$110-150**

Chestnut Flask, medium cobalt blue, 5-1/8", 22-broken rib "popcorn" pattern swirled to right, pontil-scarred base, tooled mouth, American 1815-1835 . . . .**$750-900**

Club Bottle, blue aqua, 8-1/4", 16-rib pattern swirled to left, open pontil, applied collar mouth, American 1815-1825 . . . .**$110-150**

Elongated Flask, pale green aqua, 7-1/4", 16-diamond over rib pattern, open pontil sheared lip, American 1815-1825 .**$260-350**

Club Bottle, blue aqua, 8-1/4", 16-rib pattern swirled to left, open pontil, applied collar mouth, American 1815-1825 . . . .**$110-150**

Club Bottle, blue aqua, 8-1/2", 23-broken rib pattern to right, open pontil, applied collar mouth, American 1815-1825 . . . .**$180-250**

Freeblown Chestnut Flask, aqua, 7", pontil-scarred base, sheared and tooled lip, American 1815-1835 . . . .**$120-150**

Freeblown Globular Bottle, greenish aqua, 8", open pontil, applied string lip, American 1780-1800 . . . .**$210-275**

Pattern-molded globular bottle, American, 1815-1830, **$500-800.**

Pattern-molded globular bottle, American, 1815-1830, **$600-800.**

Pattern-molded globular bottle,
American, 1815-1830, **$375-475.**

Freeblown Globular Bottle, medium green, 8-7/8", open pontil, applied string lip, American 1770-1800 . . . . **$160-200**

Freeblown Globular Bottle, medium yellow olive green, 8-1/4", open pontil, outward lip, American 1770-1800 . . . . . . **$325-400**

Freeblown Flattened Globular Bottle, bluish aqua, 9-1/2", pontil-scarred base, applied sloping collar mouth, American 1780-1810 . . . . **$85-125**

Freeblown Flattened Globular Bottle, bluish aqua, 10-1/4", pontil-scarred base, applied sloping collar mouth, American 1780-1810. . . . . **$85-125**

Freeblown Teardrop Flask, medium sapphire blue, 4-1/2", pontil-scarred base, tooled lip, European 1780-1820. . . . . . . **$120-150**

Globular Bottle, medium amber, 7-3/4", 24-rib pattern swirled to left, pontil-scarred base, rolled lip, American 1815-1835 . . . . **$525-700**

Globular Bottle, yellow amber with olive tone, 7-3/4", 24-vertical rib pattern, pontil-scarred base, outward rolled lip, American 1815-1835. . . . . **$1,300-1,600**

Globular Bottle, medium golden amber, 8-1/8", 24-rib pattern swirled to right, pontil-scarred base, outward rolled lip, American 1815-1835 . . . . **$260-350**

Midwestern Chestnut Flask, yellow amber, 24-vertical rib pattern, 4-1/2", pontil-scarred base, sheared and tooled lip, American 1915-1835 (Zanesville Glassworks). **$285-375**

Midwestern Chestnut Flask, medium golden amber, 24-rib pattern swirled to right, 5-1/4", pontil-scarred base, sheared and tooled lip, American 1915-1835 . . . . **$325-400**

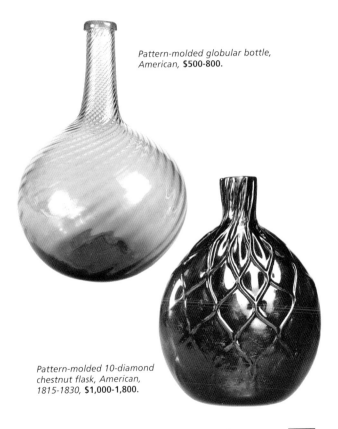

Pattern-molded globular bottle,
American, **$500-800**.

Pattern-molded 10-diamond
chestnut flask, American,
1815-1830, **$1,000-1,800**.

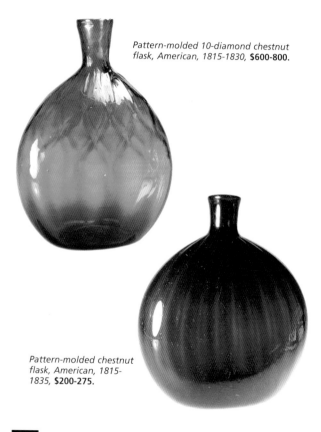

Pattern-molded 10-diamond chestnut flask, American, 1815-1830, **$600-800.**

Pattern-molded chestnut flask, American, 1815-1835, **$200-275.**

Midwestern Club Bottle, deep bluish aqua, 8-1/8", 23-rib pattern swirled to right, pontil-scarred base, applied mouth, American 1815-1835 . . . .**$185-275**

Midwestern Cruet, light green, 5-7/8", 18-rib pattern swirled to right, open pontil, tooled mouth, American 1820-1835.**$260-350**

Midwestern Elongated Chestnut Flask, light emerald green, 24-vertical rib-pattern, 5-3/4", pontil-scarred base, sheared lip, American 1815-1835 . . . .**$225-300**

Midwestern Flattened Globular Bottle, deep blue aqua, 25-swirl rib pattern to right, 9", applied mouth, American 1815-1845 . . . .**$120-140**

Midwestern Handled Globular Bottle, medium amber, 6-5/8", 24-broken rib pattern swirled to right, pontil-scarred base, applied mouth and handle, American 1820-1835 (one of the rarest and most desirable Midwestern glass items) **$25,000-30,000**

Midwestern Handled Jug, deep amber, 4-3/4", pontil-scarred base, tooled mouth, applied handle, American 1820-1835 (rare – Zanesville Glassworks) **$385-475**

Midwestern Globular Bottle, deep bluish aqua, 24-swirl rib pattern to right, 7-3/8", pontil-scarred base, outward rolled lip, American 1815-1835 . . . .**$250-300**

Midwestern Globular Bottle, medium amber, 8-1/8", pontil-scarred base, applied lip, American 1815-1835 . . . .**$385-475**

Midwestern Globular Swirl Bottle, golden yellow amber, 8-3/8", 24-rib pattern swirled to right, pontil-scarred base, rolled lip, American 1812-1835 . . . .**$550-800**

Midwestern Melon Ribbed Flask, medium blue green, 5-7/8", 16-vertical rib pattern, pontil-scarred base, tooled lip, American 1820-1835 . . . .**$210-300**

Pattern-molded pocket flask, American, 1815-1835, **$700-900.**

Rib-pattern pocket flask, European, 1818-1820, **$400-700.**

Nailsea Flask, clear glass with white opalescent loops, 8-1/8", vertical bands of applied rigaree on each side, pontil-scarred base, tooled lip, English 1850-1880 . . . . **$90-140**

Nailsea Flask, yellow amber with white looping, 5-3/8", pontil-scarred base, tooled mouth, English 1820-1850 . . . . . **$185-300**

Nailsea Flask, clear glass with white and blue alternating looping, 7-1/4", pontil-scarred base, tooled mouth, American 1850-1870 . . . . **$385-475**

Nailsea Flask – Rib Pattern, red and yellow over milk glass, 7", 12-rib pattern swirled to right, pontil-scarred base, tooled mouth, English 1860-1880 . . . . **$150-180**

Pattern Molded Bottle, light olive green, 4-1/4", 16-rib pattern swirled to right, pontil-scarred base, tooled lip, American 1820-1835 . . . . **$260-350**

Pattern Molded Oil Bottle, greenish aqua, 16-swirl rib pattern to left, 12-1/4", smooth base, deep kick-up, applied mouth, European 1850-1865 . . . . **$135-150**

Pattern Molded Chestnut, yellow amber with olive tone, 6-5/8", 15-broken rib pattern, pontil-scarred base, applied mouth, American 1820-1835 . . . . **$650-800**

Pattern Molded Flask, medium green, 7-3/4", 20-ogival pattern, open pontil, sheared lip, American 1820-1835 . . . . . . **$550-700**

Pinch Sided Spirits Bottle, clear glass, 7-3/8", pontil-scarred base with applied foot, tooled top, European 1780-1830 . . . **$225-300**

Pitkin Flask, yellow olive, 5-3/8", 36-broken rib pattern swirled to right, open pontil, sheared and tooled lip, American 1780-1820 . . . . **$625-800**

Pattern-molded cruet, American, 1810-1830, **$300-450.**

Pitkin Flask, deep emerald green, 6-3/8", 30-broken rib pattern swirled to left, pontil-scarred base, tooled mouth, American 1780-1810. . . . .**$190-275**

Pitkin Flask, medium yellow green, 6-1/4", 32-broken rib pattern swirled to right, pontil-scarred base, tooled mouth, American 1780-1810. . . . .**$660-750**

Pocket Flask, clear glass, 4-3/4", vertical rib pattern, pontil-scarred base, tooled lip, German 1780-1830 . . . .**$170-250**

Pocket Flask, clear glass, 5", overall diamond pattern, pontil-scarred base, outward rolled lip, German 1780-1830 . . . .**$160-250**

Rib Pattern Cruciform-Type Bottle/Decanter, clear glass with amethyst tint, 8-5/8", rib pattern swirled to right, pontil-scarred base, applied string lip, American 1750-1780 . . . .**$360-450**

Rib Pattern Flask, medium purple amethyst, 3-1/2", 18-vertical rib pattern, pontil-scarred base, tooled mouth, European 1815-1835 . . . .**$285-450**

Rib Pattern Pocket Flask, medium green, 20-vertical rib pattern, pontil-scarred base, applied mouth, European 1800-1830 (possibly German). **$325-400**

Rib Pattern Chestnut Spirits Flask, medium cobalt blue, 7-1/2", 24-vertical rib pattern, pontil-scarred base, tooled mouth, German 1780-1820 . . . .**$280-450**

Rib Pattern Flask, medium cobalt blue, half-pint, 5-1/2", 16-vertical rib pattern on both sides, pontil-scarred base, tooled lip, American 1840-1850 (rare in this color) **$1,100-1,500**

Fire Grenades

Fire grenades are highly prized among bottle collectors and represent one of the first modern improvements in fire fighting. A fire grenade is a bottle about the size of a baseball filled with water. Its use was simple. When thrown into a fire, it would break and spread its contents, hopefully extinguishing the flames. The fire grenades usually worked best when the fire was noticed immediately.

The first American patent on a fire grenade was issued in 1863 to Alanson Crane of Fortress Monroe, Virginia. The best-known manufacturer of these specialized bottles was the Halden Fire Extinguisher Co., Chicago, Illinois, which was awarded a patent in August 1871.

The grenades were manufactured in large numbers by companies with names as unique as the bottles themselves: Dash-Out, Diamond, Harkness Fire Destroyer, Hazelton's High Pressure Chemical Firekeg, Magic Fire, and Y-Burn. The fire grenade became obsolete with the invention of the fire extinguisher in 1905. Many of these grenades can still be found with the original closures, contents, and labels.

Babcock – Hand Grenade – Non-Freezing – Manf'd By Fire Extinguisher M'f'g Co – 325-331 S. Des Plaines St. Chicago, medium cobalt blue, 7-1/2", smooth base, sheared and ground lip, American 1875-1895 (rare) **$3,100-4,000**

Babcock – Hand Grenade – Non-Freezing-Manufactured By American-La France Fire Engine Co – Elmira, N.Y., medium amber, 7-1/2", smooth base, ground lip, American 1875-1895 (Note: rare Babcock from Elmira N.Y. These grenades were made only for a short time by the American – La France Fire Engine Co. of Elmira. Today, American La France is one of the major manufacturers of fire fighting equipment) **$2,100-3,000**

Deutsche-Loschgranate – Eberhardt, yellow amber, 14-sides, 8", smooth base (Gesetzlich-Geschutzt), sheared and ground lip, German 1910-1930 (very rare) **$430-600**

Fire Grenade – Vertical Rib-Pattern, medium green, 5-1/2", smooth base, ABM mouth, English 1910-1920 (rare) **$285-375**

Fire Grenade – Vertical Rib-Pattern, cobalt blue, 6-1/4", smooth base, tooled mouth, American 1880-1895 . . . . **$370-400**

Fire Grenade, medium amber, 6-1/2", smooth base, tooled lip, back panel is flat with center groove, American 1880-1900 (rare – had a metal holder allowing it to be hung on a wall) **$385-500**

Fire Grenade – C & NW RY (Chicago & Northwestern Railroad), clear glass, 17-3/4", smooth base, sheared lip, American 1880-1900 . . . . **$180-275**

Grenade – Extincteur – Systeme – Labbe – L'Incombustibilite Paris, yellow amber, 5", smooth base, ground lip, original contents, French 1880-1890 . . . . **$325-400**

Grenade – L'Urbaine, cobalt blue, rib-pattern, 6-1/2", smooth base, ground lip, French 1880-1900 (scarce) **$425-600**

Hayward's Hand Fire
Grenade - S.F. Hayward -
407 - Broadway - New York
- Patented Aug. 8 1871, 1871-
1890, 6-1/8", **$350-475.**

Hayward's Hand Fire
Grenade - S.F. Hayward -
407 - Broadway - New York
- Patented Aug. 8 1871, 1875-
1895, 6-1/8", **$200-300.**

Hazelton's - High
Pressure -Chemical
- Fire Keg, American,
1880-1900, **$250-300.**

Hayward Hand Grenade Fire Extinguisher – New York, pale aqua, pint, 6", smooth base (Design Patd), tooled lip, original contents, American 1875-1885 . . . . **$285-375**

Hayward Hand Grenade Fire Extinguisher – New York (Pleated Panel Grenade), cobalt blue, pint, 6", smooth base (Design Patd), tooled lip, original contents, American 1875-1885 (pleated panel is more scarce than diamond panel) **$330-400**

Hayward Hand Grenade Fire Extinguisher – New York, medium grass green, 6", smooth base (Design Patd), embossed neck foil has Trade Mark and Hayward Hand Fire Grenade tooled lip, original contents, American 1875-1885 . . . . **$650-800**

Hayward – Hand Fire – Grenade – Patented – Aug 8 1871 – S.F. Hayward – 407 – Broadway – New York, turquoise blue, 6-1/4", smooth base, tooled lip, American 1871-1895 . . **$360-450**

Harden's Improved Grenade Fire Extinguisher Patd. Oct. 7th 1884, two piece grenade wired together, half is cobalt blue, half is clear, 4-3/4", smooth base, ground lip, American 1885-1895 (rare) **$385-475**

Harden's Hand – Grenade – Fire – Extinguisher – Patented – No. 7 – Aug 8 1871 – Aug 14 1883, smoky light green, 6-1/4", smooth footed base, tooled mouth, American 1875-1895 (rare color) **$425-600**

Harden's Hand – Grenade – Fire- Extinguisher – Patented – No. 2 – Aug. 8 1871 – Aug 14 1883, turquoise blue, 5-1/8", smooth footed base, rough sheared and ground lip, American 1875-1895 . . . . **$200-250**

Harden's Hand – Grenade – Fire – Extinguisher – Patented, lavender blue, 4-7/8", smooth footed base, rough sheared lip, American 1875-1895 . . . . **$260-350**

Harden's Hand – Grenade – Fire- Extinguisher – Patented – No. 2 – Aug 8 1871 – Aug 14 1883, light sapphire blue, 5-1/4", smooth footed base, rough sheared and ground lip, American 1875-1895 . . . . **$185-250**

Harkness – Fire – Destroyer, medium sapphire blue, 6-1/4", smooth base, ground lip, original contents, American 1880-1900 . . . . **$550-700**

Harkness – Fire Extinguisher, medium cobalt blue, horizontal rib-pattern, 6-1/8", smooth base, ground lip, American 1880-1900 . . . . **$650-800**

Harkness – Fire Extinguisher, medium blue, horizontal rib-pattern, 6-1/8", smooth base, ground lip, American 1880-1900 (scarce) **$550-700**

Harkness – Fire – Destroyer (label: Patented Sept. 19th 1874 and February 1878, Improved 1881), cobalt blue, horizontal rib-pattern, 6-1/4", smooth base, ground lip, American 1871-1895 . . . . **$260-300**

HSN (Harvey S. Nutting – monogram on two diamond panels), yellow with amber tone, 7", grooved smooth base, rough sheared lip, American 1880-1890 . . . . **$190-200**

Imperial Grenade – Fire – Extinguisher, medium emerald green, 6-1/2", smooth base, ground lip, English 1880-1900. . **$385-475**

Magic – Fire – Extinguisher Co., yellow with amber tone, 6-1/4", smooth base, rough sheared lip, American 1875-1895 **$625-800**

PSH (monogram on two diamond panels), yellow amber, 7", grooved smooth base, tooled lip, American 1880-1890 **$270-350**

Rockford – Kalamazoo – Automatic and – Hand Fire Extinguisher – Patent Applied For, deep cobalt blue, 10-3/4", smooth base, tooled mouth, original contents, American 1875-1895 . . . . **$425-600**

Star (inside star) Harden Star Hand Grenade - Fire Extinguisher, Label: How To Use, Throw the Grenade into the Hottest Part of the Fire (English), 1880-1900, 7", $250-350.

Systeme - Labbe (motif of anchor) Grenade - Extincteur (diamond pattern inside four circular panels) L'Incombustibilite - Paris (French), 1880-1900, 5-7/8", $275-375.

Soda-Acid Fire Extinguisher Bottle – Acid Line – Manufactured By – Badger Fire – Extinguisher Co. – Boston, Mass. – U.S.A., clear, 6", smooth base, tooled mouth, American 1890-1900 . . . . **$110-125**

Star (inside star on flat panel) – Harden Star Hand Grenade – Fire Extinguisher, deep cobalt blue, pint, 6-1/2", smooth base (REGD – NO – 10490), ground lip, original contents, English 1884-1895 . . . . **$260-350**

Star (inside star on flat panel) – Harden Star Hand Grenade – Fire Extinguisher, brilliant green, quart, 7-7/8", smooth base (M 7 84), ground lip, original contents, American 1884-1895 . . . . **$210-250**

Star (inside star on flat panel) – Harden Star Hand Grenade – Fire Extinguisher, deep blue, pint, 6-5/8", smooth base ground lip, original contents, American 1884-1895 . . . . **$210-250**

Star (inside a star) – Harden Grenade – Sprinkler, deep cobalt blue, 17-1/4", smooth base (RD No 60064), tooled lip, English 1880-1900 (scarce) **$725-900**

Systeme – Labbe (motif of anchor) Grenade – Extincteur (diamond pattern inside four circular panels) L'Incombustibilite – Paris, golden yellow amber, 5-7/8", smooth base, ground lip, French 1880-1900 . . . . **$285-375**

The Kalamazoo – Automatic and – Hand Fire Extinguisher – Patent Applied For, cobalt blue, 10-7/8", smooth base, tooled mouth, American 1875-1895 . . . . **$325-400**

W.D. Allen Manufacturing Company – Chicago, Illinois (crescent moon), medium yellowish green, 8-1/4", smooth base, ground lip, American 1875-1895 (rare in this color) . . **$550-700**

Flasks

Flasks are popular among collectors because they display a great variety of decorative, historical, and pictorial depictions. The outstanding colors have had a major effect on the value of these pieces, more than on most other collectible bottles.

Early American flasks were first manufactured by the Pitkin Glasshouse in Connecticut around 1815, and quickly spread to other glasshouses around the country. Early flasks were free-blown and represent some of the better craftsmanship, with more intricate designs. By 1850, approximately 400 designs had been used. The bottles made during that time had black graphite pontil marks on the bottom. The pontils were coated with powdered iron, allowing the flasks' bottom to break away without damaging the glass. The flasks made between 1850 and 1870 had no such markings because of the widespread use of the newly invented snapcase.

Since flasks were designed to be refilled with whiskey or other spirits, more time and effort was taken in their manufacture than with most other types of bottles. Flasks soon became a popular item with all types of causes and promotions. Mottos were frequently embossed on flasks and included a number of patriotic sayings and slogans. One of the more controversial flasks was the Masonic flask, which bore the order's emblem on one side and the American eagle on the other. Public feelings were strong against the Masonic symbol, but the controversy soon passed. Masonic flasks are now a specialty item for collectors.

Another highly collectible flask was the Pitkin-type flasks named for the Pitkin Glassworks, where they were exclusively manufactured. While Pitkin-type flask and ink bottles are common, the bottles, jugs, and jars are very rare. German Pitkin flasks are heavier and straight-ribbed, while the American patterns are swirled and broken-ribbed with unusual colors such as dark blue.

George Washington was often depicted on the flasks, as were the candidates for the presidential elections of 1824 and 1828, which promoted John Quincy Adams and Andrew Jackson. Other events of the time also were represented on these flasks. Because of their use in promoting various political and special interest agendas, flasks created an important historical record of the people and events of the times.

Adams & Jefferson July 4 A.D. 1776 – General Washington – Bust of Washington – Kensington Glass Works Philadelphia – E. Pluribus Unum – Eagle – T.W.D., medium blue green, pint, pontil-scarred base, sheared lip, American 1825-1835 (Note: Commemorates the death of Presidents Thomas Jefferson and John Adams). **$4,600-6,500**

A – Merry – Christmas (girl on a barrel) – And A – Happy New Year – Cock on Barrel Staves (pictorial flask), light yellow amber, pint, smooth base, tooled double collared top, American 1880-1900 (extremely rare) **$550-1,000**

American System – Paddle Wheeler – Use Me But Do Not Abuse Me – Sheaf of Wheat, greenish aqua, pint, pontil-scarred base, rough sheared lip, American 1824-1828 (Note: a sought after historic flask that was blown in the Page & Bakewell Glasshouse in Pittsburgh to commemorate the passing of the Protective Tariff Act of 1824) **$15,000-20,000**

Andy Balich – 170 Pacific Ave. – Santa Cruz, Cal. – Net Contents 6 Oz., aqua, half-pint, smooth base, tooled mouth, American 1908-1918 . . . . **$80-95**

Arnett G. Smith – 14 – Fulton – St – New York (strapside flask – partial label reading Irish Whiskey – Arnett G. Smith), amber, quart, smooth base, tooled double collar mouth, American 1885-1910 . . . . **$85-100**

Baltimore – Anchor – Glassworks – Sheaf of Grain, orange amber, quart, pontil-scarred base, sheared and tooled lip, American 1865-1875 . . . . **$650-800**

Booth & Co. – Sacramento (embossed anchor), clear, pint, smooth base, tooled mouth, American 1890-1903 (rare) **$110-125**

*Baltimore Glass Works - Bust of Washington
- Classical Bust, American, 1825-1840,* **$375-500.**

Bridgeton New Jersey – Bust of Washington – Bridgeton New Jersey – Bust of Taylor, bluish aqua, quart, pontil-scarred base, tooled mouth, American 1820-1835 . . . .**$130-175**

C.C. Goodale – Full 1/2 Pt – Rochester N.Y, golden yellow amber, half-pint, smooth base, tooled mouth, American 1880-1890 (scarce) **$150-180**

C.C. Goodale – Full Pt – Rochester N.Y., medium apple green, pint, smooth base, tooled mouth, American 1885-1890 (rare in this color) **$425-600**

Civil War Period Whiskey Flask – E. Wattis Jr – Philada (on base), clear glass, pint, upper half wrapped in leather, smooth base, ground lip, American 1860-1870 . . . .**$185-275**

Cluster of Grapes – Coat of Arms, lime green, half-pint, pontil-scarred base, tooled lip, European 1850-1890. . . . .**$80-125**

Coffin Flask (unembossed), deep opalescent milk glass, pint, smooth base, tooled mouth, American 1880-1900 . . . .**$160-200**

Concentric Ring Eagle – Eagle Flask, medium yellow green, quart, pontil-scarred base, tooled lip, American 1825-1835 (rare) **$6,300-9,000**

Corn For The World – Ear-of-Corn – Monument, clear glass with amethyst tint, quart, pontil-scarred base, sheared lip, American 1825-1835 . . . .**$650-800**

Cornucopia – Urn, golden yellow amber, half-pint, pontil-scarred base, tooled lip, American 1825-1835 . . . .**$150-180**

Cornucopia – Urn, bluish aqua, pint, pontil-scarred base, tooled mouth, American 1840-1850 . . . .**$260-350**

Cornucopia – Urn, deep blue green, pint, open pontil, tooled lip, American 1835-1845 (scarce color). **$500-600**

Bust of Washington - Tree, American, 1855-1865, **$15,000-25,000** *(extremely rare - only three known to be in existence).*

Bust of Washington - Bust of Taylor, American, 1849-1855, **$800-1,500.**

Bust of Byron - Bust of Scott, American, 1825-1835, **$350-450.**

Cunninghams & Ihmsen – Glassmakers Pittsburgh, PA, bluish aqua, strapside pint, smooth base, applied mouth, American 1880-1890 . . . . **$120-150**

D. Kirkpatrick & Co – Eagle – Chattanooga – Tenn, greenish aqua, quart, smooth base, applied mouth, American 1865-1880 (extremely rare Tennessee flask) **$2,600-3,500**

Dancer – Chapman – Soldier – Balt. MD, olive green, pint, smooth base, applied ring mouth, American 1865-1875 (desirable color) **$1,900-2,800**

Dancer – Chapman – Soldier – Balt. MD, teal blue, pint, smooth base, applied mouth, American 1865-1875 . . . . **$255-350**

Eagle – Coffin & Hay – Standing Deer – Hammonton, aqua, pint, pontil-scarred base, sheared and tooled lip, American 1825-1835 (scarce - South Jersey Glasshouse) **$385-475**

Eagle – Continental – Indian Shooting Bire – Cunninghams & Co – Pittsburgh, PA, deep yellow green, quart, smooth base, applied square collar mouth, American 1865-1875 **$2,600-3,500**

Eagle – Continental – Indian Shooting Bire – Cunninghams & Co – Pittsburgh, PA, deep aqua, quart, smooth base, applied collar mouth, American 1860-1875 . . . . **$225-300**

Eagle – Geo. A. Berry & Co. – Eagle, bluish aqua, pint, smooth base, applied ringed lip, American 1860-1870 . . . . **$130-180**

Eagle – Eagle, yellow amber, half-pint, pontil-scarred base, sheared and tooled lip, American 1855-1870 . . . . **$130-140**

Eagle – Farley & Taylor – Richmond, KY, greenish aqua, gallon, open pontil, tooled mouth, American 1830-1840 . . . . **$5,100-7,000**

Dyottville Glass Works Philada. - The Father of His Country - Bust of Washington - Gen. Taylor Never Surrenders - Bust of Taylor, American, 1849-1855, **$275-450.**

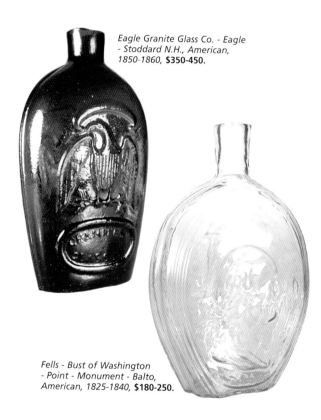

Eagle Granite Glass Co. - Eagle - Stoddard N.H., American, 1850-1860, **$350-450.**

Fells - Bust of Washington - Point - Monument - Balto, American, 1825-1840, **$180-250.**

Easley's (motif of hand) – Saloon – Huntsville – Rough & (man walking with bottle in hand) Ready – H. Easley's, aqua, half pint, 6-3/8", smooth base, applied ringed mouth, American 1860-1870 . . . . **$5,600-7,000**

Flower – Heart, blue green, quart, pontil-scarred base, sheared lip, American 1845-1860 (rare) **$2,600-3,500**

For Pike's Peak – Prospector – Eagle – Pittsburgh PA, deep bluish aqua, pint, smooth base, applied mouth, American 1965-1875. . . . . **$120-175**

French Brandy – From – F.L. Allan – 33 State Street New London, Conn (labeled whiskey flask), reddish amber, pint, smooth base, applied double collared mouth, American 1860-1866 (New London Glass Works, New London, CT) **$260-500**

Frigate – Franklin – Free Trade and Sailors Rights – Masonic Arch – Kensington Glass Works Philadelphia, pale greenish aqua, pint, pontil-scarred base, tooled lip, American 1825-1835 . . . . **$210-275**

Granite – Glass – Co. – Stoddard – N.H., olive amber, pint, pontil-scarred base, sheared and tooled lip, American 1850-1865 . . . . **$360-450**

Hendricks (bust of Hendricks) – Cleveland (bust of Cleveland), clear glass, pint pumpkinseed flask, smooth base (J.R. Hartigans – Patent, Pitts), tooled mouth American 1884 (Note: rare political flask made for 1884 presidential campaign between Grover Cleveland and James Blaine **$750-900**

Hourglass Masonic Flask, light yellow olive, swirl of amber at base, half-pint, pontil-scarred, sheared mouth, American 1814-1830 (Coventry Glass Works, Coventry, CT) **$6,200-12,000**

Horse Pulling Cart – Eagle, yellow olive, pint, pontil-scarred base, sheared and tooled lip, American 1825-1835 . . . . **$210-250**

Hunter – Hound (handled), medium amber, pint, pontil-scarred base, tooled lip and pour spout, American 1855-1870 (rare – only a few known to exist) **$7,200-8,000**

Iron Front (motif of steer's head) Neff & Duff – Austin Texas, clear glass with amethystine tint, pint, cobweb pattern, 6-5/8", smooth base, tooled mouth, American 1879-1881 (most desirable Texas flask) **$6,300-8,000**

Isabella – Anchor – Glassworks – Glass Factory, aqua green, quart, 9-3/8", open pontil, applied collar mouth, American 1865-1875 . . . . **$285-375**

Jno. F. Horne – Knoxville, Tenn (strapside flask), amber, quart, smooth base, applied mouth, American 1885-1910 . . . . . **$85-100**

Liberty – Eagle – Willington – Glass – Co – West Willington – Conn, medium blue green, half-pint, smooth base, applied double collar mouth, American 1856-1875 . . . . **$525-700**

L.N. Kreinbrook's – Bitters – Mt. Pleasant – PA (flask bitters bottle), bright yellow amber, pint, coffin-shaped form, smooth base, tooled sloping collared mouth with ring, American 1860-1890 . . . . **$800-1,500**

Log Cabin – Hard Cider (below flag, barrel, and plow), deep blue aqua, pint, pontil-scarred base, sheared lip, American 1840-1845 (made for William Henry Harrison's presidential campaign of 1840) **$6,200-8,000**

Louis Kossuth – Bust of Kossuth – Frigate – U.S. Steam Frigate – Mississippi – S. Huffsey, medium blue green, calabash, pontil-scarred base (Dolphin Mould Maker – Nth 5t St 84), applied sloping collar mouth, American 1850-1860 . . . . **$1,300-1,800**

Jenny Lind - Bust of Jenny Lind - Fislervile Glass Works - Glass Factory, American, 1855-1865, **$600-800.**

Jenny Lind - Bust of Jenny Lind - Glasshouse, American, 1855-1865, **$300-400.**

In Silver We Trust - Bust of Bryan - Bryan 1896 Sewall - United Democratic Ticket - We Shall Vote - American Eagle, American, 1896, **$600-800** *(rare political flasks made for the presidential election of 1896).*

Label-under-glass pocket flask, American, 1885-1900, **$250-350.**

Label-under-glass pocket flask, American,
1885-1900, **$250-350**.

Label-under-glass handled flask,
American, 1880-1900, **$120-180**.

LaFayette - Bust of LaFayette - S&C - Dewitt Clinton Bust of Clinton - C - T, American, 1825-1830, **$700-1,000.**

Kossuth - Bust of Kossuth - Tree, American, 1855-1865, **$180-275.**

Masonic Arch – Eagle, medium blue green, pint, pontil-scarred base, tooled mouth, American 1815-1825 (rare) . . **$3,600-4,500**

Masonic Arch – Zanesville – Eagle – Ohio (inside oval) J. Shepard & Co., bright yellow olive, pint, pontil-scarred base, tooled mouth, American 1825-1835 . . . . **$3,100-4,000**

M'Carty & Torreyson – Manufacturers – Wellsburg, VA (sunburst), light blue apple green, quart, iron pontil, sheared lip, American 1845-1855 (very rare) **$1,900-2,800**

Mohns & Kaltenbach – M & K – 29 Market Street – San Francisco, clear, pint, smooth base, tooled mouth, American 1890-1910 (rare) **$135-150**

Monument – A – Little – More – Grape – Capt Bragg, medium yellow olive, half-pint, pontil-scarred base, sheared and tooled lip, American 1825-1835 (rare color). **$2,600-3,500**

Nailsea Flask, clear glass with white loopings, 8-3/8", pontil-scarred base, tooled mouth, English 1840-1860 . . . . **$360-450**

Newmark Gruenberg & Co. – Old Judge Pony S.F., clear, pint, smooth base, tooled mouth, American 1900-1910 (rare) **$110-150**

Octopus Draped Over Silver Dollar Flask, milk glass, 4-1/2", smooth base, ground lip, metal screw-on cap, American 1901 (1901 is embossed near the base) **$600-900**

Our Choice – Bust of Cleveland Facing Bust of Stevenson – Cleve & Steve – November 8th 92 – March 4th 93 – Rooster, aqua, half-pint, smooth base, tooled mouth, American 1892 (made for the 1892 presidential campaign) **$270-350**

Pocket Spirits Flask (walking bear on one side and trees and the date 1851), clear glass with copper wheel cut decoration, pontil-scarred base, wide outward rolled lip, German 1851 . . . . . **$260-350**

Republican Gratitude – General La Fayette – Bust of La Fayette – Kensington Glass Works Philadelphia – E. Pluribus Unum – Eagle – T.W.D, aqua, pint, 6-5/8", open pontil, tooled and sheared lip, American 1825-1830 (scarce – Kensington Glassworks) **$330-400**

S (motif of palm tree) C – Dispensary, clear glass, 6-3/4", smooth base, tooled mouth, American 1893-1900 . . . .**$50-70**

SCD (monogram) – S.C. – Dispensary, clear glass, 6-3/4", smooth base, tooled mouth, American 1893-1900 . . . . . .**$50-70**

SCD (monogram) – S.C. – Dispensary, clear glass, 7-7/8", smooth base (C.F.F.C.CO.), tooled mouth, American 1893-1900 . . . .**$50-70**

Schwan – Paterson – N.J. (strapside flask), amber, quart, smooth base, tooled double collar mouth, American 1885-1910 . . . .**$85-100**

Scroll Flask (corset waist), medium blue green, pint, pontil-scarred base, sheared lip, American 1840-1850. . . . . . .**$260-300**

Scroll Flask, medium yellow apple green, quart, red iron pontil, sheared lip, American 1840-1850 (scarce color) **$650-800**

Scroll Flask, ice blue, pint, iron pontil, applied mouth, American 1840-1850 . . . .**$160-200**

Scroll Flask, deep amber, pint, pontil-scarred base, sheared and tooled mouth, American 1840-1850 . . . .**$550-700**

Scroll Flask – JR. & S. – Anchor, yellow green, half pint, pontil-scarred base, tooled mouth, American 1845-1860 (extremely rare color) **$4,200-6,000**

Scroll Flask – Louisville – Glass Works, medium yellow amber, pint, red iron pontil, ground lip, American 1845-1860 .**$450-600**

North American (inside a map of North America) - Pan American - South American (inside a map of South America), American, 1901, **$300-400**.

Seeing Eye Inside a Star - AD - Flexed Arm Inside a Star - GRJA, American, 1835-1845, **$350-450**.

Scroll flask, American, 1840-1850, **$2,000-3,000** *(rare in this color).*

Sheaf of Grain – Star, light to medium teal blue, calabash, iron pontil, applied double collar mouth, American 1850-1860 ....**$380-475**

Sheets & Duffy – Kensington, bluish aqua, strapside quart, 8-1/2", smooth base, applied ringed lip, American 1870-1880 .**$260-350**

Sitting Dog – Stag's Head with Horn and Rifle, cobalt blue, quart, pontil-scarred base, tooled lip, European 1850-1860 ....**$80-125**

Spring Garden – Anchor – Glass Works – Log Cabin, yellow olive, pint, 7-3/4", open pontil, sheared lip, American 1865-1875 ....**$1,100-2,000**

Standing Soldier – Sunflower, deep bluish aqua, calabash, iron pontil, applied mouth, American 1855-1865 (scarce) ..**$400-550**

Strapside Flask, yellow olive, quart, smooth base (A.&D.H.C.) applied ring collar mouth, American 1875-1885 (rare color) **$150-180**

Strapside Flask, dark amber, pint, smooth base, ground lip, metal screw cap, American 1875-1900 ....**$85-120**

Success to the Railroad – Locomotive, medium cobalt blue, pint, pontil-scarred base, sheared lip, American 1830-1840 ....**$5,100-7,000**

Sunburst Flask, greenish aqua, pint, pontil-scarred base, sheared lip, American 1825-1835 ....**$285-375**

Sunburst Flask, blue green, half-pint, pontil-scarred base, tooled lip, American 1820-1835 ....**$325-400**

Sunburst Flask, aqua, half-pint, 5-5/8", open pontil, sheared lip, American 1840-1850 ....**$325-400**

Sunburst Flask (wide mouth) – Keene – P & W, yellow olive amber, half-pint, pontil-scarred base, tooled expanded mouth, American 1815-1835 (rare) **$5,200-7,000**

Sunburst Flask – M'Carty & Torreyson – Manufacturers – Weburg, VA , deep bluish aqua, pint, red iron pontil, sheared lip, American 1845-1860 . . . . **$1,100-1,500**

Sunburst Flask – Schooner, aqua, half-pint, pontil-scarred base, sheared lip, American 1820-1835 . . . . **$150-160**

Token Flask (pocket flask with a United States quarter attached to an indented panel), deep teal green, 5-3/4", smooth base, tooled mouth, original metal and cork stopper with time screw shot-glass cover, American 1890-1910 . . . . **$110-150**

Sunburst flask, American, 1815-1830, $600-800.

Traveler's – Companion – Star (label: Bourbon Whisky, F. French & Son, Wholesale Druggists, Union Block, Hillsdale, Mich), medium amber in lower half shading to a pure yellow in the upper half, half-pint, iron pontil, sheared and tooled lip, American 1860-1870 . . . . **$650-800**

Tree – Tree, bluish aqua, half-pint, smooth base, applied double collar mouth, American 1860-1870 . . . . **$160-200**

Union – Clasped Hands and Mason's Compass – Eagle, bluish aqua, half-pint, smooth base, applied mouth, American 1865-1875 . . . . **$90-120**

Union – (pair of flags and three embossed bottles) Bottle – Reverse Plain Flask, clear glass, pint, smooth base, applied sloping collared mouth with ring, American 1880-1900 **$230-400**

W. Ihmsen's – Eagle – Glass – Agriculture – Sheaf of Grain and Tools, light green, pint, open pontil, sheared and tooled lip, American 1835-1845 . . . . **$1,500-1,800**

Waterford – Clasped Hands – Eagle, aqua, quart, 8-7/8", smooth base, applied double collar mouth, American 1865-1875 . . . . **$185-275**

Westford Glass Co – Westford – Conn – Sheaf of Wheat, olive green, pint, smooth base, applied double collar mouth, American 1865-1875 . . . . **$130-160**

Woman on Bicycle – Eagle – A – DHC (inside oval), bright yellow olive, pint, smooth base, applied square collar mouth, American 1865-1875 . . . . **$1,100-1,500**

Zanesville – City – Glass Works, aqua, strapside pint, smooth base, applied mouth, American 1875-1895 . . . . **$130-175**

Fruit Jars

Unlike food bottles, fruit jars were sold empty for use in home preservation of many different types of food. The use of fruit jars was predominant in the 1800s when fresh foodstuffs were not always available. Prepackaged and home canning were the only options. Although fruit jars carry no product or advertising, they aren't necessarily common or plain, since the bottle manufacturers' name is usually embossed in large lettering along with the patent date. The manufacturer whose advertising campaign gave fruit jars

their name was Thomas W. Dyott, who was in the market early selling fruit jars by 1829.

In the first 50 years, the most common closure was a cork sealed with wax. In 1855, an inverted saucer-like lid was invented that could be inserted into the jar to provide an airtight seal. The Hero Glassworks invented the glass lid in 1856 and improved on it in 1858 with a zinc lid invented by John Landis Mason, who also produced fruit jars. Because the medical profession warned that zinc could be harmful, Hero Glassworks developed a glass lid for the Mason jar in 1868. Mason eventually transferred his patent rights to the Consolidated Fruit Jar Company, which let the patent expire. In 1880, the Ball Brothers began distributing Mason jars, and in 1898 the use of a semi-automatic bottle machine increased the output of the Mason jar until the automatic machine was invented in 1903.

Fruit jars come in a wide variety of sizes and colors, commonly aqua and clear. The rarer jars were made in a variety of colors such as blue, amber, black, milk glass, green, and purple.

A.G. Smalley & Co – Patented – April 7th 1896 – Boston & New York (on base), amber, quart, smooth base, ground lip, American 1895-1910 . . . . **$50-70**

A. Stone & Co. – Philad'a, bluish aqua, half-pint, 5-7/8", smooth base, applied mouth, A. Stone & Co. – Philad'a (on closure), American 1855-1865 . . . . **$550-700**

Atlas – Strong Shoulder Mason, light green, quart, smooth base, ABM lips, American 1925-1940 . . . . **$35-45**

Atlas – Strong Shoulder Mason, light olive, quart, smooth base, ABM lips, American 1925-1940 . . . . **$30-45**

Atlas – Strong Shoulder Mason, light olive yellow, quart, smooth base, ABM lips, American 1925-1940 . . . . **$30-45**

Atlas – Strong Shoulder Mason, cornflower blue, quart, smooth base, ABM lip, American 1925-1940 . . . . **$75-100**

Bee, aquamarine, quart, smooth base, ground mouth, American 1869-1880 . . . . **$550-1,000**

Atherholt, Fisher & Co. - Philada, American, 1862-1870, **$400-600.**

Baltimore - Glass Works, American, 1855-1860, **$700-900.**

Beaver (beaver chewing a log), Canadian 1880-1895, **$150-250.**

Bloeser, American, 1868-1875, **$375-475.**

Chef – Trade Mark (Chef) – The Berdan Co., clear, half-pint, smooth base, ground mouth, glass lid, American 1910-1920 . . . . **$80-100**

Chef – Trade Mark (Chef) – The Berdan Co., clear, half-gallon, smooth base, ground mouth, glass lid, American 1910-1920 . . . . **$40-50**

Cohansey – Glass Mfg Co – Pat Mar 20 77, aqua, quart barrel, smooth base, applied groove ring wax seal, glass lid embossed (Cohansey Glass Mfg Co – Philada, Pa), American 1877-1885 . . . . **$150-160**

Columbia (monogram), aqua, quart, smooth base, ground lip, American 1884-1900 . . . . **$65-80**

Dexter (encircled by fruit and vegetables), aqua, quart, 7-1/4", smooth base (D), ground lip, original glass lid embossed "Patd Aug. 8th 1865," American 1865-1870 . . . . **$210-250**

Doane's Great Air Tight – Preserving Jar, aqua, bulbous body, quart, smooth base, applied mouth, American 1865-1870 . . . . **$3,600-4,500**

Eagle, aquamarine, quart, smooth base, ground mouth, American 1860-1870 . . . . **$170-300**

Electric – Fruit Jar (around globe), bluish aqua, pint, smooth base (Pat Apd For), ground lip, American 1885-1895 . . . . **$150-180**

Electric – Fruit Jar (around globe), bluish aqua, quart, smooth base (Pat Apd For), ground lip, American 1885-1895 . . . . **$160-225**

Eureka – A7 – Patd Dec 27th – 1864, bluish aqua with light olive green in shoulder and neck, half-gallon, smooth base, ground lip, American 1865-1875 . . . . **$75-90**

C. Burnham & Co. -
Manufacturers - Philada,
American, 1859-1865,
$500-700.

Clarke Fruit Jar Co. -
Cleveland, O, American,
1885-1895, **$100-150.**

Dexter (encircled by fruits and vegetables), American, 1865-1880, **$300-400.**

The - Doolittle - Self Sealer, pint, American, 1905-1910, **$300-$400.**

*Excelsior - Improved - 5,
American, 1875-1885,* **$60-90.**

*Franklin - R.W. King - 90
Jefferson Ave. - Detroit Mich
- Fruit Jar, American, 1865-
1875,* **$500-800.**

Figural Owl Fruit Jar, milk glass owl, smooth base, rough sheared lip, original glass insert with embossed eagle, American 1890-1910 . . . .**$110-150**

Flaccus Bros – Steer's (steer's head) Head – Fruit Jar, clear, pint, 6-1/8", smooth base, ground lip, original screw-on lid, American 1890-1910 . . . .**$260-350**

Flaccus Bros – Steer's (steer's head) Head – Fruit Jar, milk glass, pint, 6-1/8", smooth base, ground lip, original screw-on lid, American 1890-1910 . . . .**$255-350**

Gilberds (star) Jar, aqua, pint, 5-1/4", smooth base, ground lip, original clear glass lid embossed "Jas Gilberds – Patd – Jan 30, 1883 – Jamestown, N.Y.," American 1883-1885 . . . . **$1,100-1,500**

Globe, reddish amber, quart, smooth base (62), ground lip, original glass lid embossed "Patented May 25th 1886," American 1886-1895. . . . .**$155-200**

Globe, yellow amber, quart, smooth base, ground lip, original glass lid embossed "Patented May 25th 1886," American 1886-1895 . . . .**$80-125**

Globe, orange amber, quart, smooth base, ground lip, original glass lid embossed "Patented May 25th 1886," American 1886-1895 . . . .**$85-125**

Haines's – Improved – March 1st – 1870, bluish aqua, quart, smooth base, applied mouth, American 1870-1880. . . . .**$95-125**

H & S (in script), aqua, quart, smooth base, applied mouth, original attached metal yoke and lid is embossed (William Haller Patd. Aug 7 1860), American 1860-1865 (very rare) **$2,600-3,500**

The Howe - Jar - Scranton Pa, American, 1888-1895, **$150-250.**

Hoosier - Jar, American, 1882-1890, **$700-1,000.**

H.W. Pettit – Westville, N.J. (on base), aqua, pint, smooth base, applied lip, American 1870-1900 . . . . **$45-55**

Huyett & Fredley – Carisle, PA – Ladies Choice, aquamarine, quart, smooth base, ground mouth, American 1860-1870 (rare) **$550-1,000**

John F. Henry – N.Y., golden yellow amber, 4-3/8", smooth base, tooled mouth, American 1855-1875 (rare) **$150-180**

Keystone, bluish aqua, half-gallon, red iron pontil, applied mouth, American 1860-1870 . . . . **$210-300**

LaFayette (bust of LaFayette), aqua, quart, smooth base, applied mouth, original three-piece metal and glass stopper marked "Patented – Sept 21, 1994-Aug, 1885," American 1885-1895 . . . . **$1,100-2,000**

LaFayette (in script), smoky clear glass, half-gallon, smooth base, tooled mouth, original three-piece metal and glass stopper marked "Patented – Sept 21, 1994-Aug, 1885," American 1885-1895 . . . . **$1,650-2,000**

Ludlow's Patent – June 28th 1859, aqua, pint, 6-1/8", smooth base, ground lip, American 1859-1865 . . . . **$425-600**

Magic – Fruit Jar – Wm. McCully & Co – Pittsburg PA – Sole Proprietors – No. 6 – Patented – By – R.M. Dalbey – June 6th 1866, aquamarine, half-gallon, smooth base, ground mouth, American 1865-1870 (rare) **$550-1,000**

Manuafacture For – Rice & Burnett – Cleveland. O – L & W, aquamarine, quart, smooth base, applied mouth with "KLINE" stopper, American 1860-1880 (rare) **$275-500**

Mason's – C.F.J. Co. (monogram) Improved – Butter Jar, aqua, half-gallon, smooth base, rough sheared and ground lip, American 1880-1895 . . . . **$210-275**

Joshua Wright - Philada,
American, 1855-1870, **$350-500.**

The - King - Pat Nov 2, 1869,
American, 1869-1875, **$250-375.**

*Lafayette, American,
1885-1895,* **$150-200.**

*Mason's - Patent - Nov 30th
- 1858, American, 1880-1890,*
$600-900.

Mason's – Patent – Nov. 30th – 58 (on front) and "The Ball-Jar (on reverse), aqua, pint, smooth base, ground lip, American 1875-1890 . . . .**$160-200**

Mason's – Patent – Nov 30th – 1858, greenish aqua with olive amber striations, 8-3/4", smooth base, ABM lip, American 1920-1930 . . . .**$185-250**

Mastodon (wax sealer jar), bluish aqua, quart, smooth base (T.A. Evans & Co Pittsburg PA) applied groove ring wax sealer, original tin lid, American 1870-1885 . . . .**$225-300**

M.G.Co. (on base), yellow green, quart, smooth base, applied groove wax sealer, American 1870-1880 . . . .**$95-125**

M G M Co (monogram), pale amethyst, midget-pint, smooth base, ground mouth, American 1880-1900 . . . .**$275-500**

Millville – Atmospheric – Fruit Jar – Whitall's Patent – June 18th 1861, bluish aqua, pint, smooth base, applied mouth, embossed glass lid "Whitall's Patent – June 18th 1861," American 1861-1870 . . . .**$65-80**

Millville – Atmospheric – Fruit Jar – Whitall's Patent – June 18th 1861, bluish aqua, quart, smooth base, applied mouth, embossed glass lid "Whitall's Patent – June 18th 1861," American 1861-1870 . . . .**$75-90**

Millville – Atmospheric – Fruit Jar – Whitall's Patent – June 18th 1861, bluish aqua, half-gallon, smooth base, applied mouth, embossed glass lid "Whitall's Patent – June 18th 1861," American 1861-1870 . . . .**$95-110**

Millville – Atmospheric – Fruit Jar – Whitall's Patent – June 18th 1861, bluish aqua, 72 oz., smooth base, applied mouth, embossed glass lid "Whitall's Patent – June 18th 1861," American 1861-1870 . . . .**$95-110**

Mason - Patent - Nov 30th - 1880, American, 1870-1880, **$80-100.**

Queensland - Fruit Jar, Australian, 1890-1900, **$250-350.**

Millville – Whitall's Patent, bluish aqua, half-pint, smooth base (W.T.&Co. – U.S.A.), applied mouth, embossed glass lid "Whitall's Patent – June 18th 1861," American 1861-1870 . . . . . **$95-120**

Michigan Mason, aqua, smooth base, ground lip, American 1910-1920. . . . . **$25-35**

Moore's – Patent – Dec 3d 1861, bluish aqua, half-gallon, smooth base, applied mouth, American 1861-1870 . . . . **$160-200**

NE Plus Ultra Air-Tight Fruit Jar (row of squares) – Made By Bodine & Bors Wmstown, N.J. (row of circles) For Their Patent Glass Lid – (row of squares) For Their deep bluish aqua, half-gallon, smooth base, applied mouth, original glass lid embossed (PATENTED – AUG 3RD 1858), American 1858-1865 (rare) **$2,200-3,000**

Patented – Oct 19 1958, apple green, quart, smooth base, ground lip, original glass screw lid, American 1860-1870 . . . . . **$150-180**

Patented Imperial, clear glass, quart, smooth base (The G.H. Hammond Co. – Hammond, Ind – Imperial Pat – April 20th 1886), ground lid embossed "The G.H. Hammond Co. Hammond, Ind – Imperial Pat – April 20th 1886," American 1886-1890 (very rare) **$225-300**

Petal Jar, emerald green, 10 panels around shoulder, 8-3/4", red iron pontil, applied mouth, American 1850-1860 . . . . . **$1,800-2,500**

Petal Jar, deep bluish aqua, 10-3/8", iron pontil, applied mouth, American 1855-1865 . . . . **$400-475**

Porcelain – BBGM Co (monogram) Lined, aquamarine, midget-pint, smooth base, ground mouth, American 1880-1900 (rare) **$550-1,000**

Potter & Bodine's – Air-Tight – Fruit Jar – Philada – Patented – April 13th – 1858, bluish aqua, half-gallon barrel, pontil-scarred base, applied groove wax ring sealer, American 1855-1865 . . . .**$260-300**

Protector, aqua, quart, smooth base, tinned iron lid (Cohansey Mfg Co.), American 1867-1880 . . . .**$110-125**

Safety, medium yellow amber, quart, smooth base, ground lip, original glass lid embossed (Patent Applied For), American 1880-1890. . . . .**$185-250**

Safety, yellow amber, half-gallon, smooth base, ground lip, original glass lid embossed (Patent Applied For), American 1880-1890 . . . .**$225-300**

Safety Valve – HC (superimposed over triangle) Patd May 21 1895, grass green, pint, smooth base, ground lip, original lid, American 1895-1910 . . . .**$160-200**

San Francisco – Glass Works (wax sealer jar), bluish aqua, quart, smooth base, applied groove ring wax sealer, original tin lid, American 1870-1885 . . . .**$100-150**

Stevens – Tin Top – Patd July 27 1875 – Lewis & Neblett – Cincinnati. O (wax sealer jar), bluish aqua, quart, smooth base, applied groove ring wax sealer, original tin lid, American 1870-1885 . . . .**$100-150**

The Ball – Pat. Apld. For, aquamarine, quart, smooth base, ground mouth, American 1890-1900 . . . .**$260-500**

The Canton – Domestic – Fruit Jar, clear, pint, smooth base, ground mouth, glass lid, American 1889-1900 . . . .**$170-300**

The Darling, aqua, quart, smooth base, ground lip, American 1884-1900 . . . .**$65-80**

The - Puritan - LSCO (monogram), American, 1870-1880, **$150-250.**

Trade Mark - Lightning, American, 1880-1890, **$250-300.**

The Howe – Jar – Scranton – PA, aqua, quart, smooth base, ground lip, American 1888-1910 . . . . **$45-60**

The Howe – Jar – Scranton – PA, clear, pint, smooth base, ground mouth, glass lid, American 1888-1910 . . . . **$85-100**

The – King – Pat. Nov. 2, 1869, bluish aqua, quart, 7-1/2", smooth base (3), ground lip, original glass lid, American 1869-1875 . . . . **$280-375**

The Ladies Favorite (fullbodied Victorian woman holding a jar) – Wm. L. Haller – Carlisle – PA, aquamarine, quart, smooth base, ground mouth, American 1860-1870 **$3,300-6,000**

The Leader, medium amber to yellow amber, pint, 6", smooth base (3), ground lip, original amber domed lid embossed "Patd June 28 1893," American 1892-1895 (scarce in pint) **$325-400**

The Leader, yellow amber, quart, 8", smooth base (23), ground lip, original amber domed lid embossed "Patd June 28, 1892," American 1892-1895 . . . . **$310-450**

The – Paragon – Valve Jar – Patd. April 19th 1870, bluish aqua, quart, 7-3/4", smooth base (MCE & CO – 2), ground lip, American 1870-1875 (rare) **$425-600**

The – Reservoir, bluish aqua, half-gallon, smooth base (C.& I), applied mouth, glass screw-in stopper (MRS. G.E. Haller – PATD. Feb 25, 73), American 1873-1880 . . . . **$450-500**

The Rose, clear, midget-pint, smooth base, machined mouth, glass lid, American 1880-1900 . . . . **$250-400**

The – Smalley – Jar, aquamarine, quart, smooth base, ground mouth, American 1890-1900 . . . . **$200-400**

The – Van Vliet – Jar – of 1881, aqua, quart, 7-1/4", smooth base (7), ground lip, original glass lid embossed "Pat May 3d 1881," American 1881-1885 . . . . **$650-800**

Thrift – Thrift Jar Co. – Baltimore, MD, clear, pint, smooth base, metal lid, American 1913-1920 . . . . **$35-45**

Trade Mark – Lightning, golden yellow olive, half-gallon, smooth base (Putnam), ground lip, lid is embossed (Patd Jan 5. 75 Reisd. June 5. 77. Patd Apr. 25. 82), American 1885-1895 . . . . **$225-300**

Trademark – Masons – CFJ Co (mongram) – Improved, aqua, half-pint, smooth base, ABM lip, American 1870-1900. . . **$45-55**

Trade Mark – The Dandy, medium amber, half-gallon, smooth base (Gilberds), ground lip, glass lid embossed (Pat. Oct. 13th 1885), American 1885-1895 . . . . **$160-200**

U.S. Patented – May 12 1863 (wax sealer jar), bluish aqua, half-gallon, smooth base, applied groove ring wax sealer, original tin lid, American 1863-1870 . . . . **$155-200**

Union – No 4, aquamarine, quart, smooth base, ground mouth, American 1860-1880 . . . . **$350-600**

Victory – 1 – Patd Feby 9th 1864 – Reisd June 22d 1867, aqua, quart, smooth base, rough sheared and ground lip, American 1870-1895 . . . . **$75-90**

Wm. Frank & Sons Pitts, ice blue, quart, smooth base, groove wax ring sealer, American 1910-1920 . . . . **$55-70**

Woodbury Improve- WGW (monogram), aqua, half-gallon, smooth base (Woodbury Glass Work – 20 – Woodbury, N.J.), ground lip, American 1861-1885 . . . . **$95-125**

Yeoman's – Fruit Bottle – Patent – Applied For (on shoulder), aqua, half-gallon, smooth base, ground mouth, American 1870-1900. . . . . **$70-90**

Hutchinson Bottles

The Hutchinson bottle was developed in the late 1870s by Charles A. Hutchinson. Interestingly, the stopper, not the bottle itself, differentiated the design from others. The stopper, which Hutchinson patented in 1879, was an improvement over cork stoppers, since cork eventually shrank and allowed the air to seep into the bottle.

The new stopper consisted of a rubber disk held between two metal plates attached to a spring stem. The stem was in the form of a figure eight, with the upper loop larger than the lower to prevent the stem from falling into the bottle. The lower loop could pass through the bottle's neck and push the disk down to permit the filling or pouring of the contents. A refilled bottle was sealed by pulling the disk up to the bottle's shoulder, where it made a tight fit. When opened, the spring was struck, which made a popping sound. Thus, the Hutchinson bottle was the origin of the term "pop bottle," which is how soda came to be known as "pop."

Hutchinson stopped producing bottles in 1912, when warnings about metal poisoning were issued. As collectibles, Hutchinson bottles rank high on the curiosity and price scales, but pricing varies quite sharply by geographical location, compared to the relatively stable prices of most other bottles.

Hutchinson bottles carry abbreviations, of which the following three are the most common:

tbntbs - This bottle not to be sold

TBMBR -This bottle must be returned

TBINS - This bottle is not sold

Arcata Soda Works – B.P., aqua, 6-3/4", smooth base, tooled top, American 1875-1890 . . . .**$60-80**

Artic – Soda Works – Berkeley – Cal, aqua, 7", smooth base, tooled top, American 1893-1903 (extremely rare) **$120-300**

Black Diamond – A1 – Soda Works, green hue, 7", smooth base, tooled top, American 1902-1910 (scarce) **$120-200**

C. Valer & Co – Electric Bottlers – Charlotte, N.C., aqua, 6-3/4", smooth base, tooled top, American 1875-1895 . . .**$55-75**

California – S.C.&Co. – Soda Works, aqua, 6-1/2", smooth base, tooled top, American 1884 (rare) **$110-200**

Cape Argo – Soda Works – Marshfield, Ore, aqua, 6-7/8", smooth base, tooled top, American 1880-1890 . . . .**$50-65**

Crystal Bottling Co. – Charleston – W. VA., aqua, 6-3/4", mug based, tooled top, American 1880-1890 . . . .**$45-55**

Daniel Ritter – Allentown – PA, medium amber, 6-3/8", smooth base, tooled top, American 1890-1910 . . . . **$625-800**

*Claussen Bottling Works
- Charleston - S.C.,
American, 1885-1900,*
$1,200-1,800.

*C.W. Rider - Watertown -
N.Y., American, 1890-1900,*
$800-1,200.

D.W. Bostelmann – Trade Mark (anchor) Registered – Chicago Ill., deep aqua, 6-7/8", smooth base, tooled top, American 1880-1900 . . . .**$50-65**

D.W. Powell – Soda Water – Evergreen, Ala., light pink amethyst, 7-1/8", smooth base, tooled top, American 1890-1910 (rare in this color) **$385-475**

E.L. Billings – Sacramento Cal, green aqua, 7-1/8", smooth base, applied top, American 1880-1890 . . . .**$50-60**

Empire Soda Works – Weiss & Company, aqua, 6-1/2", smooth base, applied top, American 1883-1887 (extremely rare) **$550-1,000**

Eureka California (eagle) Soda Water Co. – S.F., aqua, 6-1/2", smooth base, tooled top, American 1889-1907 . . . . . . **$125-150**

Eureka Soda Works – 723 Turk St – S.F., aqua, 6-1/2", smooth base, applied top, American 1884-1898 (scarce) **$55-75**

F. Schmidt – Leadville – Colorado, clear, 6-1/2", smooth base (S), tooled top, American (Colorado Territory) 1870-1880. **$125-300**

F. Schmidt – Leadville – Colorado, clear, 6-1/4", smooth base, tooled top, American (Colorado Territory) 1870-1880. **$135-300**

H & M Eureka – Cal, aqua, 7", smooth base, tooled top, American 1875-1890 . . . .**$60-75**

H. Rummel – Charleston – W. VA., pale green, 7", smooth base, tooled top, American 1880-1900 . . . .**$30-40**

Haywards – S.J. Simons – Soda Works, light green aqua, 6", smooth base, tooled top, American 1890-1902 . . . .**$90-150**

Jas. F. Taylor – New Berne – N.C., clear, 6-1/2", smooth base (T 36), tooled top, American 1880-1890 . . . .**$55-65**

Geo. Schmuck's - Ginger Ale - Cleveland, O, American, 1885-1900, **$275-375.**

Jacob Schmidt - Pottsville, Pa, American, 1890-1900, **$350-450.**

Leadville, clear, 6-3/4", smooth base, tooled top, American (Colorado Territory) 1870-1880 . . . . **$120-300**

Leonard – Sonora – Cal., aqua, 6-7/8", smooth base, tooled top, American 1880-1907 . . . . **$85-100**

Mason & Co – Sausalito, aqua, 6-1/2", smooth base (Four "M"s embossed on base), tooled top, American 1900-1910 (extremely rare) **$550-1,000**

Mendocino – Bottling Works – A.L. Reynolds, light blue aqua, 7", smooth base, tooled top, American 1905-1910 . . . **$110-200**

Monroe Cider & Vinegar Co. – Ferndale Cal., aqua, 6-1/8", smooth base, tooled top, American 1895-1905 (rare) . . . **$80-150**

Monroe Bottling – Works – Fortuna, Cal., light green, 7", smooth base, tooled top, American 1898-1899 (scarce) . . . . **$125—250**

Montgomery – Carbonating Co. – Montogomery, W. VA., ice blue, 6-1/2", smooth base, tooled top, American 1880-1890 . . . . **$75-95**

Morgan & Co – Selma, Cal, pale aqua, 7", smooth base, tooled top, four-piece mold, American 1905-1920 (rare) **$350-600**

Nevada – Soda Water – Grass Valley – Nevada Co – Cal. (on one side) W.E. Deamer (on other side), medium aqua, 6-1/2", smooth base (embossed with gravitating stopper made by John Matthews Pat. October 11 1864 NY) tooled top, American 1880-1890 (scarce) **$70-100**

New River – Bottling Co. – Sewell, W. Va, green tinted, 7", smooth base (The Liquid), tooled top, American 1880-1890 . . . . **$40-55**

Nome – Brewing – And – Bottling Co., aqua, 7-13/16", smooth base (no embossing on base), four-piece mold, tooled top, American (Alaska Territory) 1895-1905 (very rare) **$1,000-2,000**

Otto Brandt – 287 Washington – St – Newark – N.J. (front) – Trade Mark – O.B. – This Bottle – Not To Be Sold (back), aqua, 6-7/8", smooth base (PAT 8), tooled top, American 1890-1910 . . . . **$25-35**

P.J. Fitzpatrick – Newburgh – N.Y. – PJG (monogram), bluish aqua, smooth base, (Gravitating Stopper – Made By – John Matthews – Pat – Oct 11 – 1864 – New York), tooled mouth, American 1864-1870 . . . . **$55-65**

P.J. Serwazi - Manayunk - PA, American, 1890-1900, **$350-450.**

Palmyra Bottling Works – Palmyra PA – Registered (embossed with "P" in oval slug plate), ice blue, 6-3/4", smooth base, tooled top, American 1880-1890 . . . .**$25-35**

Paul Jeenicke – San Jose, amber, 6-3/4", smooth base, applied top, American 1880-1890 (rare) **$2,200-4,000**

Pioneer – Trade (motif of anchor) Mark – Soda Works - P.O., blue aqua, 6-1/8", smooth base, tooled top, American 1880-1895 . . . . **$45-65**

Property of – Monterey Soda Works – Cal., aqua, 7", smooth base, tooled top, American 1890-1910 . . . .**$80-125**

Quinnimont – Bottling Co. – Quinnimont, W. VA., green tint, 7", smooth base (This Bottle Is Never Sold – M.G. & G. Co.), tooled top, American 1870-1880 . . . .**$55-75**

Ramona – Bottling – Works – Los Angeles, Cal., dark aqua, 6-1/2", smooth base, tooled top, American 1905-1909 (rare) **$110-200**

Registered – Biedenharn – Candy Co – Vicksburg – Miss., aqua, 7-1/4", smooth base (B.C.C.), tooled top, American 1890-1900 (the bottle that started the Coca-Cola Company) **$285-375**

Registered – Lynch & Livingston – Point Pleasant – N.J., aqua, 6-5/8", mug-based, tooled top, American 1870-1890 . . . .**$45-55**

Richmond Soda Works – R.S.W. – Point Richmond, light aqua, 7", smooth base, tooled top, American 1902-1914 (rare) **$110-300**

The Standard Bottling Works & Mfg. Co – Cripple Creek – Colo., aqua green, 6-5/8", smooth base, tooled top, American 1880-1890 . . . .**$45-65**

San Diego – Trade (star) Mark – Soda Works, light purple, 6-3/4", smooth base, tooled top, American 1888-1889 . . . . **$170-300**

Santa Rosa Bottling Co. – SRBCO (intertwined in center) – Santa Rosa, Cal., aqua, 7", smooth base, tooled top, American 1887-1910 . . . . **$65-85**

S.C. Palmer – Washington – D.Co – This Bottle – Is Never Sold, deep amber, 7-1/8", smooth base, tooled top, American 1890-1900 . . . . **$360-450**

Simon James – 27 – Brunswick St. – Jersey City, NJ – Registered, lime green, 7-3/8", smooth base, tooled top, American 1890-1910 (rare in this color) **$270-350**

Solano Soda Work – Vacaville – California, aqua, 6-1/2", smooth base, tooled top, American 1903-1910 . . . . **$50-75**

Standard – Bottling Works – Minneapolis – Minn., medium amber, 6-7/8", smooth base (H.R.), tooled top, American 1880-1890 . . . . **$65-75**

The C.C. Co. – Charleston, W. Va, ice blue, 7", smooth base, tooled top, American 1880-1890 . . . . **$45-65**

Tri-state – Bottling Co. – Huntington, W. VA. (front) – This Bottle Never Sold – M.B. & G. Co. (back), green tint, 6-1/2", smooth base, tooled top, American 1880-1910 . . . . **$55-65**

Ukiah Soda Works – Ukiah – Cal., purple tint, 7", smooth base, tooled top, American 1898-1910 . . . . **$110-150**

West Va. – Carbonating Co. – Hinton, W. VA., aqua, 6-1/2", smooth base, tooled top, American 1880-1900 . . . . **$40-55**

Winslow Junction Bottling Co. (W & R) – N.J., aqua, 8", 10 vertical panels around base, tooled top, American 1880-1890 . . . . **$55-65**

Wm. A. Kearney – Shamokin – PA – This Bottle – Never Sold, deep amber, 8-7/8", smooth base, tooled collared mouth, American 1880-1900 . . . . **$350-600**

Ink Bottles

Ink bottles have a centuries-old history, providing collectors with a wider variety of designs and shapes than any other group of bottles. People often ask why a product as cheap as ink was sold in such decorative bottles. While other bottles were disposed of or returned after use, ink bottles were usually displayed on desks in dens, libraries, and studies. It's safe to assume that, even into the late 1880s, people buying ink bottles considered the design of the bottle as well as the quality of its contents.

Prior to the 18th century, most ink was sold in brass or copper containers. The very rich would then refill their gold and silver inkwells from these storage containers. Ink sold in glass and pottery bottles in England in the 1700s had no brand name identification, and at best would have a label identifying the ink and/or the manufacturer.

In 1792, the first patent for the commercial production of ink was issued in England, 24 years before the first American patent was issued in 1816. Molded ink bottles began to appear in America around 1815-1816, and the blown three-mold variety came into use during the late 1840s. The most common ink bottle, the umbrella, features a multisided conical shape that can be found with both pontiled and smooth bases. One of the

more collectible ink bottles is the teakettle, identified by the neck, which extends upward at an angle from the base.

As the fountain pen grew more popular between 1885 and 1890, the ink bottle gradually became less decorative and soon became just another plain bottle.

Alling's – Pat'd Apl 25 1871 (label: Jet Black High School Ink, Manufactured Solely By Fred D. Alling, Rochester, N.Y.), pale blue green, 1-7/8", smooth base, tooled mouth, American 1871-1875 . . . .**$110-150**

Bank – of – England – Cottage Ink, aqua, 3-1/2", smooth base, tooled mouth, American 1880-1890 . . . .**$260-350**

Bauman's - Ink – Pittsburgh, clear, 2-3/4", smooth base, ground lip, American 1880-1890 (rare) **$160-250**

Bertinguiot, medium yellow olive, 2", pontil-scarred base, tooled mouth, American 1845-1860 . . . .**$410-500**

Blake – N.Y. Umbrella Ink, pale aqua, 3", 8-sided, open pontil, rolled lip, American 1845-1860 . . . .**$525-700**

Blake & – Herring – N.Y. – Umbrella Ink, emerald green 3", 8-sided, open pontil, rolled lip, American 1845-1860 (rare color/size/embossing) **$3,100-4,000**

Blackwood & Co. (monogram in diamond) London – Igloo Ink, pale greenish aqua, 2", smooth base, sheared lip, English 1875-1895 . . . .**$55-100**

Blackwood & Co. – 18 Bread St. Hill – London, cobalt blue, 2-1/8", 8-sided, smooth base, flared lip, English 1890-1910 . . . .**$90-120**

Blue Black Ledger, United Manufacturing Stationers, William Eden & Co. Importing Stationers' – 430 Broadway, New York, white pottery, smooth base, 98% original label, American 1890-1920 . . . . **$70-90**

Butler Ink – Cincinnati – Sided Ink, bluish aqua, 2-1/4", 12-sided, pontil-scarred base, rolled lip, American 1840-1860 . . . . **$160-250**

Carter's (on base) – Clover Ink, cobalt blue, 3", 6-sided, smooth base, ABM lip, American 1920-1930. . . . . **$150-180**

Carter's – Ink (around shoulder) – Master Ink, medium yellow green, 9-3/4", smooth base, applied sloping double collar mouth with tooled pour spout, American 1870-1885 . . . . **$110-150**

Commercial (monogram) Ink London, deep teal blue, barrel shape, 5-5/8", pontil-scarred base, tooled lip with double pour spout, English 1845-1865 . . . . **$160-250**

Davids & Black – New York, medium blue green, 5-1/4", open pontil, applied sloping collar mouth, American 1845-1860 . . . . **$285-375**

Davids & Black – New York, deep blue green, 10-1/8", open pontil, three-piece mold, applied sloping collar mouth with tooled pour spout, American 1845-1860 (rare size) **$550-700**

Davis & – D M – Miller – Umbrella Ink, bluish aqua, 2-1/2", rib pattern with two embossed panels, open pontil, rolled lip, American 1845-1860 . . . . **$450-700**

Derby – All British, deep cobalt blue, 2-3/8", triangular shape, smooth base, rough sheared mount, English 1880-1890 . **$80-140**

E. Waters – Troy – NY, light blue green, 5-1/4", iron pontil, applied mouth, American 1845-1890 . . . . **$650-900**

Blown three-mold geometric ink, American, 1815-1835, **$250-350.**

Cone ink, American, 1840-1860, **$400-700.**

Cone ink, American,
1840-1860, **$375-475**.

CA-RT-ER (embossed on
bottom of sides) main label:
Carter's - RYTO - Permanent
- Blue-Black - Ink; small label:
Hill and Kooken - Stationery
- 11 Lyman Terrace - Waltham
Mass., American, 1920-1930,
$150-$250.

Elgin – Ink, clear, 2", smooth base, tooled lip, American 1885-1895 . . . . **$85-100**

Estes – N.Y. Ink – Umbrella Ink, aqua, 4-1/8", 8-sided, open pontil, rolled lip, American 1840-1860 . . . . **$195-275**

Farley – Sided Ink, medium amber, 1-5/8", 8-sided, pontil-scarred base, rolled lip, American 1845-1860 . . . . **$320-400**

Fine – Black Ink – Made & Sold – By – J.L. Thompson – Troy N-Y, yellow olive with amber tone, 5-7/8", pontil-scarred base, flared lip, American 1840-1860 . . . . **$750-900**

Gaylord's – Superior – Record – Ink – Boston, deep olive green, 5-7/8", pontil-scarred base, flared lip, American 1835-1860 . . . . **$2,600-3,500**

G & Rs – American Writing Fluid, bluish aqua, 2", pontil-scarred base, rolled lip, American 1845-1860 . . . . **$450-600**

Government – W.B. Todd's – Writing Ink, medium teal blue, 3-1/8", smooth base, tooled mouth, American 1885-1895 . . . . **$110-150**

Harrison's - Columbian - Ink, American, 1840-1860, **$120-180.**

Granite State Ink – L.P. Farley Marlow, N.H. – Igloo Ink, bluish aqua, 1-7/8", smooth base, ground lip, American 1875-1890. . . . .**$120-150**

Harrison's – Indelible – Preparation, clear, 2-3/8", 8-sided, pontil-scarred base, rolled lip, American 1845-1860 . . .**$350-450**

Harrison's – Columbian – Ink, bluish aqua, 10-3/4" (gallon), 12-sided, pontil-scarred base, applied mouth, American 1845-1860 . . . .**$1,300-1,800**

Harrison – Tippecanoe – Cabin Ink, clear, 4-1/8", rectangular form, pontil-scarred base, rolled lip, American 1840 (very rare – made for William Henry Harrison's 1840 presidential campaign) **$16,000-25,000**

Hohenthal – Brothers & Co – Indelible – Writing Ink – N.Y., deep olive amber, 9-1/8", pontil-scarred base, applied sloping collar, American 1845-1865 . . . .**$850-1,200**

Hover – Phila – Umbrella Ink, bluish aqua, 2-3/8", 8-sided, open pontil, rolled lip, American 1845-1860 . . . .**$325-400**

Hyde – London, deep cobalt blue, 5-3/4", smooth base, tooled lip with pour spout, English 1880-1895 . . . .**$110-200**

III – IV Rd 12 6 (inside diamond) – Isaac & C L-Pool, deep purple amethyst, 5", smooth base, tooled pour spout, English 1880-1895. . . . .**$85-120**

J.E. – Peterman – Ink – Philada, greenish aqua, 3-3/4", 12-sided, open pontil, flared lip, American 1840-1860 . . . .**$385-475**

J/J. Butler – Cin, bluish aqua, 2-7/8", pontil-scarred base, rolled lip, American 1845-1855 . . . .**$110-150**

J.W. – Seaton – Louisville – KY, medium blue green, 2-1/8", 10-sided, open pontil, rolled lip, American 1840-1860 (rare with color and embossing) **$1,100-1,500**

Harrison's - Columbian
- Ink, American, 1840-
1860, **$4,500-6,500.**

Ink bottle, American,
1830-1850, **$100-150.**

James S – Mason & Co – Umbrella Ink, aqua, 2-1/2", 8-sided, pontil-scarred base, rolled lip, American 1845-1860 . . .**$285-375**

Jones – Empire – Ink – N.Y., deep olive green, 7-1/8", 12-sided, open pontil, applied mouth, American 1840-1860 **$3,600-4,500**

Josiah – Johnson – Japan – Writing – Fluid – London – Stoneware Teakettle Ink, light brown pottery, 2-1/2", 6-sided, smooth base, English 1875-1900. . . . .**$160-200**

Kirtland's – Ink – W & H – Igloo Ink, yellow with amber tone, 1-7/8", smooth base, sheared lip, American 1875-1895 . . . .**$850-1,200**

L.C. – Vertu Bordeaux – Engre De La Grange, deep amber, 2", pontil-scarred base, tooled lip, French 1845-1860 . . . .**$270-350**

Levison's – Inks – St. Louis, aqua, 2-1/2", smooth base, tooled mouth, American 1880-1895 . . . .**$350-500**

M & P – New York – Umbrella Ink, light blue green, 2-3/4", 6-sided, pontil-scarred base, rolled lip, American 1845-1860 (rare in aqua, extremely rare in other colors) **$1,100-1,500**

Pattern-Molded Handled Inkwell, light yellow green, 2-1/4", 19-rib pattern, pontil-scarred base, flared rim, applied handle, American 1825-1840 . . . . **$1,900-2,800**

Perkins – Superior – Indelible – Ink, clear, 2-5/8", open pontil, flared lip, American 1845-1860 (rare embossed ink). . .**$225-300**

Pomeroys Inks – Keystone Potter Co. – Rochester, PA – Pottery Master Ink, cream, 7-3/4", smooth base, pour spout, American 1880-1900 . . . .**$110-150**

R.B. – Snow – St. – Louis – Umbrella Ink, yellow olive, 2-1/8", 12-sided, smooth base, rough sheared and unfinished lip, American 1855-1865 . . . . **$1,600-2,500**

Runge – Tinte (motif of horse) – MF & R – Master Ink, black amethyst, 8-1/8", smooth base, tooled mouth and pour spout, German 1880-1910 . . . . **$150-180**

Saltglaze Stoneware Bulk Ink Jug, (embossed), "Harrison's Patent Columbian Ink", gray pottery, 11", applied handle, American 1840-1860 . . . . **$750-900**

S. Fine – Blk. Ink, medium amber, 3-1/4", open pontil, rolled lip, American 1845-1860 (extremely rare color for this ink) **$185-275**

S.I. – Comp, milk glass, 2-3/8", barrel shape, smooth base, tooled mouth, American 1870-1890 . . . . **$425-600**

S.O. Dunbar – Taunton – Mass (Label: Dunbar's Black Ink, Superior To Any Other Ink In Use, S.O. Dunbar, Taunton, Mass), aqua, 3-7/8", 8-sided, open pontil, flared lip, American 1850-1860 . . . . **$325-400**

Stafford's Carmine Non-Copying – Master Ink, clear, smooth base, 98% label, American 18901920 . . . . **$70-90**

Stafford's – Ink – Made In U.S.A – Master Ink, amber, 9-1/8", smooth base, tooled mouth, American 1890-1910 . . . . . **$40-55**

Superior Black Ink Preparte By Stretch, Bennett & Co. Philadelphia – Labeled Umbrella Ink, medium sapphire blue, 2-3/4", 8-sided, smooth base, tooled mouth, American 1875-1895 . . . . **$285-375**

Teakettle Ink – China, white bisque china with red, gold, and black Japanese flower, bird, and tree decoration, 3", applied frond on top and applied bird on original stopper, European 1875-1890 . . . . **$450-600**

Teakettle Ink – Double Font, milk glass, 2-1/4", 8-sided, smooth base, ground lips, applied mother-of-pearl panels, American 1875-1895 . . . . **$750-900**

Teakettle Ink – Miniature, medium green, 1-1/8", 8-sided, polished pontil, polished lip, American 1875-1890 . . . . **$435-600**

T. Davids & Co (along the edge of an English registry stamp) – Pottery Master Ink, cream, 8-1/4", smooth base, pour spout, English 1880-1900. . . . . **$45-60**

T. Davids & Co (along the edge of an English registry stamp) – Pottery Master Ink, cream, 7-1/2", smooth base, pour spout, English 1880-1900. . . . . **$40-60**

T.K. Hibbert – Pittsburgh, cobalt blue, 5-5/8", open pontil, applied mouth, American 1840-1860 . . . . **$2,600-3,500**

Thacker – London – Domed Ink, blue green with amber streaks, 1-5/8", smooth base, tooled top, English 1885-1895 . . . . . **$35-45**

Unoco Fast Black Writng Ink – Umbrella Ink, yellow olive green, 2-3/4", 8-sided, smooth base, tooled mouth, 97% label, American 1870-1885 . . . . **$260-350**

Ward's Ink, emerald green, 4-3/4", smooth base, applied mouth with tooled pour spout, American 1860-1870 . . . . **$160-200**

Warrens – Congress – Ink-sided Ink, medium olive green, 2-7/8", 8-sided, pontil-scarred base, rolled lip, American 1845-1860 . . . . **$850-1,200**

W.E. Bonney – Barrel Ink, light blue green, 2-1/2", pontil-scarred base, rolled lip, American 1845-1860 (rare in this color) **$450-700**

Wood's – Black Ink – Portland, deep olive amber, 2-3/8", pontil-scarred base, tooled lip, American 1845-1860 . . . . **$1,100-1,500**

Writing – Fluid – Petroleum – P.B. & Co. – Barrel Ink, aqua, 2-1/2", smooth base, applied mouth, American 1875-1895 . . . . **$325-400**

*Umbrella ink, American,
1840-1860,* **$700-1,000.**

*Umbrella ink, American,
1840-1860,* **$300-450.**

*Umbrella ink, American,
1840-1860,* **$1,200-1,600.**

*Umbrella ink, American,
1840-1860,* **$1,500-2,500.**

Figural Inks

Ink – Adrien Maurin – Depose – Locomotive, bluish aqua, 2-1/8", smooth base, ground lip, American 1875-1890 . . . . **$850-1,200**

Ink – Building (1776-1876), clear glass, 3-1/2", (Patented – April) smooth base (Patented – April 11 1876), ground lip, American 1876. . . . . **$450-600**

Ink – BF – House, milk glass, 4-7/8", smooth base, tooled mouth, American 1875-1890 . . . . **$625-800**

Ink – Liberty Bell – 1776-1926, clear, 2-5/8", smooth base, tooled mouth, American 1926 (made for the 50th anniversary of the signing of the Declaration of Independence) **$185-275**

Inkwell – Ma & Pa Carter Inkwells – Carter's Ink, bisque pottery with multicolored paint, both 3-3/4", smooth base (Pat'd Jan 6 1914, Germany), American 1914-1920 . . . . **$210-300**

*Ma & Pa "Carter's Inx" set, American, 1890-1891, **$120-160**.*

Teakettle Ink – Benjamin Franklin, cobalt blue, 2-3/4", smooth base, ground lip, American 1875-1895 . . . . **$750-1,000**

Teakettle Ink – Figural Cat, clear glass, 2-1/8", smooth base, ground lip, American 1875-1890 . . . . **$450-600**

Teakettle Ink – Figural Foot Wearing a Sandal, clear glass, 1-1/2", smooth base, rough sheared and ground lip, French 1875-1900 . . . . **$285-375**

Teakettle Ink – Snail, clear glass, 1-5/8", smooth base, ground lip, English 1875-1900 . . . . **$325-400**

Inkwell – E. Mauring (on back of shoe), deep cobalt blue, 2-1/8", smooth base, sheared and ground lip, French 1880-1900 . . . . **$1,100-1,800**

Medicine Bottles

The medicine bottle group includes all pieces specifically made to hold patented medicines. Bitters and cure bottles are excluded from this category, however, because the healing powers of these mixtures were very questionable.

A patent medicine was one whose formula was registered with the U.S. Patent Office, which opened in 1790. Not all medicines were patented, since the procedure required the manufacturer to reveal the medicine's contents. After the passage of the Pure Food and Drug Act of 1907, most of these patent medicine companies went out of business after they were required to list the ingredients of the contents on the bottle. Public demand quickly diminished as consumers learned that most medicines consisted of liquor diluted with water and an occasional pinch of opiates, strychnine, and arsenic. I have spent many enjoyable hours reading the labels on these bottles and wondering how anyone survived the recommended doses.

One of the oldest and most collectible medicine bottles, the embossed Turlington "Balsam of Life" bottle, was manufactured in England from 1723 to 1900. The first embossed U.S. medicine bottle dates from around 1810. When searching for these bottles, always be on the lookout for embossing and original boxes. Embossed "Shaker" or "Indian" medicine bottles are very collectible and valuable. Most embossed medicines made before 1840 are clear and aqua. The embossed greens, amber, and various shades of blues, specifically the darker cobalt blues, are much more collectible and valuable.

A.L. Scovill – Dr. A. Rogers – Liverwort Tar – & Canchalagua – Cincinnati, deep bluish aqua, 7-1/2", open pontil, applied mouth, American 1840-1860 . . . .**$160-200**

Althrop's – Constitutional Tonic – Chicago – & – New York, aqua, 9-7/8", smooth base (D.S.G.CO), applied mouth, American 1870-1880 . . . .**$110-150**

American – Eagle – Liniment, bluish aqua, 5-1/8", 6-sided, smooth base, flared lip, American 1850-1860 . . . .**$150-180**

American Quinine – Elixir – Chicago – Ills, medium amber, 9-3/8", smooth base, tooled mouth, American 1880-1890 . . . .**$165-200**

Anderson's – Dermador, pale aqua, 4-1/8", open pontil, rolled lip, American 1880-1890 . . . .**$45-70**

Atkins – Tonic – Syrup, light green, 4-1/4", 8-sided, open pontil, inward rolled lip, American 1830-1845 (extremely rare)**$550-700**

Atwood's Vegetable Dysentery Drops, Manufactured By Moses Atwood, Georgetown, Mass, olive amber, 6-1/4", pontil-scarred base, applied sloping collar mouth, American 1835-1850 . . . .**$275-350**

Ayers – Ague – Cure – Lowell – Mass, aqua, 7", pontil-scarred base, applied mouth, American 1840-1855 (scarce) . . .**$160-200**

Bach's – American – Compound – Auburn, N.Y., aqua, 5-3/8", pontil-scarred bases, applied sloping collar mouth, American 1840-1865 . . . .**$35-40**

Balm – of – X Thousand – Flowers – Merchant – New York, aqua, 5-1/8", pontil-scarred base, applied mouth, American 1845-1855 (rare) **$160-200**

Barnes Magnolia Water – Nueva York – Ph.H. Drake Y.CIA., milk glass, 7-1/2", smooth base, tooled lip, American 1880-1900 . . . .**$110-150**

Brant's Indian – Purifying Extract – M.T. Wallace – Proprietor, bluish aqua, 6-3/4", open pontil, applied sloping collar mouth, American 1840-1860 . . . .**$150-180**

Bringhurst's – King's – Mixture – Wilmington, aqua, 6-1/8", open pontil, applied mouth, American 1840-1860 . . . .**$375-450**

Brown's – Blood Cure – Philadelphia, medium green, 6-3/8", smooth base (M.B.W. – U.S.A.), tooled mouth, American 1890-1910 . . . .**$160-200**

B.W. Fetters – Druggist – Philadelphia – Patented August 1, 1876, medium blue green, 8-5/8", smooth base, tooled mouth, American 1880-1890 (rare) **$225-300**

C. Brinckerhoffs – Health Restorative – Price 1.00 – New York, yellow olive green, 7-1/4", pontil-scarred base, applied mouth, American 1840-1860 . . . . **$1,100-1,500**

Christian Xander's – Melliston – Wild Cherry Cordial – Washington, D.C., clear, 9-3/8", smooth base, tooled mouth, American 1890-1910 . . . .**$90-100**

Cibil's Fluid Extract of Beef, Cibils Co Importers, New York, emerald green, 4", smooth base, tooled mouth, American 1890-1925 . . . .**$45-60**

Citrate of Magnesia – Sanford-frazier – Drug Co. – Enid, Okla, bright green, 7-3/4", smooth base, tooled mouth, original porcelain stopper, American 1890-1910 . . . .**$160-200**

Clemens Indian (motif of Indian) Tonic – Prepared By – Geo. W. House, aqua, 5-5/8", open pontil, folded lip, American 1840-1860 . . . .**$850-1,200**

Connell S. Brahminical – Moonplant – East Indian – Remedies (motif of feet surrounded by stars) Trade Mark, medium amber, 8-1/2", smooth base, applied double collar mouth, American 1880-1890 . . . .**$185-225**

Damascus (motif of an Arab, city, and camel) San Francisco – Cor. Geary & Mason Sts. – Trade Mark – Stoddart Bros, yellow amber, 4-1/2", smooth base (W.T. & CO.), tooled lip, American 1890-1900 . . . . **$160-200**

Dandelion & Tomato – Panacea – Ransom & Steven – Druggists Boston, aqua, 9", open pontil, applied sloping collar mouth, American 1840-1855 . . . . **$550-700**

Davison & Son – Fleet Street, yellow olive green, 6", pontil-scarred base, applied string lip, English 1770-1790 . . . **$225-300**

Ditchett's – Remedy For – The Piles N.Y., olive green, 9", smooth base, applied sloping double collar mouth, American 1855-1865 (extremely rare) **$3,200-4,000**

Doct. – Harrison's – Tonic – Chalybeate, medium emerald green, 9", smooth base, applied mouth, American 1865-1875 (rare) **$300-550**

Doctor – Warren's (backward "S") – Cough – Mixture, clear, 4", pontil-scarred base, flared lip, American 1840-1855 (rare) **$160-200**

Dr. Bell's – British Liniment – S.M. Shaw & Co – Alfred ME U.S.A., bluish aqua, 6-1/8", open pontil, rolled lip, American 1845-1855 (extremely rare). **$370-450**

Dr. Birmingham's – Antibillious – Blood Purifier, medium teal blue, 8-5/8", smooth base, applied square collar mouth, American 1865-1875 . . . .**$450-600**

Dr. C.W. Roback's – Scandinvaian – Blood Purifier – Purely Vegetable – Dyspepsia – Liver Complaint, deep aqua, 8-1/2", iron pontil, applied double collar mouth, American 1840-1860 (scarce) **$375-450**

Davis Vegetable Pain Killer, American, 1840-1860, **$180-250.**

Dr. Browder's Compound Syrup of Indian Turnip, American, 1840-1860, **$400-600.**

Dr. Davis's – Departure – Phila, medium blue green, 9-1/2", iron pontil, applied sloping collar mouth, American 1840-1860 . . . . **$1,600-2,000**

Dr. E. Blecker's – Tonic Mixture – For – Chills & Fever, deep bluish aqua, 6-7/8", pontil-scarred base, applied sloping collar mouth, American 1840-1855 (rare) **$650-800**

Dr. Edward's – Tar Wild Cherry – & Naptha – Cough Syrup, aqua, 5-1/8", open pontil, rolled lip, American 1840-1860 . . . . **$225-300**

Dr. F. Houck's – Panacea – New York, bluish aqua, 8-1/2", smooth base, applied sloping double collar mouth, American 1855-1865 . . . . **$165-200**

Dr. Fenner's – Kidney & Backache – Cure, medium amber, 10-1/4", smooth base, tooled mouth, American 1880-1895 **$55-75**

Dr. Friend's – Cough Balsam – Morristown N.J., bluish aqua, 6-3/8", open pontil, applied sloping collar mouth, American 1840-1860 (very rare) **$385-475**

Dr. Geo. W. Fisher's – Catarrh Cure – Baltimore, MD, golden yellow amber, 5-7/8", smooth base, tooled lip, American 1890-1910 (rare colored cure bottle) **$150-180**

Dr. H. Van Vleck's – Family Medicine – Pittsburgh PA, cornflower blue, 8-1/8", pontil-scarred base, applied sloping collar mouth, American 1845-1855 . . . . **$2,300-3,200**

Dr. H.W. Bergner's – Stomachic – Reading, PA, aqua, 4-3/4", open pontil, rolled lip, American 1840-1860 . . . . **$160-200**

Dr. H.W. Swartz – Cancer Specialist – New Oxford, PA, clear, 6-1/2", smooth base, tooled mouth, American 1885-1900 (very rare) **$110-150**

Dr. H. James – No. 19 Grand St. – Jersey City – N.J. – Also No 14 Decil St – Strand – London, bluish aqua, 8-1/8", open pontil, applied mouth, American 1840-1860 . . . . **$190-275**

Dr. J.A. Goodale – Newton & Dover – N.J., bluish aqua, 3-7/8", open pontil, rolled lip, American 1840-1860 . . . . **$160-200**

Dr. Jackson's – Pile – Embrocation – Phila, pale green aqua, 3-7/8", pontil-scarred base, wide flared out lip, American 1845-1855 . . . . **$225-300**

Dr. Jacob Webber's – Invigorating Cordial – T. Jones Agent & Proprietor – New York, aqua, 9-3/4", smooth base, applied double collar mouth, American 1855-1865 . . . . **$160-175**

Dr. Jayne's – Alternative – Philada, aqua, 5-3/4", pontil-scarred base, applied sloping collar mouth, American 1840-1865 . **$35-40**

Dr. Jones – Red (motif of three-leaf clover) – Clover – Tonic – E.Y. Griggs – Ottawa, Ills, medium amber, 9", smooth base, tooled mouth, American 1880-1890 . . . . **$75-90**

Dr. Kilmer & Co – Catarrh – Dr. Kilmer's – Cough Cure – Consumption Oil – Specific – Binghamton, N.Y., aqua, 8-5/8", smooth base, tooled mouth, American 1880-1895 . . . . **$560-700**

Dr. King's – Croup – & – Cough – Syrup, pale aqua, 5", open pontil, applied double collar mouth, American 1840-1860 (scarce) **$130-160**

Dr. Mann's – Celebrated – Ague Balsam – Galion, Ohio, deep aqua, 7", iron pontil, applied double collar mouth, American 1840-1860 . . . . **$370-450**

Dr. Markley's – Family – Medicine – Lancaster, PA, aqua, 6-1/2", open pontil, applied double collar mouth, American 1854-1860 . . . . **$285-375**

Dr. Mann's Celebrated Ague Balsam - Galion Ohio, American, 1840-1860, **$400-700.**

Dr. Townsend's - Sarsaparilla - Albany - N.Y., American, 1840-1860, **$300-400.**

Dr. Ordway's Celebrated Pain Destroyer (Label: Dr. Ordway's Celebrated Pain Destroyer, Ordway & Wadleigh Sole Proprietors, Lawrence, Mass), clear, 5-1/8", 12-sided, open pontil, flared-out lip, American 1835-1850 . . . . **$80-100**

Dr. S.A. Weaver's – Cerate, aqua, 2-3/4", open pontil, rolled lip, American 1840-1860 . . . . **$260-350**

Dr. S.F. Stowe's – Ambrosial Nectar (motif of stemmed glass inside vine frame) – Patented May 22, 1866, light yellow green (citron), 8", smooth base, applied mouth, American 1885-1895 (scarce) **$160-200**

Dr. S. Hart – New York – Vegetable – Extract, aqua, 7-1/4", open pontil, applied tapered mouth, American 1840-1860 (rare) **$325-400**

Dr. Sage's – Catarrh – Remedy – Buffalo – Dr. Pierce's – Buffalo – N.Y., emerald green, 2-1/8", smooth base, tooled mouth, American 1880-1890 . . . . **$85-100**

Dr. Swayne's – Panacea – Philada, clear with amethyst tint, 8", smooth base, tooled lip, American 1880-1890 . . . . **$150-180**

Dr. Taylor's Chronothermal – Balsam of – Liverwort – For Consumption – Asthma & C.G.J.L., bluish aqua, 8-1/8", pontil-scarred base, applied sloping collar mouth, American 1840-1855 (rare) **$285-375**

Dr. W. Eaton Boynton's Blood Cure and Humor Destroyer (labeled medicine bottle), bluish aqua, 7-1/2", pontil-scarred base, applied sloping collar mouth, American 1830-1850 . . . . **$150-180**

Drink – Wm Radam's – Microbe – Killer (around shoulder), medium amber, 10-3/8", smooth base, tooled mouth, American 1895-1905 (one of the rarest of the Radam bottles) . . . **$260-350**

E.C. Allen - Concentrated Electric Paste - OR - Arabian Pain - Extractor - Lancaster PA, American, 1840-1860, **$600-800.**

Dr. Wistar's Balsam of Wild Cherry - Philada, American, 1840-1860, **$170-250.**

Duffy's Formula, amber, 9-7/8", smooth base, applied mouth, American 1875-1890 . . . . **$110-150**

Extract – Valaria – Shaker – Fluid, bluish aqua, 3-3/4", open pontil, flared lip, American 1845-1855 . . . . **$130-150**

Fairchild's – Sure – Remedy, bluish aqua, 7-7/8", pontil-scarred base, applied sloping collar mouth, American 1840-1860 (extremely rare) **$850-1,200**

Fisher's – Seaweed – Extract – Manx Shrub (motif of shrub) – Registered – Company – Ulverston – Quarrie's Patent, yellow green, 5-1/4", triangular form with bulged neck, smooth base, tooled lip, American 1890-1910 . . . . **$260-350**

Forestine Kidney Cure, medium amber, 9-3/8", smooth base, tooled mouth, American 1880-1895 . . . . **$55-75**

From – Dr. H.C. Porter – & – Son's – Drug Store, clear, 7-5/8", smooth base, tooled mouth, American 1885-1900 . . . . **$180-275**

Gell's – Dalby's Carminative, pale blue green, 3-7/8", open pontil, flared out lip, American 1825-1835 . . . . **$225-300**

Germ Bacteria or – Fungus Destroyer – Wm Radams – Microbe (man beating a skeleton) Registered Trade Mark Dec. 13, 1887 – Cures – All – Diseases, amber, 10-1/4", smooth base, tooled lip, American 1887-1895 . . . . **$225-300**

Gu Wa's – Chinese – Herb – & – Vegetable – Remedies, amber, 6-3/4", smooth base (H), tooled lip, American 1890-1900 . . . . **$325-400**

Guinn's Pioneer – Blood Renewer – Macon Medicine Co. – Macon GA, reddish amber, 11-1/8", smooth base, applied double collar mouth, American 1875-1885 . . . . **$360-450**

For Colds - Coughs Croup & C - Immediate Relief & Speedy Cure, American, 1875-1885, **$500-700.**

Follansbee's - Elixir - of Health, American, 1840-1860, **$500-700.**

G.W. Merchant – Lockport – N.Y., blue green, 5-1/8", open pontil-scarred base, applied sloping collar mouth, American 1840-1860 . . . .**$260-350**

H. Lake – Indian – Specific, aqua, 8-1/4", open pontil, applied mouth, American 1840-1860 . . . . **$875-1,400**

Hermanu's – Germany's Infallible – Dyspepsia Cure, yellow amber, 2-7/8", smooth base, tooled lip, American 1880-1890 . . . . **$85-100**

Hoffman's Mixture – For – Gonorrhea Gleet & C. – Solomons & Co. – Savannah, Geo, aqua, 5-7/8", smooth base, tooled lip, American 1880-1890 (rare) **$85-120**

Holden's – Dysentery – & – Diarrhoea – Cordial, aqua, 5-1/4", open pontil, applied mouth, American 1840-1860 (rare) . . . **$360-450**

Holme & Kidd, deep bluish aqua, 6-1/2", pontil-scarred base, rolled lip, American 1840-1860 . . . . **$225-300**

Hop – Tonic (on 4 roof panels) Hop Tonic, medium amber, 9-7/8", smooth base, tooled mouth, American 1880-1890 . . . . **$185-250**

Hurd's Cough – Balsam, bluish aqua, 4-5/8", open pontil, rolled lip, American 1840-1860 . . . . **$45-70**

Improved – Distilled – Microbe Killer, clear, 9-3/4", smooth base (I.G.CO), tooled lip, American 1890-1910 . . . . **$160-200**

Indian – Specific – For Coughs – Prepared By – Dr. C. Freeman, bluish aqua, 5", pontil-scarred base, flared lip, American 1835-1850 . . . .**$385-500**

James L. Bispham – No. 710 – So 2d St – Philada, teal green, 8-1/4", smooth base, applied mouth, American 1865-1875 . . . .**$150-160**

Indian Clemens (standing Indian) Tonic - Prepared By Geo. W. House, American, 1840-1860, **$600-800.**

Jelly of Pomegranate - Preparate By - Dr. Gordak - Only, American, 1840-1860, **$200-300.**

Jas. Tarrant – Druggist – New York, aqua, 5-1/2", pontil-scarred base, applied sloping collar mouth, American 1840-1865 . . . . **$35-45**

J.B. Hicks – Reading, PA, aqua, 4-1/8", open pontil, flared out lip, American 1840-1860 . . . . **$85-100**

Jelly of – Pomegranate – Preparate – By – Dr. Gordak – Only, aqua, 6-3/4", pontil-scarred base, flared lip, American 1840-1860 (scarce) **$325-400**

J.W. Bull's – Recto – Mistura – Baltimore, aqua, 5-7/8", open pontil, applied mouth, American (extremely rare) **$435-600**

JNO Sullivan – Pharmacist (JS monogram) – Boston, milk glass, 5", smooth base, tooled lip, American 1880-1900 . . . . . **$110-150**

John C. Baker Co – Cod Liver Oil – Philadelphia, clear, 9", smooth base, tooled mouth, American 1900-1910 . . . . **$125-140**

John A. Jones – Baltimore – No 1, pale aqua, 3-3/8", open pontil, flared lip, American 1845-1855 . . . . **$75-100**

Jos. Fleming – Druggist – Cor. Market & Diamond – Pittsbg PA, ice blue, 7-5/8", iron pontil, applied double collar mouth, American 1845-1855 (extremely rare) **$185-275**

Log Cabin – Hops and Buchu – Remedy, amber, 10-1/8", smooth base (Pat. Sept. 6/87), applied blob type mouth, American 1887-1895 . . . . **$110-125**

Longlely's – Panacea, olive green, 6-3/4", pontil-scarred base, applied double collar mouth, American 1840-1860 **$3,600-4,500**

Lyon's – Power – B & P – N. Y., medium blue green, 4-1/4", smooth base, tooled lip, American 1860-1880 . . . . **$150-180**

Lyon's – Power – B & P – N. Y., deep reddish puce, 4-1/8", open pontil, inward rolled lip, American 1860-1880 . . . . **$160-250**

*John Gilbert &
Co - Druggists
- 177 North 3D. St.
- Philad, American,
1855-1865,*
$275-325.

*Log Cabin Sarsaparilla - Rochester, N.Y.,
American, 1887-1895,* **$250-350.**

L.P. Dodge Rheumatic - Liniment - Newburg, American, 1840-1860, **$1,800-2,750.**

Mrs. E. Kidder- Dysentery Cordial - Boston, American, 1840-1860, **$800-1,200.**

L.Q.C. Wishart's Pine Tree – Tar Cordial – Phila – Trade (motif of tree) Mark, blue green, 10-1/4", smooth base, tooled mouth, American 1885-1895 . . . .**$160-200**

Mad. M.J. Goodman's – Excelsior – Pearl – Drops, milk glass, 4-5/8", smooth base, rolled lip, American 1880-1895 . .**$160-200**

Magnes – Carbonic, amber with white and blue enameled background, black lettering, 9", smooth base, tooled lip, original glass stopper, American 1890-1910 . . . .**$150-180**

Magnetic – Aether By – Halsted & Co, aqua, 4-3/8", 9-sided, open pontil, flared out lip, American 1840-1860 (extremely rare) **$425-600**

M.B. Riberts's – Vegetable – Embrocation, light emerald green, 5", pontil-scarred base, applied sloping collar mouth, American 1840-1860 . . . .**$225-300**

McDonald's – Annihilator – Bronchitis – Coughs & Colds, medium amber, 7-3/4", smooth base, tooled mouth, American 1880-1890 . . . .**$110-150**

M.K. Paine Druggist – & Apothecary – Windsor, VT, milk glass, 6-1/2", smooth base, applied mouth, American 1880-1895 . . . .**$160-200**

Morley's – Liver and Kidney – Cordial, medium amber 9", smooth base, tooled mouth, American 1880-1890 . . . . . .**$75-90**

Mother's – Worm Syrup (side of building with windows and doors) – Edward Wilder & Co – Wholesale Druggists, clear, 4-5/8", smooth base, tooled mouth, American 1885-1900 . . . .**$150-180**

Mrs. E. Kidder – Dysentery – Cordial – Boston, aqua, 7-7/8", open pontil, applied mouth, American 1840-1860 . . . .**$185-225**

Murray & Lanman – Chemists & Druggists – No 69 Water St – New York, medium apple green, 10-1/2", open pontil, applied sloping double collar mouth, American 1845-1855 .... **$1,600-2,500**

Myers – Rock Rose – New Haven, aqua, 8-7/8", iron pontil, applied mouth, American 1840-1860 .... **$425-600**

N.W. Seat (letter "S" is backwards on bottle) MD – Negative – Electric Fluid – New York, aqua 3-1/4", open pontil, rolled lip, American 1840-1860 .... **$160-200**

Normal Liquid – Ipecac – Parke, Davis & Co – Detroit Michigan, U.S.A., amber, 4-1/2", smooth base, tooled mouth, American 1890-1925 .... **$45-60**

Owl Drug Co. (owl on mortar) San Francisco, deep yellow green, 9-3/4", smooth base, tooled mouth, American 1900-1915 .... **$225-300**

Paul G. Schuh – Rattle Snake Oil (inside a coiled snake) Cairo, Ill, clear, 5-1/2", smooth base, tooled mouth, American 1885-1895 .... **$225-300**

Prairie Weed – Balsam – Austin Bros & Steere – Boston (sheaf of weeds), aqua, 7", smooth base, tooled mouth, American 1885-1900 .... **$75-90**

Primley's – Iron & Wahoo – Tonic – Jones & Primley Co. – Elkhart, Ind, yellow olive amber, 9-1/2", smooth base (F.C. Mfg. Co), applied mouth, American 1870-1880 ...... **$260-350**

Purcell – Ladd & Co – Druggist – Richmond, VA, aqua, 3-7/8", open pontil, rolled lip, American 1840-1860 .... **$325-400**

Querus – Cod Liver Oil – Jelly, bluish aqua, 5-3/8". Wide mouth jar, pontil-scarred base, folded rim, American 1845-1855 (scarce) **$225-300**

Mrs. S.A. Allen's - Worlds
Hair - Restorer - New York,
American, 1865-1875,
$300-400.

Myers - Rock Rose - New Haven,
American, 1840-1860, **$350-450.**

*Mystic Cure - For - Rheumatism - and - Neuralgia
- Mystic Cure, American, 1890-1900,* **$150-200.**

No 1 Shaker Syrup - Canterbury, N.Y., American, 1840-1860, **$180-250.**

The Owl Drug Co. - Trade Mark - San Francisco, American, 1890-1915, **$100-150.**

R.A. Boyd – Belvidere. N.J., aqua, 6-1/4", open pontil, applied double collar mouth, American 1840-1860 (very rare) . **$185-275**

R.E. Sellers – Druggist – Pittsburgh, clear, 4-3/4", pontil-scarred base, rolled lip, American 1840-1860 . . . . **$55-75**

Rhode's – Antidote – To – Malaria – Fever & Ague Cure, deep bluish aqua, 8-1/4", pontil-scarred base, applied sloping collar mouth, American 1845-1855 (rare pontiled cure bottle) **$385-475**

Richards & Perkins – Druggists – Bangor ME, deep bluish aqua, 7-1/4", pontil-scarred base, applied sloping collar mouth, American 1840-1860 (very rare) **$160-200**

Robbins – Anod. Drops – Balto, aqua, 4-1/4", open pontil, applied mouth, American 1840-1860. **$235-300**

Rogers – Vegetable – Work Syrup – Cincinnati, deep aqua, 4-7/8", open pontil, applied mouth, American 1840-1860 (very rare) **$205-300**

Rohrer's – Expectoral – Wild – Cherry – Tonic – Lancaster, PA, medium golden amber, 10-3/4", smooth base, applied mouth, American 1865-1870 . . . . **$210-300**

Rothe – Boston – No 1, aqua, 3-5/8", open pontil-scarred base, rolled lip, American 1840-1860 . . . . **$85-125**

R.W. Davis Drug Co – Chicago, U.S.A., milk glass, 11-1/8", smooth base, tooled mouth, American 1890-1910 . . . . **$105-150**

Samuel Simes – Pharmacien – Chestnut St. Phil, aqua, 8-7/8", open pontil, applied mouth, American 1845-1855 . . . . . **$75-100**

Scarpa's – Oil For – Deafness, aqua, 2-1/2", 6-sided, open pontil, flared out lip, American 1840-1860 (very rare) **$460-550**

Selden's – Wigwam – Liniment – N.Y., aqua, 7-7/8", open pontil, applied mouth, American 1840-1860 (rare). **$325-400**

Proctor & Gamble - Glycerine, American, 1850-1860, **$250-300.**

Rohrer's - Expectoral - Wild Cherry - Tonic - Lancaster, PA, American, 1855-1865, **$375-500.**

Schwartz & Haslett – C.F. Galton's – Dyspepsia Remedy – Pittsburgh, PA, amber, 7-3/4", smooth base, applied mouth, American 1870-1880 . . . .**$130-150**

Shaker – Anodyne – Nth Enfield – N.H., bluish aqua, 4", smooth base, tooled mouth, American 1875-1885 . . . .**$85-120**

Shaker Cherry – Pectoral Syrup – Canterbury – N.H. No. 1, aqua, 5-3/8", open pontil, applied mouth, American 1840-1860 . . . .**$160-200**

S.S. Ryckman – Sole Mfg Hamilton – Ont (Label: Ryckman's SRS Kootenay Cure, S.S. Ryckman Medicine Co, Hamilton, Canada), medium amber, 10-1/8", smooth base, tooled mouth, Canadian 1880-1890 . . . .**$105-125**

Swaim's – Panacea – Philada, medium olive green, 7-3/4", smooth base, applied mouth, American 1855-1865 . . . .**$160-200**

Sweet Spirits, Nitre, Put Up By N. Wood & Son, 428 & 430, Fore Street, Portland, ME (labeled medicine bottle), yellow olive, 5", open pontil, flared out lip, American 1835-1855 . . . .**$155-175**

T. Morris Perot & Co – Druggists – Philada, aqua, 4-7/8", open pontil, rolled lip, American 1850-1880 . . . .**$255-300**

T. Morris Perot & Co – Druggists – Philada, sapphire blue, 4-7/8", open pontil, rolled lip, American 1850-1880 . . .**$250-300**

Tarpant – Druggist – New York, bluish aqua, 5", pontil-scarred base, rolled lip, American 1840-1860 . . . .**$55-75**

Telsier-Prevost – A Paris, medium blue green, 7-3/4", pontil-scarred base, applied sloping collar mouth, American 1840-1860 . . . .**$260-400**

Rumford - Chemical Works, American, 1885-1900, **$200-300.**

Sparks - Kidney & Liver - Cure - Trade Mark (Upper Torso of Man) - Perfect Health - Camden, N.J., American, 1880-1890, **$800-1,200.**

The Great European Cough Remedy, Prepared By Rev. Walker Clark, Minot, Maine (labeled medicine bottle), olive amber, 4-5/8", pontil-scarred base, applied mouth, American 1835-1855
....**$160-200**

The Great – Shoshonees – Remedy Of – Dr. Josephus, deep bluish aqua, 9-1/4", smooth base, applied sloping collar mouth, American 1870-1880.............................**$85-100**

The River Swamp – Chill and (motif of alligator) Fever Cure – Augusta, GA, yellow amber, 6-1/4", smooth base, tooled lip, American 1880-1890............................**$550-700**

Thompsonian – Appetizer – Trade Mark (motif of portly man) – Prepared By – JJ. Vogt & Co – Cleveland O, medium yellow amber, 9-1/8", smooth base (B.F.C. CO), applied sloping collar mouth, American 1875-1885 (rare)...............**$160-200**

Thron's – Compound – Syrup of – Cod Liver – Oil, deep aqua, 7-3/8", 8-sided, open pontil, applied mouth, American 1840-1860 (extremely rare)...**$425-600**

Trade Mark – Est 1842 – (motif of castle) Duffy's Tower Mint, amber, 9", tower with windows and doors, smooth base, applied mouth, American 1875-1885......................**$525-700**

Trade Mark – Sparks – Perfect Health (upper torso of a man) For – Kidney & Liver – Diseases – Camden, deep amber, 9-1/2", smooth base, tooled lip, American 1885-1895..**$260-350**

U.S.A. – Hosp. Dept, yellow amber with olive tone, 9-1/2", smooth base, applied double collar mouth, American 1860-1870 (used during the Civil War by the Union Army Medical Corps)
....**$530-800**

Vaughn's – Vegetable – Lithontriptic – Mixture – Buffalo, deep bluish aqua, 8-1/8", smooth base, applied sloping collar, American 1855-1870.................................**$150-180**

Thompson's - Hygeia -
Wild Cherry - Phosphate
- Chicago American, 1880-
1895, **$375-450.**

U.S.A. - Hosp. Dept, American,
1863-1870, **$800-1,200.**

U.S.A. - Hosp. Dept, American, 1863-1870, **$150-250.**

W.C. Montgomery's - Hair - Restorer - Philada, American, 1865-1875, **$275-375.**

Western – Moxie – Nerve Food Co. – Chicago, aqua, 9-7/8", smooth base, tooled blob top, American 1890-1910 . . .**$160-160**

White & Hill – Dr. Warren's – Expectorant – Nashua, N.H., aqua, 6-3/8", open pontil, applied double collar mouth, American 1840-1860 . . . .**$225-250**

Whitwell's – Patent – Volatile – Aromatic & – Headache – Snuff, clear, 3-5/8", pontil-scarred base, inward rolled lip, American 1830-1850 . . . .**$225-350**

Wild Cherry Tonic – Wm. F. Zoeller – Pittsburgh, PA, amber, 10-3/4", smooth base, applied mouth, American 1870-1880 (very rare) **$325-400**

Winans Bros (Motif of Indian) Indian – Cure – For The – Blood – Price $1.00 – Winans Brothers – Indian Cure, bluish aqua, 9-1/4", smooth base, tooled mouth, American 1880-1890 . . . .**$160-250**

U.S.A. - Hosp. Dept, American, 1865-1875, **$250-300.**

Milk Bottles

In recent years, many collectors have taken a renewed interest in collecting milk bottles. The first patent date for a milk bottle was issued in January 1875 to the "Jefferson Co. Milk Assn." The bottle featured a tin top with a spring clamping device. The first known standard-shaped milk bottle (pre-1930) had a patent date of March 1880 and was manufactured by the Warren Glass Works of Cumberland, Maryland. In 1884, A.V. Whiteman patented a jar with a dome-type tin cap to be used along with the patent of the Thatcher and Barnhart fastening device for a glass lid. There is no trace of a patent for the bottle itself. Among collectors today, the Thatcher milk bottle is one of the most prized. There are several variations on the original.

Very early bottles were embossed with a picture of a Quaker farmer milking his cow while seated on a stool. "Absolutely Pure Milk" is stamped into the glass on the bottle's shoulder.

An important development in the design of the milk bottle was the patent issued to H.P. and S.L. Barnhart on September 17, 1889, for their method of capping and sealing. Their invention involved the construction of a bottle mouth adapted to receive and retain a wafer disc or cap. It was eventually termed the milk bottle cap and revolutionized the milk bottling industry. Between 1900 and 1920, there weren't many new patents or bottles.

With the introduction of the Owens semi-automatic and automatic bottle machines, milk bottles became a mass-produced product. Between 1921 and 1945, the greatest number of milk bottles were manufactured and used. After 1945, square milk bottles and paper cartons were commonly used.

Two types of milk bottles are of particular interest to the collector. These are the "baby tops," which had an embossed baby's face on the upper part of the neck, and the "cop-the-cream" bottles that had a policeman's head and cap embossed into the neck. In 1936, Mike Pecora Sr. of Pecora's Dairy in Drums, PA, created the baby top design. Pecora's Dairy used quart, pint, and half pint round bottles with pyro printing. Fifteen years after the original baby face was produced, a "twin face" baby top was made with two faces, back to back, on opposite sides of the bottle. Both of these clear-colored bottles, along with their tin tops, are very rare and valuable.

Note: The color mentioned in the following bottle descriptions is the color of the lettering on the bottle.

Baby Tops

Dressel Dairy Co – Granite City, IL, red $109

Edgewood Dairy – Beloit, WI, orange and black (semi-rare) $110

Embassy Dairy – Washington, DC, red. $55

Fox Dairy – Fostoria, O – Home Owned, red $80

Frozen Gold – Safe Milk – Sheboygan, WI, black (rare) . . $80

J.J. Brown Dairy – Troy, NY, orange. $85

Lemke's Deluxe – Wausau, WI, camel tan $80

North Jersey – Irvington, NJ, orange $55

Page's – Pittsburgh, PA, orange. $55

Pecora's – Hazleton, PA, red. $55

Rando Milk Co – Quality Milk For The Baby – Endicott, NY, orange (semi-rare) $80

Springfield Plantation Dairy – Savannah, GA, orange . . . $105

Swayer Farms – Gilford, NH – For Health, orange and black (semi-rare) $155

Sunnyhurst Dairy – Reading, MA, orange (semi-rare) $150

United Farm – Albany, NY, red. $105

Upton's Farm – Bridgewater, MA, black $60

Cop the Cream

Crombie Guernsey Dairy – Joliet, IL, red (semi-rare) $160

Fountain Head Dairy – Hagerstown, MD, tan (semi-rare) $155

Furman Bros – Ithaca, NY, orange. $155

Baby Top, Rando - Milk Co. - Endicott, NY, **$75.**

Hillside Dairy Milk – Whately, MA, black (semi-rare) $165

Hy-Point Dairy – Wilmington, DE, orange (rare) $155

Leighty Pure Milk Co – Connelleville, PA, red $80

Morningcrest Farms – Eau Claire, WI, orange (semi-rare) . . . $155

Pitstick Farm – Dairy – Ottawa, IL, red (semi-rare) . . $155

Royal Farms Dairy – Baltimore, MD, orange (semi-rare) . . $160

Silver Hill Dairy – Portland, OR, red (semi-rare) $155

West Side Dairy – Albans, VT, red (semi-rare) $160

Cream Tops

Burg's – Model Dairy – Clintonville, WI, orange $55

Consumers Dairy Co. – Westerly, RI, black $55

Greenville Dairy Banquet Products – Greenville, PA, green
. . . . $50

Green Meadow Farm – Rye, NY, green (semi-rare) $75

Larose Dairy – So. Hadley Falls, MA, red $65

McAdams Dairy Products – Chelsea, MA, orange $55

Queen City Dairy – Cumberland, MD, orange $25

Shamrock Dairy – Tucson, AZ, black $50

Tru-li-pure – Nashville, TN, red $35

Week's Dairy – Laconia, NH, red $35

Quarter Pints

Almida County – Oakland, CA, orange $35

Bay City Creamery – San Leanadro, CA, red $30

El Camino Creamery – San Bruno, CA, black $30

Elkhorn Farm – Watsonville, CA, orange $25

Hygionic Dairy Co. – Watertown, NY, orange $15

Pratt's Dairy – Visalia, CA, black $30

Rivera Dairy – Santa Barbara, CA, green $35

Virginia Dairy – The Home of Better Milk – Richmond, VA,
red (semi-rare) $55

Wildwood Dairy – Santa Rosa, CA, green $35

Zenda Farms – Clayton, NY, orange $25

Cream Top, Greenville - Dairy - Banquet - Greenville, Pa, $50.

Gallons

Bolin Dairy Farm – Bradford, PA, red. $55

Carron Country Creamery – Rawlins, WY, yellow. $60

Guernsey Milk – Champaign, IL, orange $60

Harmony Dairy – Country Style – Buttermilk – Pittsburgh, PA, red. $55

Ka-vee – Best By Test – Milk, Belleville, PA. $55

Lewis Dairies Inc – Grove City, PA, green $60

Marburger Farm Dairy – Evans City, PA, black. $50

Otto's Milk – Pittsburgh, PA, red $55

Purity Milk Co. – Phillipsburg, PA, red $55

Sanitary Milk Co – Rantoul, IL, orange $50

Square Quarts

Armstrong Dairy Inc – Locust Valley, NJ, orange (semi-rare) $35

Big Boy Milk – Rochester, NY, amber $15

Blue Spruce Dairy – Freehold, NJ, blue $25

Broadway Farms Dairy – New York City, NY, red $25

Fitchett Bros – Lake View Dairy – Poughkeepsie, NY, orange $25

Harrisburg Milk – Harrisburg, PA, green and orange $50

Hy Vita Milk Co – Ship Bottom, NJ, orange (semi-rare) . . . $55

J.D. Poole & Sons – Minford, OH, red $25

J & J Dairy Products Inc. – Jersey City, NJ, red $15

Little Dairy – Let Us Serve You – Namog, ID, green $35

Model Dairy – Huron, SD, red (semi-rare) $30

Momence Dairy – Momence, IL, purple $15

Rutland Hills Co-op Inc – Watertown, NY, orange $25

Seegert's Milk – Forestville, NY , orange $20

University Of New York – Delhi, NY, green $35

Square Quart, J.D. - Poole - & - Sons - Minford, Ohio, **$10.**

Coffee Creamers

Carrigan's – Niagara Falls, NY, green $40

Dart's Dairy – Manchester, CT, orange $30

Girton Dairy Equipment – Girton Mfg. – Illville, PA, orange (semi-rare) $75

Johnson's Dairy – Cooperstown, NY, black (semi-rare) $80

Kyles Dairy – Mackeyville, PA, orange $35

Lincoln Trail – Motel And Restaurant – Highway 66 – Tell City, IN, red $55

*Coffee Creamer, Dart's Dairy - Manchester, Conn., **$30.***

Neidig's Dairy – Sunbury, PA, orange $25

N. Mex Milk Prods. Inc – Belen, NM, orange (rare) $100

Picket's Pasteurized Products – Sheridan, IN, orange $45

Ramon's – Hickory – Foods – Florence, AL, green $55

Richard Dairy – Neward, NE, orange (semi-rare) $55

Sharpes Dairy – Jackson, MI, green $55

Strickler's – It's Better – Cream – Huntingdon, PA, orange
. . . . $25

Twin Cedar Dairy – McClure, PA, red $35

Waynesburg Sanitary Dairy Co – Waynesburg, PA, orange $30

Miscellaneous

A.G.S. & Co. – Patented – April 5, 1898, clear, quart, smooth base, tooled mouth, American 1890-1900 . . . . **$80-100**

Arborvitae – Lodge Farm – Succasunna – N.J. – This Bottle – To Be Washed – And Returned, clear, 6-7/8", smooth base, tooled mouth, American 1910-1920 . . . . **$110-150**

Country Store Countertop Milk Jar, deep bluish aqua, 17-1/2" h, 12" dia., smooth base, ABM lip, American 1920-1935 (made by Owens Illinois Glass Co.) **$700-800**

Ferme – Des – Vauzillons (on lid), milk glass encased in clear quart, pontil-scarred base, tooled mouth, French 1910-1920 . . . . **$170-250**

Greenfield – Dairy Co – Jersey City, clear, 1/4 pint, smooth base, ABM lip, American 1915-1925 . . . . **$110-150**

One Quart – Liquid – E.F. Mayer – Phone – Glen'd 3887R – 289 Hollenbeck St., amber, quart, smooth base (M), American 1920-1935 . . . . **$130-160**

This Bottle – The Property of and Filled By – The Page Dairy Co. – Toledo – Ohio – Sealed – One Quart – No. 5, deep amber, quart, smooth base, ABM lip, American 1920-1935 . . . . **$120-150**

Trade Mark – Union Milk Company (cow's head) Milk & Cream – Registered – The Publick Cautioned – Not To Use This Bottle, clear, quart, smooth base, tooled lip, American 1915-1925 . . . . **$90-120**

One Quart - Liquid - Carrigan's - Niagara - Dairy Co. - Reed, American, 1920-1930, **$375-450** (rare in this color).

Weckerle - Reg - Weckerle - 1 Qt, American, 1820-1930, **$275-375.**

Patriotic Bottles

With the beginning of World War II, the bottling industry, specifically the milk bottling manufacturers, began a campaign of patriotism in America that had never been experienced before at any time of history. World War II resulted in some of the most collectible bottles with war slogans depicting tanks, soldiers, fighter planes, "V" signs, and saying and slogans about Pearl Harbor. While many of the bottles, especially milk bottles, were colorful with many detailed graphics, many war slogans are basic and plain with sayings like "Buy War Savings Bonds — Keep It Up" on the wings of bombers and fighter planes and "Buy Bonds and Stamps."

The Applied Color Label (ACL) soda pop bottle was conceived in the 1930s when Prohibition forced brewing companies to experiment with soda pop. Bottlers throughout the United States created bottle labels that will forever preserve unique patriotic moments and figures in

American history such as the American flags, the Statue of Liberty, the "V" symbol, fighter planes, fighter pilots, soldiers, and the Stars and Stripes. Bottles with images of Uncle Sam and the American Flag are the most popular.

Other groups of bottles such as historical flasks, figurals, and Jim Beam bottles have depicted patriotic figures, embossed images, and paintings of important patriotic milestones in the history of America. There are 25 different types of flasks representing the American flag in various forms such as symbols of patriotism, a rallying cry for winning the war, and the re-establishment of the Union following the Civil War.

Beer Bottles

"Buy U.S. War Bonds", 9-1/2", Metz Brewing Co. **$30-35**

Pioneer "Victory" Beer, 9-1/2" **$30-35**

Uncle Sam Beer – Glencoe Brewing Company, Glencoe, Minnesota – 1918, amber, 9-1/4", two paper labels with picture depicting Uncle Sam holding a bottle of beer next to the brewery, 14 oz. **$135-150**

Figurals

Canteen – 25th Annual Encampment – GAR – Department of Ohio – 1891 – Steubenville (bust of man on one side and filson on reverse side), white pottery with maroon transfer and gold trim, 3-1/4", smooth base, original mouth ring, American 1891 . . . . **$160-250**

Canteen – Souvenir – Twenty Sixth Grand Annual – Encampment – Washington, Dc Sept. 20th To 23rd 1892, Reverse Side: GAR 1861 To 1865 1892 – Patented April 16, 1885, stamped metal canteen with stamped copper embossing, 5", original cork stopper on chain, American 1892 . . . . . . **$160-200**

Independence Hall Bank – "Bank of Independence Hall 1776-1876 – Patent Pending, pressed clear glass, 7-1/4", tin base sliding closure, American 1876 (rare souvenir candy container from the Philadelphia Centennial Exposition of 1876) . **$400-475**

Liberty Bell Candy Container – "Proclaim Liberty Throughout The Land – 1776/Centennial Exposition/1876", clear, 3-1/2", smooth base, sheared and ground lip, American 1875-1876 . . . . **$200-275**

Liberty Dollar Coin Flask – on one side "United States Of America/In God We Trust" (American eagle)/one dollar, on other side "E. Pluribus Unum"/(bust of Columbia), clear, 4-1/2", smooth base, ground lip, American 1885-1895 . . . . **$275-350**

Military Hat Candy Container, clear, cap reading "U.S. Military Hat, Pla-Toy Company, Greensburg, PA, American 1930-1940 . . . . **$90-140**

Statue of Liberty Jars (2), both clear glass, 12-1/2", smooth base, ground rims, American 1886-1890 (brought from France in 1885 and unveiled on October 28, 1886, President Cleveland received this gift from France for the American people) **$300-375**

Statue of Liberty, milk glass base with cast metal Statue of Liberty, 15-1/2" (including statue), smooth base, sheared and ground lip, American 1890-1900 . . . . **$425-500**

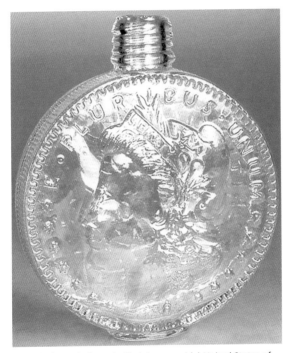

Figural Liberty Dollar coin flask (on one side) United States of America - In God We Trust (American eagle) - One Dollar (on other side) E. Pluribus Unum (bust of Columbia) 1885, 1885-1895, 4-1/2", **$250-350.**

Uncle Sam Candy Container, clear glass with 50% or original red, white, and blue paint - Uncle Sam standing next to container, American 1915-1925 . . . .**$325-400**

Uncle Sam, clear, 9-1/2", smooth base, tooled top, "Tall Hat" screw on cap, American 1890-1910. . . . .**$90-120**

Flasks & Bottles

Ceramic G.A.R. Presidents Flask, white with multicolored transfers of G.A.R. medal on one side depicting Lincoln April 14th, 1865; Garfield July 2nd, 1884; and McKinley Sept 6th, 1901 on reverse, 5-3/4", (rare flask showing the three Presidents who were assassinated while in office). **$375-450**

Eagle with Banner, medium yellow olive green quart, smooth base, applied top, American 1855-1860 . . . .**$575-800**

Eagle – Eagle, greenish aqua pint, pontil-scarred base, sheared lip, American 1835-1845 . . . .**$160-200**

Eagle – Furled Flag – "For Our Country", medium yellow green pint, pontil-scarred base, tooled lip, American 1825-1835 (rare) **$1,600-2,500**

Eagle – "Liberty" Tree, light green half-pint, pontil-scarred base, tooled top, American 1820-1835 . . . .**$750-900**

Franklin D. Roosevelt Flask – bust of Roosevelt on one side above an American eagle, reverse side has image of hydro-electrical dam and hand grasping a lightning bolt with TVA…1936, Tennessee Valley Authority, aqua, 10", smooth base, tooled top, American 1936. . . . .$125-200

Eagle – Morning Glory – Stoneware Flask, tan pottery with dark brown Bennington-type glaze, pint, pontil-scarred base, applied double collar mouth, American 1840-1845 . . . .**$750-1,000**

Eagle - Cornucopia, 1825-1835, 7", $150-200.

Eagle - Eagle, 1855-1865, pint, Ohio Glasshouse, **$3,000-4,500 (Rare).**

Eagle – Morning Glory – Stoneware Flask, tan pottery with dark brown Bennington-type glaze, pint, pontil-scarred base, applied double collar mouth, American 1840-1845 . . . . **$750-1,000**

"Liberty"/Eagle – Willington Glass Co. – West, Willington – Conn, deep olive green pint, smooth base, applied sloping collar top, American 1865-1875 . . . . **$225-300**

Teddy Roosevelt & Cabinet Whiskey Bottle – "Cabinet (three – eagle picture – star) Whiskey – A Blend Bottled By – Robert & Lindley – Salt Lake City, Utah, medium amber, 9", smooth base, tooled top, American 1905 (label depicts President Theodore Roosevelt with Vice President Charles Fairbanks presiding with full cabinet) **$325-400**

U.S. Patented Applied For – E. Puribus Unum – C. Packman Jr. & Co. Baltimore, MD – label-under-glass flask, clear glass with multicolored label depicting an eagle with crossed flags, shield, and cannons, smooth base, ground lip, original metal cap and strap rings, American 1885-1900 . . . . **$400-475**

Jim Beam Bottles

American Bald Eagle – 1966, white head, golden beak, and rich brown plumage, yellow claws grip on a branch of a tree . . **$30-35**

Amvets – 1970, commemorates the 25th anniversary of the Veterans of American Wars; World War II, Korea, and Vietnam. Gold metal eagle designed for stopper above the red, white, blue, and yellow bottle. Embossed war scene is on the reverse. 11-3/4" . . . **$30-35**

Bald Eagle – 1985, bald eagle with spread wings **$30-35**

Boots and Helmet – 1984, army helmet sitting on top of combat boots, (very collectible among military personnel and collectors). . . . **$20-35**

Label-under-glass flask, U.S. - Patented Applied For - E. Pluribus Unum - C. Packman Jr. & Co. Baltimore, Md, 1885-1900, 5", **$375-475.**

Selection of flasks: Eagle (reverse plain), 1830-1845, 2-1/2 quart, **$4,000-6,000 (extremely rare size);** *Eagle - Eagle, 1835-1845, quart,* **$175-250;** *Eagle - Eagle, 1835-1845, pint,* **$150-200.**

Crispus Attucks – **1976**, picture of Crispus Attucks, American Revolutionary War hero with American flag in background **$15-20**

Franklin Mint – **1970**, Liberty Bell on one side and blue and white shield with Liberty on other side **$15-20**

Pearl Harbor – **1972, Dec 7 1941 – Pearl Harbor – Pearl Harbor Survivors Association**, bald eagle sitting on top of bottle **$30-35**

Statue of Liberty – **1975**, "Give me your tired"....on back **$25-30**

Statue of Liberty – 1985, "Give me your tired"....on back
....$25-35

U.S. Open – Pebble Beach, Cal – June 12-18 1972, red, white, and blue Uncle Sam hat doubling as a gold bag $30-35

Washington State Bicentennial – 1976, Revolutionary War drummer on red and white base with a gold Liberty Bell reading "1776-1976" and round blue sign with stars reading "200 Years"
....$20-25

Milk Bottles

Quarts 1942-1945

Anderson Erickson Dairy, Des Moines, IA, picture of Abraham Lincoln, "That Freedom shall not perish from the earth!", Buy War Bonds..$110-135

Clarksburg Dairy, Clarksburg, WV, Conserve "V" For Victory – Buy War Bonds and Stamps $95-110

Cloverleaf Dairy, MD, red stars around bottle, bomber with "Buy War Savings Bonds" on wings – "Keep It Up" $85-110

Compston Bros. Dairy, Corning, CA, black lettering, Milk for Victory with "V" symbol $85-110

Crane Dairy, Utica, NY, red lettering, Buy War Bonds and Stamps For Victory $50-60

Dykes Dairy, Warren, PA, The United States is a Good Investment (Picture of Statue of Liberty) Buy War Bonds and Stamps . $85-95

Elmwood Dairy, Oxbridge, MA, We Need Your Help (Uncle Sam Pointing) It's Your Right – It's Your Responsibility – Buy More Bonds..$65-78

*Buy - Everybody
- Every Pay Day - 10c
- War - Bonds,* **$150.**

Ferry Hills Farms, Praire View, IL, It's Patriotic to Save (Fighter Plane) Buy War Bonds and Stamps **$85-95**

Geneva Dairy, Geneva, NY, "V" For Victory – sailor standing by battleship **$85-110**

Golden Crest, Bordens, Buy War Bonds **$85-100**

Hansen Dairy, Deer Lodge, MT, black lettering, Bonds Buy Bombs **$85-100**

Haskels Dairy, Augusta, CA, Back Their Attack – Buy More War Bonds – Drink Milk For Health. **$55-65**

Haskels Dairy, Augusta, CA, Milk Helps To – Keep 'Em Flying – Do Your Part – Buy War Bonds and Stamps (Picture of Pilot) **$85-95**

Heisler's Cloverleaf Dairy, Tamaqua, PA, Armaments and Good Health – For Victory – Drink More Milk. **$110-135**

Hygrade Dairy, Buffalo, NY, Give A Pint of Blood And Help Save A Life (rare) **$190-210**

Illinois Valley, Strator, Ottawa IL, orange lettering, Revenge Pearl Harbor **$85-100**

Kentucky Acres Dairy, Crestwood, KY, Buy War Bonds, Everybody – Every Payday (on arrow pointing to target) **$55-65**

Lavine's Dairy, Potsdam, NY, Victory – Picture of soldier in middle of "V" **$85-105**

Melrose Dairy, Dyersburg, TN, red lettering, fighter plane "Keep 'Em Flying, Buy War Bonds Today" **$110-130**

Perry Creamery, Tuscalocsa, AL, National Defense Starts – Buy Defense Bonds – With Health Defense. **$65-80**

Shamrock Dairy, Tuscon, AZ, America Has A Job To Do! "V" symbol with picture of pilot **$85-110**

Shums Dairy, Jeanette, PA, (picture of eagle) National – Defense Starts With Good Health – Build America's Future – Drink More Milk **$40-50**

Sunshine Dairy, St. Johns, Newfoundland, Canada, black & orange lettering, victory sign with Churchill, Tanks, and Ships **$220-260**

Thatchers Manufacturing Glass Co. – Series of (8) Slogans (Ea) **$110-160**
  • Victory – Comes A Little Closer Every Time You Buy A – War Bond (fighter plane)

- We Need Your Help – It's Your Fight – It's Your Responsibility – Buy War Bonds (Uncle Sam pointing)

Anderson Erickson Dairy, Des Moines, IA

- "That Freedom Shall Not Perish From the Earth!" – Buy War Bonds (Abraham Lincoln)
- Think – Act – Work (picture of eagle) – Victory
- You Can Keep 'Em Flying By Buying (fighter plane) U.S. War Bonds – Stamps

For Victory - Buy - United States - Savings Bonds - and Stamps, **$70.**

Milk - The First Line - of - Health Defense, **$50.**

My - War Stamps - Are - Adding Up, **$150.**

- Action Speaks Louder Than Words – What Are You Doing to Help Uncle Sam?

Royale Dairy, Elmira, NY

- Keep Them Rolling (Tank) Buy Bonds and Stamps
- You Owe It To Your Country – Buy War Bonds – You Owe It To Your Health – Drink Milk

The Navy - Our Protector, **$250.**

V - for - Victory - M - for - Milk, **$250.**

We're All Pulling For - Uncle Sam, **$75.**

Common Quarts

A Healthy Nation Is A Strong Nation – Uncle Sam Holding A Glass Of Milk $40-50

America Is A Great Place To Be – Lets Keep It That Way $40-45

Buy Defense Bonds And Stamps For Victory – "V" Symbol $50-60

Food Fights Too – (Picture Of Uncle Sam) Conserve What You Buy – Plan All Meals For Victory $50-55

For Our Defense – Battleship – 1,200 Men $55-60

God Bless America – Pearl Harbor Remembered (Made For Collectors Market) – 1992 . . . . $18-22

Help Save The Life Of A Soldier Or Sailor (picture of Red Cross) Donate To The Blood Plasma Program Of The Red Cross (Rare) $210-250

It's Great To Be An American, Picture Of Uncle Sam And Eagle $40-45

Invest In Victory (picture of bombers) War Savings – Bonds – Stamps $85-100

Remember Pearl Harbor – Safe Guard Your Country – By Doing Your Bit Now – Be Prepared – "V" Symbol $130-150

Uncle Sam Pointing To Signs: Your Country First, Your Family Second, Yourself Last $50-60

U.S. Savings Bonds And Freedom Shares $25-30

We Cherish Liberty – Health – Let's Protect Them – 1943 . . . . $40-50

50th Anniversary Of Pearl Harbor (made for collectors market – 1992) **$20-25**

Cream Tops

Common Bottle, Food For Victory – Careful Wartime Meal Planning Will Help Us Win **$85-100**

Common Bottle, Uncle Sam Prescribes Milk For The Army (rare) **$160-200**

Common Bottle, V For Victory – Guernsey Milk For Health **$85-95**

Common Bottle, Making It Together (Picture of Uncle Sam and Milk Man) An American Tradition **$40-50**

Gateway Dairy, My War Stamps Are Adding Up **$90-100**

Shamrock Dairy, Tucson, AZ, America Has A Job To Do, "V" symbol with fighter pilot **$85-105**

Walnut Grove Dairy, Alton, IL, Buy War Bonds and Stamps For Victory **$80-95**

Half-Pints

Alden's Dairy, Speed Victory **$30-35**

Common Bottle, Do Your Part Too! Buy War Bonds & Stamps **$40-45**

Common Bottle, You Can Keep Them Flying By Buying U.S. War Bonds and Stamps **$35-40**

Common Bottle, War Bonds For Victory **$25-30**

Dairylea Dairy, Buy Bonds For Victory **$40-50**

Live Oak Riviera Farms, Santa Barbara, CA, USA Food Emblem – red and blue, flying eagle surrounded by stars **$40-45**

War Slogans

Action Speaks Louder Than Words, Help Uncle Sam, round red quart $85

Air – Land – Sea (in circle with large V in background) Sanida Dairy, Erie PA, round red gallon $85

Buy War Bonds & Stamps, round red quart $55

Conserve For Victory, round red quart $110

Do Your Part Too! Buy War Bonds & Stamps, round half pint $40

For Freedom Buy War Bonds, Wrightwood Dairy, Chicago, IL, round red quart $55

For Our Defense, Pete Miller's Dairy, Sauquoit, NY, round red quart $105

Make America Strong, Mountain Gold Dairy, Walsenberg, CO, round red quart $40

My War Stamps Are Adding Up, Gateway Dairy, round green and red cream top quart $90

Pledge Of Allegiance, square red two-quart $40

Prepared And Ready For Orders, Are You?, round green quart $80

Remember Pearl Harbor, Be Prepared, High Grade Dairy, Harrington, DE, round red quart $100

Soldier, Sailor, Marine, They Guard Your Home (photos of soldiers), round cream top quart $50

Speed Victory, Alden's Dairy, round red half pint $30

Turner & Wescott V For Victory, Morse Code For V, round black quart $80

U.S. Savings Bonds And Freedom Shares, round orange quart
.... **$25**

War Bonds For Victory (Uncle Sam in center), green round
quart.. **$40**

We Cherish Liberty, Let's Protect Them (pyro), round maroon
quart.. **$35**

We Need Your Help, It's Your <u>Fight</u>, It's Your <u>Responsibility</u>,
Buy More Bonds, Elmwood Dairy, Oxbridge, MA**,** round green
quart.. **$65**

**Your Country First, Your Family Second, Yourself Last (picture
of Uncle Sam),** round red quart **$50**

Shot Glasses & Stir Sticks
Blown Glass Uncle Sam Top Hat with blown glass stir sticks (set
of six), hat 2" x 2-1/4", stir sticks 5-1/4" (ea) (set)..... **$135-150**

Soda Bottles
Dunn's Beverages – Statue Of Liberty In Front Of Clouds
–1954, clear glass, 10 oz., Sedalia, MO **$17-20**

Liberty Bottling Co – Statue Of Liberty – 1950, green glass, 12
oz., Memphis, Tenn. **$70-85**

**My Pic – 1949 – Statue Of Liberty With Stars Erupting From
Torch**, clear glass, 10 oz., Alexandria, LA **$30-35**

**Uncle Sam's Beverage (picture of Uncle Sam on yellow label)
– 1947**, clear glass, 7 oz., Houston, TX **$90-100**

Victory Beverage – 1944, dark glass, 9-1/2" **$30-35**

Victory Root Beer (picture of stars and stripes) – 1947, dark
glass, 10 oz. **$55-65**

Whiskey Bottles

Royal Doulton Dewars White Label Bottle, high-glazed porcelain with a dark brown base and dark brown top fading to a light brownish gold center, picture of Uncle Sam smoking a pipe, 7-1/4" x 6-1/2" x 2-3/4", English, 1907 . . . . **$325-400**

Whiskey Nipper - Uncle Sam - Your Health, 1930s, **$45-55.**

Miscellaneous

Opalescent milk glass with Uncle Sam seated between the smokestacks of the ship U.S.S. Olympia. Bottom of boat has an eagle on the bow with portholes and guns on the sides, 6-1/2" x 3" x 4-5/8", American 1898 . . . .**$130-150**

Franklin D. Roosevelt Glass Goblet – top of glass: "1933 – Franklin D. Roosevelt – 32nd President of The United States of America. Inaugurated March 4, 1933"; front of glass: (bust of Roosevelt) – reverse side of glass: (image depicting birds on a grape vine) – Repeal of the 18th Amendment Dec 7th 1933; base of glass: "Asst. Sec. of Navy 1915-20, Gov. of New York State 1929-1933", frosted glass, 6-1/4", smooth base, American 1933. . . . .**$225-300**

Gilbert Stuart Portrait of George Washington on Liverpool Pitcher, white pottery, 7-1/2", smooth base ("Herculaneum" imprint), English 1790-1905 (extremely rare). Gilbert Stuart (1755-1828) painted all the notable American figures of the Federal period and was considered "Father of American Portraiture." This famous Herculaneum image of George Washington imprinted on the base of the pitcher identifies it as a product of one of the more renowned pottery manufacturers of the period for the Liverpool region of England. **$1,000-1,200**

Gravy Boat, Union Porcelain Works (Green Point) Brooklyn, NY, fine porcelain gravy boat with Uncle Sam and John Bull reclining on top of boat, 7-1/2" x 3-1/2" x 5-1/8", American 1868 . . . . . **$1,250-1,500**

McKinley – Bryan Campaign Bottles (2) – Bottle 1: "In Bryan We Trust – Free Silver 16-1 (bust of Williams Jennings Bryan); Bottle 2: "In McKinley We Trust" – Gold Standard (bust of William McKinley), clear glass, 6-1/2", smooth base, tooled tops, American 1896 (extremely rare) **$500-700**

*Barber bottle, blue stars and stripes pattern, 1885-1925, 7", **$250-350.***

*Barber bottle, red stars and stripes pattern, 1885-1925, 7", **$250-350.***

*For Pike's Peak
- Traveler - Eagle,
1870-1875,
6-1/8", $80-120.*

*Patriotic Shaving Mug,
Made for William
Parilla, 1885-1925,
3-7/8", $140-180.*

McKinley – Roosevelt Campaign Flask – "Our Candidates" **(bust of William McKinley and Teddy Roosevelt)**, clear glass, 5", smooth base, screw-on metal cap, blue and white support rope for hanging purposes, American 1900 . . . . **$550-700**

Occupational Shaving Mug Made for "Adolph Market," picture on mug depicting a flexed arm holding a hammer in front of the American flag, maroon wrap with a gold gilt edge, American 1880-1920 . . . . **$325-400**

St. Louis World's Fair Ceramic Mug, ceramic mug, 4-1/2", logo depicting Washington, Jefferson, Lafayette, Napoleon and St. Louis, 1904. Crossed American flags, shield, and eagle, smooth base (Sinclair Art. Co, Decorators of China, East Liverpool, O), American 1904. . . . . **$130-150**

Woodrow Wilson Royal Staffordshire Caricature Toby Jug, red, white, and blue, 11", smooth base, English 1918. In 1918, an English political cartoonist designed a set of Toby jug caricatures to honor the leaders of World War I, manufactured by Royal Staffordshire Pottery, Staffordshire, England. President Woodrow Wilson is depicted astride a biplane in a flying position wearing a Colonial hat. **$425-500**

Perfume and Cologne Bottles

At the request of many bottle collectors in the United States and Europe, I am adding a chapter on perfume and cologne bottles in this second edition. I couldn't have done so without a lot of help from Penny Dolnick, who provided the background and pricing information, and Randy Monsen and Rodney Baer for providing the great photographs.

Penny's credentials speak for themselves as a past President of the International Perfume Bottle Association (IPBA), author of the *Penny Bank Commercial Perfume Bottle Price Guide*, 7th Edition, the *Penny Bank Miniature Perfume Bottle Price Guide*, 2nd Edition, and the *Penny Bank Solid Perfume Bottle Price Guide*, 3rd Edition. Penny, who can be contacted at alpen@gate. net, is willing to help fellow collectors identify and date bottles, but not conduct actual appraisals.

The International Perfume Bottle Association is an organization of 1,500 perfume bottle collectors in several countries. Its main objective is to foster education and comradeship for collectors through its quarterly full color magazine, its regional chapters, and its annual convention. Collectors can obtain further information from the organization's Web site at www.perfumebottles.org.

In addition, every year, the IPBA convention plays host to the Monsen and Baer Perfume Bottle Auction, featuring approximately 400 perfume bottles and related items. A full color 128 page hardbound catalogue entitled "The World of Perfume"

is available by contacting Randall Monsen and Rodney Baer at monsenbaer@errols.com.

Collectors look for two types of perfume bottles—decorative and commercial. Decorative bottles include any bottles sold empty and meant to be filled with your choice of scent. Commercial bottles are sold filled with scent and usually have the label of a perfume company. Since there are thousands of different perfume bottles, most collectors specialize in a subcategory.

Popular specialties among decorative perfume bottle collectors include ancient Roman and Egyptian bottles; cut glass bottles with or without gold or sterling silver trim or overlay; bottles by famous glassmakers such as Moser, Steuben, Webb, Lalique, Galle, Daum, Baccarat, and Saint Louis; figural porcelain bottles from the 18th and 19th century or from Germany between 1920 and 1930; perfume lamps (with wells to fill with scent); perfume burners; laydown and double-ended scent bottles; atomizer bottles; pressed or molded early American glass bottles; matched dresser sets of bottles; and handcut Czechoslovakian bottles from the early 20th century.

Collectors of commercial perfumes specialize in categories such as the following: bottle of particular colors; bottles by a single parfumer (Guerlain, Caron, or Prince Matchabelli); bottles by famous fashion designers (Worth, Paul Poiret, Chanel, Dior, Schiaparelli or Jean Patou); bottles by a particular glassmaker or designer, (Lalique, Baccarat, Viard or Depinoix); giant factice bottles (store display bottles not filled with genuine fragrance); small compacts, often figural, that hold solid (cream) perfume; tester bottles (small bottles with long glass daubers); and figural, novelty, and miniature perfumes (usually replicas of regular bottles given as free samples at perfume counters).

The novice perfume bottle collector may be surprised to learn that the record price for a perfume bottle at auction is over $80,000, and the little sample bottles that were given free at perfume counters in the '60s can now bring as much as $300 or $400! New collectors may also be surprised to discover that European collectors are more interested in miniature bottles than their full-size counterparts, and that bottles by American perfume companies are more desirable to European collectors than to Americans, and vice-versa. Also, most collectors of commercial perfume bottles will buy empty examples, but those still sealed with the original perfume carry a premium, and the original packaging can raise the price by as much as 300%! The rubber bulbs on atomizer bottles dry out over time but the lack of one or the presence of a modern replacement does not really affect the price.

Collecting perfume bottles is a hobby that can begin with little or no investment. Just ask a friend who wears Shalimar to save her next empty bottle for you. But beware! Investment quality perfume bottles can be very pricey! The rules for value are the same as for any other kind of glass—rarity, condition, age, and quality of the glass.

There are, however, some special considerations when collecting perfume bottles.

1. You do not have an investment quality bottle (one that will appreciate in value over time) unless the bottle has its original stopper and label. (This rule only applies to commercially made perfume bottles.)

2. An investment quality bottle must have high quality glass (must not be a lower-end eau de cologne or eau de toilette bottle) and must have no corrosion on any metal part.

3. In 1963, small plastic liners were added to the dowel end of stoppers on commercial bottles. Before that, the all-glass stoppers had to be individually ground to match the neck of its bottle. Bottles without the plastic liners (pre-1963) are preferred to those that have them.

Perfume Bottle Values
Note: All dates given are for the introduction of the scent (if applicable), not for the issue of the particular bottle.

Decorative Perfume Bottles

German Ceramic Crown Top of Dutch Boy Holding Flowers, 4.2, c1920 . . . . **$150**

German Ceramic Crown Top of Seated Kewpie Doll, 2.9" c1930s **$125**

Baccarat Signed Atomizer for Marcel Franck, 3.75", c1930s **$90**

Ruby Cut Glass w/Sterling Neck and Elaborate Stopper, French, 3.8", c1855 . . . . **$575**

English Ruby Glass Double-Ended Scent w/Sterling Mounts, signed, 4.5", 1905 . . . . **$350**

R. Lalique "Myosotis #3", green stain, nude stopper, signed, 9.0", c1928. . . . . **$4,000**

R. Lalique "Sirenes" Perfume Burner, blue stain, nude figures, signed, 7.0", c1920 . . . . **$2,200**

Webb Red Glass w/Sterling Stopper and White Cameo Overlay, unsigned, 4.4", c1910. . . . . **$1,250**

Limoges Enameled w/Lady, enameled overcap, inner stopper, 2.5", c19th c. **$800**

Benoit Nuit de Paques [Easter Evening], 1925, 4.4", **$3,500-4,500** *(extremely rare in flask form with only five known to exist of this model – the back molded H. Benoit Paris).*

Clear glass bottle, sterling silver top, 1897, 8", $450-650 (Birmingham, England).

Houbigant La Belle Salson [The Beautiful Season], 1926, 3.9", $4,000-6,000 (signed in the mold R. Lalique).

Volupte Atomizer Enameled w/Art Deco Motifs, unsigned, 9.3", c1930s **$1,150**

Devilbiss Black Glass w/Gold Mica "Lady Leg" Atomizer, label, 6.8", c1930s **$275**

Devilbiss Perfume Lamp, enameled w/dancing girls, metal cap and base, 7.5", c1930s **$460**

Austrian Square Metal Filigree Over Glass, w/glass jewels, 2.1", c1920s **$115**

Czech Pale Blue Cut Glass, w/matching keyhole stopper, 5", c1920s **$175**

Birmingham Engraved Sterling Laydown w/Glass Liner, hinged cover, 4.5", 1885 . . . . **$475**

Ingrid Czech Lapis Lazuli Glass Atomizer, cut w/roses, label, 5", c1920s **$350**

Moser Amber w/Gold Frieze of Female Warriors, signed, 6", c1920s **$250**

Hoffman Clear w/Amber Lady and Cherub Stopper, many jewels, signed, 6.8", c1920s **$1,600**

Czech Clear w/Pale Blue Nude Figure Dauber, blue jewels, unsigned, 5.7", c1920s **$6,300**

Shuco Mohair Monkey Figure, w/perfume tube inside, 5", c1930s **$265**

American Molded Paperweight Bottle, w/bird stopper, unsigned, 5.3", c1940s **$25**

American Clear Bottle, w/elaborate silver overlay, ball stopper, 5.1", c1930s **$100**

Kosta Faceted Bottle and Stopper, signed V Lindstand, 3.5", c1950 . . . . **$40**

Galle Atomizer, yellow w/maroon berry and leaf overlay, cameo signed, 7.36", c1910 . . . . **$2,200**

Daum Nancy, peach w/amber leaf and flower overlay, cameo signed, 6.5", c1915. . . . . **$1,000**

Baccarat Two Dolphins Bottle, ball stopper, signed, 6", c1925 . . . . **$300**

Fenton Blue Opalescent Coin Dot Atomizer for Devilbiss, 4", c1940s **$75**

Steuben Blue Aurene Atomizer, acorn finial, for DeVilbiss, 9.5", c1930 . . . . **$1,050**

Cambridge Pink Foot Urn, stopper w/long dauber, label, 4.75", c1940s **$75**

Commercial Perfume Bottles

Elizabeth Arden It's You, MIB, Baccarat white figural hand in dome, 6.5", c1938 . . . . **$4,300**

Babs Creations Forever Yours Heart, in composition hands w/ dome, 3.5", c1940 . . . . **$233**

Bourjois Evening in Paris, cobalt w/fan stopper, banner label, 4.5", c1928. . . . . **$265**

Bourjois Evening in Paris, cobalt bullet-shape laydown, good label, tassel, 3.5", c1928 . . . . **$22**

Hattie Carnegie, blue clear head and shoulders bottle, label, 3.25", c1944. . . . . **$123**

Caron Nuit De Noel, MIB, black glass, gold label, faux shagreen box w/tassel, 4.36", c1922 . . . . **$98**

Chanel #5, glass, giant factice, 10.5", c1921. . . . . **$595**

Mary Chess Souvenir D'un Soir, MIB, replica of Plaza Hotel fountain, 3.62", c1956. . . . . **$2,875**

Colgate Cha Ming, glass stopper, flower label, box, 3", c1917. . . **$46**

Corday Toujours Moi, MIB, clear bottle w/gold trim, glass stopper, 2.5", c1924. . . . . **$81**

Corday Tzigane R Lalique Tiered Bottle and Stopper, label, 5.5", c1940s **$291**

Coty Ambre Antique R Lalique, w/gray stained maidens, 6", c1913. . . . . **$1,380**

Coty L'Origan, MIB, Baccarat, flat rectangle, sepia stained moth stopper, 3.25", c1903. . . . . **$285**

D'albert Ecusson Urn, w/gold label, box, 3.87", c1952. . . . . . **$52**

Jean Desprez Votre Main Sevres, porcelain hand w/applied flowers, 3.2", c1939. . . . . **$1,900**

Dior Diorissimo, MIB, clear amphora, glass stopper, 3.87", c1956 . . . . **$148**

Dior Diorissimo Urn, w/gilt bronze flowers stopper, box, 9", c1956. . . . . **$1,850**

D'Orsay Toujours Fidele, Baccarat, pillow shape w/bulldog stopper, box, 3.5", c1912. . . . . **$520**

Duchess of Paris Queenly Moments, Queen Victoria bottle on wood base, 3.5", c1938 . . . . **$33**

Faberge Woodhue, oversize upright logo stopper, 3.5", c1940. **$75**

Forvil Relief R Lalique, round bottle w/swirl pattern, no label, 6.87", c1920. . . . . **$475**

Dorothy Gray Savoir Faire Bottle, w/enameled mask, gold stopper, 4", c1947 . . . . **$460**

Jacques Griffe Griffonage, square bottle, flat top glass stopper, box, 2.25", c1949 . . . . **$23**

Guerlain Shalimar Baccarat, signed classic winged bottle, blue stopper, 5.5", c1921 . . . . **$155**

Guerlain Shalimar, MIB, donut-shaped cologne, pointed glass stopper, 11", c1921 . . . . **$36**

Houbigant Parfum Ideal, Baccarat, faceted stopper, gold label, box, 4.2", c1900 . . . . **$80**

Isabey Bleu De Chine Viard, gray stain w/enameled flowers, 5.75", c1926 . . . . **$1,325**

Andrew Jergens Ben Hur, rounded bottle, frosted stopper, black label, 5.25", c1904 . . . . **$50**

Lander Gardenia, dime store bottle w/orange plastic tiara stopper, 4.75", c1947 . . . . **$19**

Lanvin Arpege, MIB, black boule w/gold logo, gold raspberry stopper, 3.5", c1927 . . . . **$255**

Lucien Lelong Indiscret, draped bottle, glass bow stopper, label, 4.75", c1935 . . . . **$50**

Prince Matchabelli Added Attraction, MIB, red crown, velvet case, 2.12", c1956 . . . . **$394**

Prince Matchabelli Crown Jewel, MIB, clear crown, cross stopper, chain, 2", c1945 . . . . **$51**

Molinard Xmas Bells, MIB, black glass figural bell, gold lettering, 4.25", c1926 . . . . **$460**

Solon Palmer Gardenglo, sample bottle, glass ball stopper, label, 4.75", c.1913 . . . . **$20**

Raphael Replique, MIB, R logo stopper, red seal, 3.25", c1944 . . . . **$50**

Guerlain Le Mouchoir de Monsieur [A Gentleman's Handkerchief] clear glass and stopper, 1902, 5", $300-400 The bottle, known as the Escargot or "Snail," by Pochet et du Courval, dates from 1902.

Guerlain Rose du Moulin, 1907, 1.7", $125-175.

Luxor Lybis, clear glass and blue glass stopper, 1924, 5.4", $500-750.

Porcelain handpainted bottle, no stopper, 2.4"; Opaque glass scent bottle with décor of leaves and silver cap with hallmarks for London, 1903, 5.2"; Porcelain honeycomb bottle with a green bee on both sides, 4.1", Opaque white glass bottle and stopper, 3.2"; **$400-600.**

Nina Ricci L'Air Du Temps, MIB, Lalique, double dove stopper, 4.5", c1948. . . . . **$250**

Elsa Schiaparelli Shocking Torso, w/flowers, tape measure, dome, 4", c1936 . . . . **$185**

Tre Jur Suivez Moi Lady, figure bottle w/long dauber, 2.5", c1925 . . . . **$215**

Vigny Golliwogg, MIB, black face stopper w/seal fur hair, 3.5", c1919. . . . . **$347**

Worth Dans La Nuit R Lalique, matte blue boule, name on stopper, 5.75", c1920. . . . . **$865**

Ybry Femme De Paris, Baccarat, green opaque w/enameled overcap, 2.25", c1925 . . . . **$500**

Miniature Perfume Bottles

Elizabeth Arden Blue Grass, blown bottle w/blue horse figure inside, box, 2.2", c1934 . . . . **$870**

Bourjois Evening in Paris, cobalt mini in green bakelite shell, 2", c1928. . . . . **$280**

Bourjois On The Wind, peach label and cap, 1.5", c1930 . . . **$26**

Hattie Carnegie A Go Go, square mini in hat box, 1.36", c1969 . . . . **$55**

Caron Nuit De Noel, tester, black cap and label, full, 1.75", c1922. . . . . **$31**

Ciro Chevalier De La Nuit, frosted figural knight, black head, 2.36", c1923. . . . . **$250**

Colgate Caprice, worn label, twisted screw cap, 2", c1893 . . . **$18**

Corday Toujours Moi, shield shape label, pink plastic cap, 1.75", c1923. . . . . **$25**

Coty A'suma Boule, with embossed flowers, no label, 1.5", c1934 . . . . **$87**

Jean Desprez Sheherazade, MIB, tall spire stopper, 3", c1960s **$155**

Dior Diorama, round laydown "pebble," black label, 1", c1950 **$71**

Dior, Miss Dior round laydown "pebble," white label, 1", c1953 **$33**

D'Orsay Intoxication, draped bottle, gold label, gold pouch, 1.62", c1942 . . . . **$29**

Evyan Great Lady, laydown heart bottle, full, 2.25", c1958. . . . **$8**

Guerlain Chamade, green plastic pagoda cap, 1.25", c1969 . **$275**

Guerlain L'Heure Bleu, tester, black cap w/dauber, horse label, 2.25", c1912. . . . . **$160**

Guerlain Mitsouko, replica mini, glass stopper, full, 1.5"c, 1919 . . . . **$22**

Richard Hudnut Le Debut Bleu, MIB, blue w/gold raspberry stopper, 1.25" c1927 . . . . **$255**

Richard Hudnut Le Debut Noir, MIB, black w/gold raspberry stopper, 1.25", c1927 . . . . **$778**

Karoff Buckarettes, set of two, cowboy and cowgirl w/wooden heads, 1.87", c1940 . . . . **$91**

Lanvin Arpege, tiny black boule w/logo, 1.2", c1927 . . . . **$545**

Le Galion Sortilege, tiny mini w/ship cap & gold label, 1.25", c1937 . . . . **$29**

Lucien Lelong Passionment, tiny mini w/pearl cap, label, 1.12", c1940. . . . . **$14**

Germain Monteil Laughter, blown bottle, blue threaded stopper, full, 1.5", c1941 . . . . **$52**

Raphael Replique, MIB, Lalique acorn in plastic case, 2", c1944 .... **$145**

Revillon Detchma, MIB, urn-shaped, metal cap, 2.25", c1955 **$14**

Nina Ricci, set of three: sunburst, leaf and heart minis in box, 1.25-1.5", c1952 .... **$663**

Rochas Femme, round laydown "pebble," gold label, 1.5", c1945 .... **$48**

Elsa Schiaparelli Shocking Torsos, set of three torsos in Jack in Box w/flowers, 1.36", c1936 .... **$1,100**

Rose Valois Canotier, figural mini wearing hat in plastic case, 2.3", c1950 .... **$256**

Weil Cobra, MIB, ball stopper, worn box, 1.5", c1941 ...... **$34**

Weil Secret of Venus (Antilope), waisted bottle, blue cap, full, 1.36", c1942 .... **$32**

Miscellaneous Perfume/Cologne/Scent Bottles

Blown Cologne Bottle, opalescent sapphire blue, 6-1/8", swirl line throughout bottle, pontil-scarred base, rolled lip, American 1855-1865 .... **$250-350**

Bunker Hill Monument Cologne (label: Cologne Water For The Toilet), deep purple amethyst, 6-1/2", smooth base, rolled lip, American 1875 (rare in this color) **$700-900**

Cologne Bottle, purple amethyst, 4-5/8", 8-sided, corset waist shape, smooth base, rolled lip, American 1865-1875 .. **$600-800**

Cologne Bottle (label: Eagdi Cologne Paris), aqua, 6-3/8", plume and vine design on three panels, open pontil, thin flared-out lip, American 1840-1860 .... **$70-100**

Sterling silver covered perfume bottle with inner stopper, 2.8";
Bottle with ornate sterling silver top, hallmarked Birmingham,
1892; sterling silver covered bottle, 3.6", hallmarked London
1907, **$200-300. (all)**

Cologne bottle, 1860-1880, 9-3/4", $275-375.

Cologne bottle, 1860-1880, 5-3/4", $175-275.

Cologne bottle, 1845-1865, 12", $200-300.

Cologne Bottle (label: Eau De Cologne) – Label Under Glass, clear glass, 6-7/8", copper wheel- cut decoration reading "Sarah", label under glass is red, blue, gold with black and white photo of a woman, smooth base (J. QUINLAN-NEW YORK), tooled mouth, American 1880-1910 . . . .**$400-500**

Cologne Bottle (label: Cologne Water For Toilet), clear glass, 5-5/8", obelisk with herringbone corners and stars on two side panels, smooth base, tooled lip, American 1870-1880. .**$140-180**

Cologne Bottle (label: Double Extract D'Eau De Cologne), deep cobalt blue, 4-1/4", 12-sided with sloped shoulder, smooth base, rolled lip, American 1865-1885 . . . . **$300-400**

Cologne Bottle (label: Double Extract D'Eau De Cologne Perfectionee), medium cobalt blue, 6-3/8", 12-sided, pontil-scarred base, rolled lip, American 1860-1880 . . . . **$300-400**

Cologne Bottle – Perfume – Aimee – Richard Hudnut – New York, porcelain with light blue glazing and blue lettering, 10", smooth base (This Bottle Is The Property Of R. Hudnut's Pharmacy New York), tooled top, American 1890-1920 . . . . **$200-300**

Fancy Cologne Bottle, milk glass, 5", embossed Indians on two panels, pontil-scarred base, tooled mouth, American 1845-1865 (rare in this color) **$1,800-2,800**

Fancy Cologne Bottle, medium sapphire blue, 5-7/8", pontil-scarred base, flared lip, American 1825-1845 . . . . **$2,000-3,000**

Pattern Molded Cologne Bottle, medium purple amethyst, 4-1/2", 12-vertical rib-pattern swirled to left, pontil-scarred base, flared lip, American 1820-1835 . . . .**$400-600**

Scent Bottle, deep cobalt blue, 3-1/4", swirl pattern, pontil-scarred base, tooled mouth, American 1840-1860 . . . .**$100-150**

Fancy cologne bottle, 1850-1870, 9-7/8 ", **$800-1,200.**

*Label-under-glass cologne bottle - Eau De Cologne, J. Quinlan - New York (on base), 1880-1910, 6-7/8 ", **$400-500**.*

Sandwich cologne, 1850-1870, 3-3/8", **$140-180**.

Sandwich cologne, 1870-1880, 4", $275-375.

Sandwich cologne, 1870-1890, 4-7/8", **$275-375.**

*Seahorse scent bottle,
1820-1835, 2-3/4",*
$100-150.

*Scent bottle, 1850-1880,
2-1/2",* **$150-250.**

Sunburst Scent Bottle, medium cobalt blue, 2-7/8", pontil-scarred base, rolled lip, American 1820-1835 . . . .**$400-600**

Teardrop Cologne Bottle, clear glass with alternating blue, white, and pink vertical strips, 4-3/4", pontil scared base, tooled mouth, American 1840-1870 . . . .**$175-275**

Poison Bottles

Poison bottles are a unique category for collecting by the very nature of their contents. While most people assume that poison bottles are plain, most are actually very decorative, making their toxic contents easily identifiable. In 1853, the American Pharmaceutical Association recommended laws for identification of all poison bottles. In 1872, the American Medical Association recommended that poison bottles be identified with a rough surface on one side and the word "Poison" on the other. As so often happened during that era, passing of these laws was very difficult and the manufacturers were left to do whatever they wanted. Because a standard wasn't established, a varied group of bottle shapes, sizes, and patterns were manufactured, including skull and cross-bones, or skulls, leg bones, and coffins.

These bottles were manufactured with quilted or ribbed surfaces and diamond/ lattice-type patterns for identification by touch. Colorless bottles are very rare since most poison bottles were produced in dark shades of blues and browns, another identification aid. When collecting these bottles, caution must be exercised, since it is not uncommon to find a poison bottle with its original contents. If the bottle has the original glass stopper, the value and demand for the bottle will greatly increase.

Brecklein, cobalt blue, 7-1/2", irregular hexagon form, smooth base (C.l.G.Co. Patent Appl'd For), tooled lip, American 1890-1915 (rare) **$2,100-3,000**

Champion – Embalming Fluid – The Champion – Chemical Co. – Springfield – Ohio – Poison, clear glass, 8-1/2", smooth base, tooled mouth, American 1890-1915 . . . . **$160-200**

(Motif of skull and crossed bones inside triangle) De – Dro – Giftflasche – Des – Deutschen – Drogisten – Verbandes – Ddv (monogram) – (motif of skull and crossed bones inside triangle) De – Dro – Giftflasche – Des – Deutschen – Drogisten – Verbandes – DDV (monogram), medium green, 9-5/8", triangular form, smooth base (750), ABM lip, German 1910-1930 (scarce) **$285-375**

Durfee – Embalming – Fluid Co. – Grand Rapids – Mich – Poison, medium amber, 8-1/2", smooth base, tooled mouth, American 1890-1915 . . . . **$160-200**

(Motif of skull and crossed bones on 6 panels) Federation Francaise Droguistes Merchands De Couleurs, light yellow green, 10-3/4", 6-sided, smooth base (1 Litre Depose Modele), ABM lip, French 1910-1930 (rare) **$320-400**

Gift (skull and crossbones) – Gift, medium amber, 5-1/2", smooth base (200), tooled lip, German 1900-1920 . . . . **$325-400**

*Brecklein, 1890-1915, 7-1/2", **$2,000-3,000** (very rare).*

Columbian Pharmacy, Inc. - 461 State St. Perth Amboy, N.J., 1890-1915, 5", $1,200-1,800 (one of only two known examples).

Corrosive Sublimate - Poison, 1890-1910, 2-7/8"; Antiseptic Tablets - Poison, 1890-1910, 3-1/4", **$100-150** *(both).*

Gray & Pearse – Druggist – Poison – Take Care – Cheyenne – Wyo, cobalt blue, 3-5/8", smooth base (W.T. & CO), tooled lip, American 1890-1915 (extremely rare Western poison) **$850-1,200**

Hydrarg Salicyl Poison, amber, 4-1/8", smooth base (Pat. Apr. 2, 1889 – W.T.CO), tooled lip, American 1880-1910 . . . . . . **$75-90**

Jacob Hulle – Not To Be Taken – Strychnine, deep cobalt blue, 3-5/8", smooth base, tooled mouth, American 1890-1915. **$40-50**

(Skull and crossed bones) Poison – Jacobs – Bichloride – Tablets, yellow amber, 2-1/4", 8-sided, smooth base, tooled mouth, American 1890-1910 . . . . **$825-1,200**

Lattice and Diamond Pattern – Poison, deep cobalt blue, 7", smooth base, tooled lip, original glass "Poison" stopper, American 1890-1910 . . . . **$285-375**

Lattice and Diamond Pattern – Poison, medium cobalt blue, 9-3/8", smooth base, tooled lip, original glass "Poison" stopper, "Posion" embossed on label panel, American 1890-1910 . . . . **$1,300-1,800**

Melvin & Badger – Apothecaries – Boston, Mass, cobalt blue, 3-3/8", smooth base (C.L.G. CO. – Patent Applied For), tooled mouth, American 1890-1920 (scarce in this size) **$135-150**

Nicoticide, cobalt blue, 4", smooth base, tooled mouth, English 1890-1915 . . . . **$45-55**

Phenol Poison, amber, 6-5/8", smooth base, tooled lip, original ground glass stopper, American 1880-1910 . . . . **$75-90**

Poison (motif of star above and below skull and crossed bones) Poison, yellow amber, 4-3/4", smooth base, tooled mouth, American 1890-1910 (scarce) **$525-700**

F. & E. Bailey & Co. - Lowell, Mass, 1890-1915, 5", **$300-400.**

For - External - Use Only - Prescriptions - Reese Chem. Co - 1000 - External - Use 4 Times Daily - Mfg. By - Reese Chem. Co - Cleveland - O, 1915-1925, 5-1/2", **$80-120.**

Figural Grim Reaper Poison Bottles, 7"; (4) skull shot glasses, 1-7/8", 1900-1920, $200-250 (all).

Figural Skull Poison - Poison - Pat. Appl'd For, 1880-1910, 2-7/8", $2,500-3,500 (rare).

Gift (skull & crossed bones) - Giftglasche - Gift, 1910-1930, 7-3/4", **$150-200.**

Gift - Flasche (skull & crossed bones) & Skull & Crossed Bones; Giftflasche (skull & crossed bones) (both German), 1890-1930, 6-1/4" & 5-1/4", **$120-160** *(Both).*

Gray & Pearse - Druggist - Poison - Take Care - Cheyenne - Wyo, 1890-1915, 3-5/8", **$800-1,200.**

Jacob Hulle - Not To Be Taken - Strychnine; Poisonous - Not To Be Taken; Not To Be Taken; Owbridge's Embrocation - For Outward - Application - Only; Usage Externe - Not To Be Taken - Use With Caution; Oval Poison; Poision - Not To Be Taken; Not To Be Taken; Triangular Poison; Not To Be Taken (foreign), 1895-1920, 3-1/2"-7-3/4", **$100-150 (all).**

Label-under-glass jar - Hydrarg. - Ammon. - Poison, 1890-1910, 3-5/8", **$150-250.**

Lattice-and-diamond pattern poison, 1890-1920, 7", 3-3/4", 3-1/2", **$250-450** (All Three).

Poison – Poison (label: Poison Caution), medium golden amber, 2-3/4", smooth base, tooled mouth, American 1890-1910 (scarce) **$160-200**

Poison (on shoulder), deep cobalt blue, 3-1/2", smooth base (Patent – T & L CO), tooled mouth, American 1890-1910 (scarce) **$160-250**

Poison (embossed on two sides), medium amber, smooth base, ABM lip, Australian 1920-1930 (scarce) **$285-375**

Poison – Bowker's Pyrox (on base), clear glass, 5", smooth base, ABM lip, American 1895-1900 . . . . **$15-20**

Poison – Davis & Geck (monogram) Brooklyn, N.Y. – Germicidal Tablets, cobalt blue, 3-1/8", smooth base, tooled lip, American 1890-1915 . . . . **$620-800**

Poison (on neck) – Electric Balm – G.M. Rhoades – Grand Rapids – Mich, clear glass, 6-5/8", smooth base, tooled mouth, American 1885-1895 . . . . **$160-200**

Poison – H.K. Mulford Co – Chemist – Philadelphia – Poison, cobalt blue, 1-7/8", smooth base, tooled mouth, American 1890-1900 . . . . **$15-20**

Poison – (label: Coffinoids, Manufactured By Crystal Chen Co., New York City, deep cobalt blue, 3-1/4", coffin shape, smooth base, tooled top, American 1890-1910 . . . . . . **$425-600**

Poison – F.A. – Thompson – & Co – Detroit – Poison, medium amber, 3-1/8", coffin form, smooth base, tooled mouth, American 1890-1910 . . . . **$625-900**

Poison – (figural grim reaper), bisque with brown and tan glaze, 7", smooth base, original stoppers, American 1900-1920 . **$40-45**

Poison – Nit.Strychnia, Chas. Pfizer & Co. New York, cobalt blue, 2-3/8", smooth base, tooled top, American 1895-1910 **$15-20**

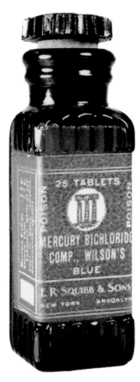

Mercury Bichloride - Comp. Wilson's - Blue - E.R. Squib & Sons - New York Brooklyn, 1890-1910, 3-1/8", **$50-75.**

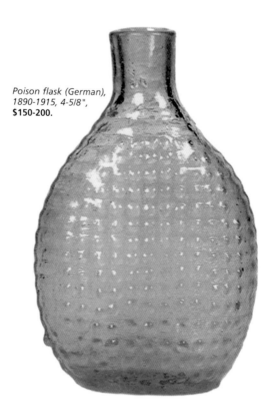

Poison flask (German), 1890-1915, 4-5/8", **$150-200.**

*Poison (Lot of 8), 1890-1910, 2" to 8-1/4", **$100-200** (all).*

Poison - Poison, 1890-1910, 5-1/8"; Melvin & Badger - Apothecaries - Boston, Mass, 1890-1910, 5-3/8", **$200-300 (both).**

Poison - Diamond - Antiseptics - Lilly - Poison - Poison, 1890-1910, 10-1/2", **$200-300.**

Poison (skull & crossed bones) Poison; (skull & crossed bones) Poison - Tinct - Iodine; (skull & crossed bones) Poison - Tinct - Iodine; Poison (motif of star above and below skull and crossed bones) Poison, 1910-1925, 2-1/2", 6-5/8", $100-150 (all).

Poison – Pat Appl'd For (figural skull poison), cobalt blue, 4-1/8", smooth base, tooled mouth, American 1890-1910 . . . . . .**$725-900**

Poison – Poison Phosp.Strychnia, clear glass, 3-1/4", smooth base, tooled top, American 1890-1910 . . . .**$15-20**

Poison Flask, ice blue with overall hobnail pattern, 4-5/8", pontil-scarred base, tooled mouth, German 1890-1915 . . . . . .**$160-200**

Poison Flask, medium olive green, 5-5/8", overall hobnail pattern, pontil-scarred base, sheared lip, American 1820-1835. . .**$155-200**

Poison – (submarine-shaped poison), deep cobalt blue, 2-1/2", smooth base (Registered No 336907), tooled lip, English 1890-1915. . . . .**$425-600**

Poison – The Owl Drug Co (motif of double winged owl on mortar and pestle), medium cobalt blue, 5", triangular form, smooth base, ABM lip, American 1915-1925 . . . . **$150-180**

Poison – The Owl Drug Co (motif of double winged owl on mortar and pestle), medium cobalt blue, 8-1/2", triangular form, smooth base, tooled mouth, American 1915-1925 . . . . **$320-400**

Poison – The Owl Drug Co (motif of owl on motar and pestle) – Aqua Ammonia, Poison, deep cobalt blue, 9-5/8", triangular form, smooth base, tooled mouth, American 1890-1910 (scarce) **$735-900**

Poison – Use with Caution – 16 Oz., cobalt blue, 8-3/4", smooth base, tooled mouth, Canadian 1890-1910 . . . . **$225-300**

Poison – O.K. Is Absolutely Sure – Special – Is King of All (embalming fluid bottle), clear glass, 11", smooth base, tooled mouth, American 1880-1920 . . . . **$45-60**

Poison – Poison (label: Poison – Diamond – Antiseptics – For External Use Only – Lilly – Eli Lilly and Company), Indianapolis, U.S.A., medium amber, 10-1/2", smooth base, tooled mouth, American 1890-1910 . . . . **$225-300**

Poison – Poison (label: Coffin Shape – Corrosive – Mercuric Chloride – The Norwich Pharmacal Co, Norwich, New York), medium cobalt blue, 7-1/2", smooth base (Norwich -16A), tooled mouth, American 1890-1910 . . . . **$1,100-1,500**

Rat – Poison, clear glass, 2-3/8", smooth base, tooled mouth, American 1890-1920 . . . . **$45-80**

Ser C Sol – Elliott – Poison – Poison – Not To Be Taken – Ser C Sol – Elliotts – Poison – Not To Be Taken, medium amber, 5-1/8", triangular form, smooth base (L), tooled mouth, French 1890-1920 . . . . **$85-120**

Strychnia – Poison, clear glass, 2-1/2", oval form, smooth base, tooled mouth, American 1890-1910 . . . .**$110-150**

Strychn – Pulv (above an orange enameled skull and crossbones) – Apothecary Jar, medium amber with gold, red, white, and black enamel label, 5", smooth base, tooled mouth, original glass hollow blown stopper, European 1900-1925 . . . .**$220-300**

The – Egyptian – Chemical – Company Poison – Boston – Mass (embalming fluid), clear glass, 8-5/8", smooth base, tooled mouth, American 1890-1910 . . . .**$45-60**

The – Oriental – Embalming – Fluid – Poison – The – Egyptian – Chemical Co. – Boston – Mass, clear glass, 11-1/2", smooth base, tooled mouth, American 1890-1920**$45-60**

Contents – 16 Fl. Oz. – The – JMF. Hartz Co. – Limited – Toronto (inside embossed heart), deep cobalt blue, 7-3/4", smooth base, tooled mouth, Canadian 1890-1925 . .**$750-1,000**

Usage Externe, medium golden amber, 9", 6-sided, smooth base (500), tooled mouth, German 1890-1920 . . . .**$160-250**

Zewnetrznie, aqua, 8-1/2", 6-sided, smooth base (500), tooled top, German 1890-1920 . . . .**$225-300**

Soda Bottles

After years of selling, buying, and trading, I think soda bottles support one of the largest collector groups in the United States. Even collectors who don't normally seek out soda bottles always seem to have a few on their tables for sale.

Soda bottles aren't unique in design, since manufacturers had to produce bottles as cheaply as possible to keep up with demand. The only way to distinguish among bottles is by the lettering, logos, embossing, or labels (not very common). With the use of carbonated water, the bottle manufacturers had to provide a stronger type of bottle, which led to the heavy glass-walled blob-type soda bottle.

Soda is artificially flavored or unflavored carbonated water. In 1772, an Englishman named Joseph Priestley succeeded in defining the process of carbonation. Small quantities of unflavored soda were sold by Professor Benjamin Silliman in 1806. By 1810, New York druggists were selling homemade seltzer as a cure-all for stomach problems, with flavors added to the solution in the mid-1830s. By 1881, flavoring was a standard additive in these seltzers.

With the advent of the soda bottle and the use of carbonation, the problems of the corks blowing out due to the increased pressures brought about the invention of many types of closures. Some of these more common closures were the Hutchinson-type wire stoppers, lightning stoppers, and cod stoppers.

A. Schroth – Sch.ll Haven – Superior – Mineral Water – Union Glass Works, cobalt blue, 7-1/4", mug base, iron pontil, applied blob top, American 1840-1855 (rare) **$1,300-1,600**

Albert Fischer – Atlantic City, N.Y., deep amber, 7", smooth base, tooled mouth, American 1865-1876 .... **$160-200**

B. Carter – West Chester (in slug plate), medium blue green, 7", iron pontil, applied mouth, American 1840-1860 (scarce) **$325-400**

Bridgeton Glass Works – N.J. medium blue green, 7-3/8", smooth base, applied mouth, original metal band closure stamped "John Allender, Patent July 24 1855", American 1855-1865 (scarce) **$160-200**

Buffums – Sarsaparilla & Lemon – Mineral Water – Pittsburgh, bluish aqua, 10-sided, 8", iron pontil, applied tapered collar mouth, American 1840-1855 .... **$550-700**

C. Maick's – Phillipson – Reading, PA – M & P, light green, 7-1/2", smooth base, applied mouth, American 1875-1885 .... **$75-100**

Blanchard & Defreest - Troy, N.Y. - Superior - B & Soda Water, American, 1840-1860, **$375-550.**

C. Cleminshaw - Soda & - Mineral Water - Troy N.Y., American, 1840-1860, **$375-475.**

Carl H. Schultz – C-P M-S – Pat. May – 1868 – New York, medium green, 6-3/4", smooth base, applied blob top, American 1880-1890 . . . . **$75-90**

Carpenter – & Cobb – Knickerbocker – Soda Water – Saratoga – Springs, blue green, 7-3/8", 10-sided, iron pontil, applied blob top, American 1840-1855 (rare). **$525-700**

City Bottling Works – Toledo, Ohio, medium sapphire blue, 6-3/8", smooth base, large applied mouth, American 1875-1885 . . . . **$285-375**

Clarke & Co – New York, medium amber with olive tone, pint, pontil-scarred base, applied sloping collar mouth, American 1855-1865 . . . . **$130-150**

Crystal Palace – Premium – Soda Water – W. Eagle – New York (motif of Crystal Palace) – Union Glass Works, deep teal blue green, 7-3/8", iron pontil, applied blob top, American 1845-1860 . . . . **$550-700**

Crump & Fox – Bernardston – Mass – Superior – Soda Water, deep blue green, 7-1/4", iron pontil, applied blob top, American 1840-1855 . . . . **$850-1,200**

Dean & Paxton – Newark – N.J., deep cobalt blue, 7-1/8", iron pontil, applied blob top, American 1840-1855 (very rare) **$260-350**

Deer Park – L.I., cobalt blue, 8-sided, 7-1/4", iron pontil, applied blob top, American 1840-1855 (rare). **$1,100-1,500**

Dr. Brown N.Y. – B, medium blue green, 6-3/4", iron pontil, applied sloping collar mouth, American 1840-1860 . . . . **$380-475**

Dyottville Glass Works – Philada, medium cobalt blue, 7-1/2", smooth base, applied blob top, American 1850-1860 . . . **$85-120**

Carpenter & Cobb Knickerbocker Soda Water - Saratoga Springs, American, 1840-1860, **$400-700.**

Chas. Grove - Cola. PA. (in a slug plate) - Brown - Stout, American, 1840-1860, **$300-400 (Rare).**

Early Sided Soda Bottle (unembossed), dark amber, 8-3/8", 8-sided, smooth base, applied mouth, American 1855-1865 . . . .**$210-300**

E. Roussel – Philada – Cyottville Glass Works – R – Philada – This Bottle – Is Never Sold, medium cobalt blue, 7-1/2", iron pontil, applied sloping collar mouth, American 1840-1860 . . . .**$110-150**

E. Smith – Elmira – N.Y., deep cobalt blue, 7-1/8", smooth base, applied blob top, American 1855-1865 . . . .**$550-700**

E.S. Hart – Canton – CT – Superior – Soda Water – Union Glass Works, bluish aqua, 7-5/8", pontil-scarred base, applied blob top, American 1845-1855 . . . .**$85-120**

Empire Bottling Works – Reading PA, aqua, 6-5/8", smooth base, applied mouth, American 1875-1885 . . . .**$65-80**

Excelsior – Ginger Ale – 1852 – John Ryan – Savannah GA, medium amber, 7-1/4", smooth base, applied blob top, American 1875-1890 . . . .**$260-350**

Francis Dusch – This Bottle Is Never Sold, deep cobalt blue, 7-1/2", smooth base, applied blob top, American 1865-1885 . . . .**$210-250**

G.A. Sammis – Hempstead – L.I., medium aquamarine blue green, 7-3/8", iron pontil, applied sloping collar mouth, American 1845-1855 (scarce) **$270-350**

G. Gent – New York, greenish aqua, 7-1/8", iron pontil, applied blob top, American 1845-1855 (scarce) **$225-300**

G.H. Hausburg – Blue Island – ILL – I.G.CO. 3 1-1/2, deep yellow green, 8-1/2", smooth base, tooled mouth, American 1890-1910 . . . .**$110-150**

D. Harkins - Richmond - PA (in a slug plate), American, 1840-1860, **$400-600.**

Eagle With Shield and American Flags, American, 1840-1860, **$400-600.**

Embossed Eagle (in a slug plate), American, 1850-1860, **$250-350.**

Fairbanks & Beard - Howard St. - Boston - F&B, American, 1855-1865, **$250-350.**

G. Lauter – Reading – PA – Walater – L – Reading, PA, aqua, 7", smooth base, applied mouth. $75-100

American 1875-1885

Ghirardelli's – Branch – Oakland, cobalt blue, 7-1/2", smooth base, applied mouth, American 1855-1870 . . . .$110-150

Gleason – & Cole – Pittsbg – Mineral Water, cobalt blue, 7-3/4", 10-sided, iron pontil, applied sloping collar mouth, American 1840-1855 (rare) $750-1,000

Hamilton Glass Works – N.Y., aquamarine, 7", iron pontil, applied mouth, American 1840-1860 . . . .$120-150

Hoxsie Jeffers & Co – Albany, blue green, 7", smooth base, applied mouth, American 1855-1870 . . . .$150-180

Hutchinson & Co – Celebrated – Mineral – Water – Chicago, medium cobalt blue, 7-1/4", iron pontil, applied blob top, American 1840-1855 . . . .$650-800

J.A. Dearborn – New York (in slug plate), medium teal blue, 6-3/4", iron pontil, applied sloping collar mouth, American 1840-1855. . . . .$225-300

J.B. Bryant – Wilmington (in slug plate) – Porter – Ale Cider, medium emerald green, 7", iron pontil, applied sloping double collar mouth, American 1840-1855 . . . .$750-900

J. Boardman – New York, medium yellow olive green, 7-1/4", iron pontil, applied sloping collar mouth, American 1845-1855 . . . .$225-300

J.D. Ludwick – Pottstown, PA – This Bottle – Not To – Be Sold – Registered 1889, deep green, 7-1/4", smooth base, tooled lip, American 1890-1910 . . . .$75-100

Fields Superior Soda Water - Charleston - S.C., American, 1840-1860, **$400-600 (scarce).**

J. & H. Casper - Lancaster - PA - Cold Cream Soda, American, 1870-1880, **$100-150.**

J.H. Magee (in slug plate) – Vine St – Philada, medium cobalt blue, 7-3/8", iron pontil, applied sloping double collar mouth, American 1840-1860 . . . .**$150-200**

J. Johnston – Superior – Soda Water – New York – Union Glass Works – Phila, teal blue, 7-1/4", iron pontil, applied mouth, American 1845-1855 (scarce) **$150-180**

J. Lampin – Utica – Mineral Waters – L – This Bottle – Is Never Sold, cobalt blue, 7-5/8", iron pontil, applied sloping collar mouth, American 1840-1855 (scarce) **$650-800**

J. Schweinhart – Pittsburgh – PA – 10th Ward – Bottling Works – A.&D.H.C., cobalt blue, 7", smooth base (J.S.), applied blob top, American 1870-1885 . . . .**$130-150**

J.T. Brown – Chemist – Boston – Double – Soda – Water, medium blue green, 8-3/4", torpedo shape, smooth base, applied blob top, American 1850-1860 . . . .**$385-475**

J. Voelker & Bro. – Cleveland. O – V & Bro, medium cobalt blue, 10", smooth base, applied mouth, American 1875-1885 . . . .**$450-600**

J.W. Harris – Soda – New Haven – Conn, cobalt blue, 8-sided, 7-5/8", iron pontil, applied blob top, American 1845-1855 . . . .**$260-350**

J & W. Coles – Superior – Soda & – Mineral Water – Staten Island, blue green, 7-1/2", iron pontil, applied sloping collar mouth, American 1840-1855 (rare) **$380-475**

James Wise – Allentown – PA – This Bottle – Belongs To – James Wise, cobalt blue, 7", smooth base, applied mouth, American 1855-1870 . . . .**$80-100**

John Clarke – New York, medium yellow olive amber, pint, pontil-scarred base, applied sloping collar mouth, American 1845-1860
. . . .**$160-200**

L. Gahre – Bridgeton – N.J. – G, blue green, 7", smooth base, applied sloping collar mouth, American 1855-1870 . . .**$130-160**

Lancaster – Glass Works – N.Y., cobalt blue, 7-1/8", iron pontil, applied sloping collar mouth, American 1840-1860 . . .**$160-200**

M. Monju & Co – Mobile, aqua, 7-3/8", pontil-scarred base, applied blob top, American 1840-1860 . . . .**$125-175**

M. Monju & Co – Mobile, teal blue, 7-3/8", pontil-scarred base, applied blob top, American 1840-1860 . . . .**$135-175**

Neptune – Glass Works, pale green, 7-3/8", pontil-scarred base, applied sloping blob top, American 1840-1860 (rare) . .**$360-450**

Owen Casey – Eagle Soda – Works – Sac City, cobalt blue, 7-1/2", smooth base, applied blob top, American 1870-1880
. . . .**$160-200**

P. Conway – Bottler – Philada – No 8 Hunter St – & 108 Filbert St – Mineral Waters, cobalt blue, 7-1/4", iron pontil, applied blob top, American 1840-1860 . . . .**$130-175**

P. Divine – Bottler – Philada., light green, 7-1/2", smooth base, applied mouth, American 1855-1870 . . . .**$60-80**

Quinan & Studer – 1888 – Savannah – GA, deep cobalt blue, 7-7/8", smooth base, tooled top, American 1880-1890 .**$160-175**

Robert Portner – Brewing Co – Tivoli (inside diamond) Alexandria VA – This Bottle – Not To – Be Sold, olive green, 9", smooth base, applied mouth, American 1885-1900 . . .**$75-90**

Roland & Upp – Reading, PA, aqua, 6-5/8", smooth base, applied mouth, American 1875-1885 . . . .**$65-80**

Knickerbocker Mineral Water - Bottle Registered - According to Law - Boughton & Chase - Rochester, N.Y., American, 1840-1860, **$500-$800 (Rare).**

L. Schmitt Columbia (in a slug plate), American, 1840-1860, **$300-400 (Very Rare).**

Owen Casey - Eagle Soda - Works - Sac City, American, 1870-1880, **$250-350.**

San Francisco - Glass Works, American, 1870-1876, **$150-200.**

S. Keys – Burlington – N.Y. – Union Glass Works Philad. – Superior – Mineral Water, cobalt blue, 7-3/8", mug base, iron pontil, applied tapered collar mouth, American 1840-1855 (extremely rare) **$850-1,200**

S. Smith – Auburn – 1857, medium cobalt blue, 10-sided, 7-3/4", iron pontil, applied blob top, American 1840-1855 . . . . **$650-800**

S.S. – Knicker – Bocker – Soda – Water, deep cobalt blue, 8-sided, 8", iron pontil, applied blob top, American 1840-1855 . . . . **$450-600**

Seitz Bros. – Easton, PA – S, medium teal blue, 6-3/4", smooth base, applied blob top, American 1865-1875 . . . . **$50-70**

Sloper & Frost, medium cobalt blue, 7-1/2", iron pontil, applied mouth, American 1845-1860 . . . . **$325-400**

Smith & – Fotheringham – Soda Water – St. Louis – This Bottle – Is Never Sold, deep cobalt blue, 7-1/2", 10-sided, iron pontil, applied sloping collar mouth, American 1845-1855 (scarce) **$225-300**

Smith's – Mineral – Soda Water – New York – Premium – S, pale blue green, 7-1/2", iron pontil, applied slopping collar mouth, American 1855-1875 . . . . **$50-60**

Soda Water, emerald green, 7-3/4", torpedo shape, smooth base, applied mouth, American 1850-1860 . . . . **$550-700**

Soda Water – Von – Dr. Struve, olive green, 7-3/4", smooth base, applied mouth, German 1850-1870 . . . . **$130-150**

Steinke & – Kornahrens (in slug plate) – Soda Water – Return This Bottle – Charleston S.C., deep cobalt blue, 8-1/4", 8-sided, iron pontil, applied sloping collar mouth, American 1845-1855 . . . . **$550-700**

Seitz & Bro. - Easton, PA - S, American, 1840-1860, **$180-275.**

Smedley & Brandt (in a slug plate), American, 1840-1860, **$300-400 (Very Rare).**

Suydam & Dubois – N.Y. – Union Glass Works – Superior – Mineral Water, cobalt blue, 7-1/2", mug base, iron pontil, applied tapered collar mouth, American 1840-1855 (rare) **$1,600-2,500**

T.S. Waterman – 11 St Paul St – N.O. – W. Mineral Water, deep aqua, 7-1/4", iron pontil, applied mouth, American 1840-1860 .... **$160-200**

Torpedo Soda – Unembossed, medium blue green, 8-1/2", smooth base, applied sloping collar mouth, American 1850-1865 .... **$150-180**

Twitchell – T – Philada (reverse same), light green, 7", smooth base, applied mouth, American 1855-1870 .... **$60-80**

W. Dean – Newark – N.J., deep blue aqua, 6-3/4", iron pontil, applied blob top, American 1840-1855 .... **$160-200**

Waring – Webster – & Co – 192 West St. N.Y. – Soda Water, deep cobalt blue, 8-sided, 7-3/8", iron pontil, applied blob type mouth, American 1840-1855 .... **$160-200**

W.H.H. – Chicago, medium cobalt blue, 7-1/2", iron pontil, applied blob top, American 1845-1855 .... **$160-200**

W. Morton – Trenton – N.J. – W, medium emerald green, 7-1/8", iron pontil, applied mouth, American 1845-1855 (scarce) **$150-180**

Willis & Ripley – Portsmouth – W & R, deep sapphire blue, 7-3/8", iron pontil, applied sloping collar mouth, American 1840-1855 .... **$450-600**

Wm. Heiss Jr – Manufacturer Of – Superior Mineral – and Soda Waters – No 213 North 2d St – Philada – This Bottle – To Be Returned, medium cobalt blue, 7-3/8", 8-sided, iron pontil, applied sloping collar mouth, American 1840-1860 .... **$225-350**

**W.P. – Knicker – Bocker – Soda Water – 164 18th St. N.Y.
1848**, deep cobalt blue, 7-1/4", 10-sided, iron pontil, applied blob
top, American 1840-1855 . . . .**$450-600**

**Wm.W. Lappeus – Premium – Soda or – Mineral – Waters
– Albany**, deep cobalt blue, 7-1/8", 10-sided, iron pontil, applied
blob type, American 1840-1855 (scarce) **$550-700**

Youngblood (large letters around bottle), light green, 7-1/2",
smooth base, applied mouth, American 1855-1870 . . . . . .**$60-80**

*Tweddle's - Celebrated - Soda
or Mineral - Water - Courtland
Street - 38 - New York,
American, 1840-1860,* **$275-375.**

Target Balls

Target balls are small round bottles filled with confetti, ribbon, and other items. They were used for target practice from the 1850s to the early 1900s. They gained considerable popularity during the 1860s and 1870s with the Buffalo Bill Cody and Annie Oakley wild west shows. Around 1900, clay pigeons started to be used in place of target balls. Because they were made to be broken, they are unfortunately extremely difficult to find and have become very rare, collectible, and valuable.

A.J. Legorone (range target ball), light cobalt blue, 2-1/4", rough sheared mouth, English 1880-1900 (rare) **$330-400**

Bo't. of — Jas. Brown & Sons — 136 Wood St. — Pittsg. PA — Manufacturers — And — Dealers In — Fire Arms, medium amber, 2-3/4" dia., rough sheared mouth, American 1880-1900 (rare) **$3,200-4,000**

E. Jones Gunmaker Blackburn Lanc (target ball), medium cobalt blue, 2-3/4", diamond pattern, rough sheared mouth, English 1880-1900. . . . .**$260-350**

Freeblown Target Ball, medium pink amethyst, 2-1/2" dia., sheared mouth, American 1880-1900 . . . .**$130-160**

Grafl — Zu — Solms — Glasfab — Andreashutte (target ball), medium amber, 2-5/8", diamond pattern, sheared mouth on unusually long neck, German 1880-1900 (extremely rare, made by German Glasshouse Andreashutte founded in 1858 in Schlesien, Germany, now part of Poland) **$1,500-1,800**

Grafl – Zu – Solms – Glasfab – Andreashutte (target ball), clear glass, 2-5/8", diamond pattern, sheared mouth on unusually long neck, German 1880-1900 (extremely rare, made by German Glasshouse Andreashutte founded in 1858 in Schlesien, Germany, now part of Poland) **$1,450-1,800**

Greene – London (range target ball), medium sapphire blue, 2-1/4" dia., rough seared mouth, English 1880-1900 . . **$280-375**

Gurd & Son – 185 Dundas Street – London Ont, medium yellow amber, 2-3/4" dia., square pattern, rough sheared mouth, Canadian 1880-1900 (rare variant with embossed squares above and below the center band) **$1,100-1,600**

For Hockey Patent Trap (English), 1880-1900, 2-1/2" dia., **$500-700.**

Target Ball (Czechoslovakia), 1890-1910, 2-1/2" dia., **$150-200.**

From J. Palmer O'Neil – & Co – Pittsburgh (target ball), medium amber, 2-3/4", rough sheared mouth, American 1880-1900 (extremely rare – one of only two known to exist – J. Palmer O'Neil was president of Pittsburgh Firearms Company from 1878 to 1886 and bought the Pittsburgh Pirates in 1891) **$4,600-6,500**

Made By Rutherford & Co Hamilton Ont, golden yellow amber, 2-5/8" dia., diamond pattern, rough sheared mouth, Canadian 1880-1900 (rare) **$2,600-3,500**

N.B. Glass Works Perth – N.B. Glass Works Perth, cobalt blue, 2-5/8" dia., diamond pattern, rough sheared mouth, English 1880-1900 (variant with backward "S") **$160-200**

Range Target Ball, dark emerald green, 1-1/4" dia., rough sheared lip, English 1880-1915. . . . . **$110-150**

Range Target Ball, deep emerald green, 1-1/2" dia., rough sheared lip, American 1880-1910 . . . . **$75-100**

Range Target Ball, medium emerald green, 1-1/2", rough sheared mouth, American 1880-1910 . . . . **$50-70**

Range Target Ball, clear glass, 2" dia., sheared mouth, American 1880-1910 . . . . **$75-100**

Range Target Ball – BMP – London, deep cobalt blue, 2-1/4", long neck to fit over a wooden peg, sheared mouth, English 1880-1900. . . . . **$225-300**

Sophienhutte In Ilmeenau (Thur), bluish aqua, 2-5/8" dia., diamond pattern, rough sheared mouth, German 1880-1900 (extremely rare) **$750-900**

Sophienhutte In Ilmeenau (Thur), reddish amber, 2-5/8" dia., diamond pattern, rough sheared mouth, German 1880-1900 (rare) **$550-700**

*Target Ball (Czechoslovakia),
1890-1910, 2-1/2" dia.,*
$150-200.

*Target Ball (German),
1890-1910, 2-5/8" dia.,*
$150-200.

Stacey & Co – London, medium cobalt blue, 2-5/8", square pattern, rough sheared mouth, English 1880-1900 (extremely rare) **$450-600**

Target Ball, bright yellow green, 2-1/2" dia., overall diamond pattern, sheared lip, Czechoslovakia 1890-1910 . . . . **$160-200**

Target Ball, Persian blue, 2-1/2" dia., overall fern, star, and pinwheel pattern, sheared mouth, English 1880-1900 (unique) **$2,600-3,500**

Target Ball – F.B.H. (at base) – Two Unembossed Circular Panels, medium cobalt blue, 2-5/8", diamond pattern, rough sheared mouth, Australian 1880-1900 (made by Fredric Bolton Hughes, owner of South Australian Glass Bottle Company from 1896 to 1913) **$550-700**

Target Ball, black amethyst, 2-5/8" dia., overall diamond pattern, sheared and ground lip, German 1890-1910 . . . . **$160-200**

Target Ball, deep cobalt blue, 2-5/8" dia., overall square pattern, rough sheared lip, Australian 1880-1900 (only a few types of target balls were made in Australia) **$1,500-1,800**

Target Ball, cobalt blue, 2-5/8" dia., square pattern above and below a plain center band, rough sheared and outward flared lip, French 1880-1900 . . . . **$160-200**

Target Ball, yellow amber, 2-5/8" dia., horizontal ribs down both mold seams, overall pimple design, rough sheared mouth, American 1880-1900 (extremely rare) **$1,600-2,000**

Target Ball, light cobalt blue, 2-5/8" dia., blown-in three-part mold, rough sheared mouth, American 1880-1900 . . . . **$150-180**

Target Ball, yellow amber, 2-3/4" dia., 6 raised beads on shoulder near the lip, rough sheared lip, blown-in three-part mold, American 1880-1900 . . . . **$160-200**

Target Ball, medium yellow amber, 2-3/4", three sizes of embossed circles around entire ball, rough sheared mouth, American 1880-1900 (extremely rare – referred to as the nickel, dime, quarter ball) **$1,600-2,000**

Target Ball (motif of man shooting), medium purple amethyst, 2-5/8" dia., diamond pattern, rough sheared mouth, American 1880-1900 . . . . **$150-180**

Target Ball (motif of man shooting), deep purple amethyst, 2-3/4" dia., diamond pattern, rough sheared mouth, English 1880-1900 . . . . **$550-700**

Target Ball (motif of man shooting), medium green, 2-5/8", diamond pattern, rough sheared mouth, English 1880-1900 . . . . **$360-450**

Target Ball (composite), pale aqua, 2-3/4" dia., impressed on bottom (Patented Sept 3, 1879, March 3, 1880, Lockport, N.Y.), hollow with roughly formed mouth, American 1880-1910 (very rare) **$425-600**

Van Cutsem – A St. Quentin, deep cobalt blue, 2-5/8", diamond pattern, sheared flared out mouth, French 1880-1900 . **$110-150**

WW Greener St Marys Works Birmm & 68 Haymarket London, medium yellow amber, 2-5/8" dia., diamond pattern, rough sheared mouth, English 1880-1900 . . . . . . **$1,500-1,800**

Target Ball (Australian), 1880-1900, 2-5/8" dia., **$1,400-1,800.**

Whiskey Bottles

Whiskeys, sometimes referred to as spirits, come in an array of sizes, designs, shapes, and colors. The whiskey bottle dates back to the 19th century and provides the avid collector with numerous examples of rare and valuable pieces.

In 1860, E.G. Booz manufactured a cabin-shaped whiskey bottle embossed with year 1840 and the words "Old Cabin Whiskey." According to one theory, "booze," the nickname for hard liquor, was derived from his name. The Booz bottle is also given the credit of being the first to emboss the name on whiskey bottles.

After the repeal of Prohibition in 1933, the only inscription that could be found on any liquor bottles was "Federal Law Forbids Sale or Re-use of This Bottle," which was continued through 1964.

A.P. Hotaling & Co's – Old Bourbon Whisky (motif of kangaroo inside a shield) **Barron, Moxhah & Co – Sydney – Sole Agents For – Australia**, medium orange amber, 11-3/4", smooth base, applied sloping double collar mouth, American 1885-1895 (rare) **$7,300-9,000**

Albro & Bro's – 156 – Bowery – N.Y. – Strapside, medium olive amber, quart, smooth base, applied mouth, American 1880-1890 . . . . **$160-175**

Ambrosial – B.M. & F. AW Co (on applied seal), deep amber, 9", pontil-scarred base, applied mouth and handle, American 1860-1870 . . . . **$225-300**

Belle – of – Anderson – Old – Fashion – Hand Made – Sour – Mash, milk glass, 8-1/4", smooth base, tooled mouth, American 1885-1895 . . . . **$85-100**

Bennett & Carrol – 120 Wood St – Pittsburgh, medium golden amber, 9-1/2", barrel shape, smooth base, applied mouth, American 1865-1975 (rare whiskey barrel) **$850-1,200**

Bininger's Nightcap – No 19 – Broad St. N.Y., golden amber, 8-1/4", smooth base, applied collared mouth with internal screw threads, American 1860-1880 . . . . **$160-300**

Bottle For – Truet Jones – & – Arrington – Eichelberger – Dewdrop (label: Superior – Old Rye – Whiskey), deep reddish amber, 10", smooth base, applied square collared mouth, American 1860-1870 (rare – Stoddard Glasshouse, Stoddard, New Hampshire) **$1,200-2,000**

B.M. & E.A. Whitlock & Co – New York, bluish aqua, 8-1/8", barrel shape, open pontil, applied mouth, American 1855-1865 (scarce) **$550-700**

C.A. Richards & Co – 99 Washington St. – Boston, medium amber, 9-1/2", smooth base, applied sloping collar mouth, American 1865-1875 . . . . **$160-200**

Casper's Whiskey – Made By Honest – North – Carolina People, medium cobalt blue, 12", smooth base, tooled mouth, American 1880-1900 . . . . **$425-600**

Chestnut Grove – Whiskey – G.W. (on seal) – Handled Whiskey, orange amber, 8-7/8", open pontil, applied seal, handle, and mouth, American 1860-1875 . . . . **$270-350**

Distilled In 1848 – Old Kentucky – 1849 – Reserve – Bourbon – A.M. Bininger & Co 19 Broad St. N.Y., amber, 8-1/8", barrel shape, pontil-scarred base, applied double collar mouth, American 1855-1865 . . . . **$425-600**

Durham (standing steer) Whiskey, orange amber, 11-1/2", smooth base, applied mouth, blown-in four-piece mold, American 1880-1890 . . . . **$670-900**

E.G. Booz's – Old Cabin – Whiskey – 120 Walnut St – Philadelphia – (1840) E.G. Booz's – Old Cabin – Whiskey, deep amber, 7-3/4", cabin shape, smooth base, applied sloping collar mouth, American 1860-1875 (earlier and rarer of the E.G. Booz cabin bottles). **$3,600-4,500**

Evans & Ragland – Old – Ingledew – Whiskey – LaGrange GA, medium amber, 10-1/4", smooth base, tooled mouth, American 1870-1880 . . . . **$225-300**

Ewyssons – Denver – Colo. – U.S.A., medium amber, 10-5/8", smooth base, ground lip, original screw-on cap, American 1890-1910 . . . . **$85-120**

A. M. Bininger & Co - No 375 Broadway N.Y., American, 1865-1875, **$1,400-1,800.**

Casper's Whiskey - Made By Honest - North - Carolina People, American, 1885-1900, **$400-600.**

Applied Handle Whiskey, Chestnut Grove - Whiskey - C.W., American, 1859-1870, **$375-475.**

Charles - London - Cordial - Gin, American, 1860-1870, **$180-220.**

Combination lock whiskey bottle, Hayner Whiskey - Stopper Patent - Hayner's Patent Combination Lock Stopper, The Hayner Distilling Company, American, 1897-1910, **$140-180.**

Crane & Brigham - San Francisco, American, 1880-1890, **$500-800.**

E.G. Booz's - Old Cabin Whiskey - E.G. Booz's - Old Cabin Whiskey - 120 Walnut St. Philadelphia, American, 1865-1875, **$2,750-4,000.**

Forest – Lawn – J.V.H., medium olive amber, 7-1/4", pontil-scarred base, applied sloping collar mouth, American 1855-1875 . . . .**$425-600**

G.O. Blake's – KY – Whiskey – GOB and G.O. Blake's – Bourbon Co – KY – Whiskey (inside barrels) Adams, Taylor & Co – Proprietors – Boston & Louisville, deep sun-colored amethyst, 12-1/2", smooth base, tooled mouth, American 1880-1890 . . . . **$60-75**

Golden Eagle Distilleries Co (picture of eagle) San Francisco, Cal, amber, 11", smooth base, tooled top, American 1904-1910 . . . .**$260-350**

Greeting – Theodore Netter – 1232 Market St. – Philadelphia, deep cobalt blue, 6", barrel shape, smooth base, tooled mouth, American 1890-1910 . . . .**$375-550**

Griffith Hyatt & Co – Baltimore – Handled Whiskey Jug, amber, 7-1/2", globular with flattened label panels and applied handle, tubular pontil scar, applied square collared mouth, American 1840-1860 . . . .**$475-800**

H. Rickett's & Co Glassworks Bristol (on base) and Patent (on shoulder), medium green, 10-1/4", pontil-scarred base, applied sloping double collared mouth, three-piece mold, American 1835-1855 . . . .**$125-150**

H.A. Graef's Son Canteen – N.Y., deep yellow olive, 6-1/2", canteen shape, smooth base, applied square collared mouth, applied handle, American 1860-1880 . . . .**$250-400**

Hilbert Bros – Wine – And – Liquor – Merchants – 101 Powell St – San Francisco, Cal, amber, 12", smooth base, glob top, American 1892-1901 . . . . **$2,200-3,000**

Imperial – Levee – J. Noyes Hollywod, MI (cluster of grapes on stump), medium golden yellow amber, 9-3/8", red iron pontil, applied mouth, American 1865-1875 (considered by many collectors to be the State of Mississippi's No. 1 bottle) **$2,700-4,500**

J.N. Kline & Co – Aromatic – Digestive Cordial, medium amber, pumpkinseed flask, 5-1/2", smooth base, applied mouth, American 1860-1870 . . . . **$450-600**

J.T. Bickford & Bartlett – Boston – Handled Whiskey, medium amber, 8-3/4", open pontil, applied seal, handle and mouth, American 1865-1875 (rare) **$385-475**

Joseph Fetz – Importer – 3rd & – Mission Sts – S.F., clear, 12", smooth base, tooled top, American 1885-1890 . . . . **$80-100**

L.L. Lyons – Pure Ohio – Catawba Brandy – Cini, golden amber, 13-3/4", smooth base, applied mouth with ring, American 1860-1880 (rare) **$225-400**

Lindley & Co – (monogram) – Sacramento, Cal, clear, 11-7/8", smooth base, tooled top, American 1895-1905 . . . . **$40-50**

Mansion House – 478 – 4th Ave. N.Y. – Wm. Brandes & Co Props – Strapside Flask, medium amber, half-pint, smooth base, applied mouth, American 1880-1900 . . . . **$45-60**

(American Eagle) M.G. Landsberg – Chicago – 1771-1876, medium amber, 11", smooth base, applied mouth, American 1876 (bottled for the 1876 Centennial) **$1,600-2,500**

Mist of The Morning – SM – Barnett & Company, dark amber, 10", barrel shape, smooth base, applied sloping double collar mouth, American 1865-1875 . . . . **$160-200**

Mohawk Whiskey – Pure – Rye – Patented – Feb 11 1868 (Indian Queen), medium golden amber, 12-1/2", smooth base, inward rolled lip, American 1868-1875 (rare) **$2,600-3,500**

*Griffith Hyatt & Co.
- Baltimore, American,
1860-1875,* **$275-400.**

*J.N. Kline & Cos
Aromatic Digestive
Cordial, American,
1870-1880,* **$275-375.**

London - Royal - Imperial Gin, American, 1865-1875, **$600-900.**

Milton J. Hardy - Old - Bourbon - Trade Mark (eagle) - Wellington A. Hardy - Manufacturer - Louisville, KY, American, 1878-1880, **$5,000-8,000.**

Myers & Company Dist's – Pure – Fulton – Whiskey – Patap. – Covington, KY. U.S.A., aqua, 9-1/8", smooth base, tooled mouth, American 1885-1895 . . . .$110-150

N. Van Bergen & Co – Gold Dust Kentucky Bourbon – N. Van Bergen & Co. – Sole Propts, clear, 11-3/4", smooth base, applied top, American 1880-1882 . . . . $825-1,000

Nathan Bros – Philad, medium golden amber, 7-1/2", smooth base, applied water seal above crescent-shaped label panel, applied mouth, American 1855-1870 (rare) $325-400

Net Contents 25 Oz. – McCleod – Hatje Co – Wine & Liquor – M Co L – Merchants – San Francisco, orange amber, 11-3/4", smooth base, tooled lip, American 1900-1905 . . . **$55-80**

Old Bourbon – Whiskey – For Medicinal – Purposes – Wilson Fairbank & Co – Sole Agents, bluish aqua, 10", smooth base, applied mouth, American 1865-1875 . . . .$260-350

Old Continental – Whiskey (standing Continental soldier) 1776, medium yellow amber, 9-1/2", smooth base, applied mouth, American 1865-1875 . . . . **$2,600-3,500**

Patrick Smith – 1313 – Sec. Ave – NW Corner 69th St – New York – One Half-Pint – Full Measure, amber, half-pint, smooth base (L & MC – A82 FULTON ST – N.Y.) tooled mouth, American 1890-1910 . . . .$85-150

Perrine's – Apple – Ginger – Phila – Perrine's (motif of apple) Ginger, amber, 10", smooth base, tooled mouth, American 1880-1890 . . . .$225-275

Phoenix – Old (picture of bird) Bourbon – Naber, Alfs & Brune – S.F. – Sole Agts., amber, 11-3/4", smooth base, applied top, American 1880-1895 . . . . $1,100-2,000

Pure Malt Whiskey – Bourbon Co. Kentucky, amber, 8-3/4", open pontil, applied handle and mouth, American 1860-1875 (scarce) **$450-600**

R.B. Cutter – Pure – Bourbon, deep cherry puce, 8-1/2", pontil-scarred base, applied mouth and handle, American 1855-1870 . . . .**$825-1,200**

Reed's Old Lexington Club, medium golden amber, 11", smooth base, applied sloping collar mouth, American 1870-1880 . . . . . .**$150-180**

Robinson & Lord – 88 & 90 – Lombard St – Baltimore, deep amber, barrel shape, 10-1/8", iron pontil, applied mouth, American 1860-1870 (rare) **$825-1,200**

Roehling & Schutz, Inc. – Chicago, amber, 9-5/8", cabin shape, smooth base, tooled lip, American 1880-1890 . . . .**$285-375**

Salem – THD (monogram) – Mass – Strapside Flasks, aqua, half-pint, smooth base, tooled mouth, American 1880-1900 . . . .**$45-60**

Silas F. Miller & Co – Galt House – Louisville, medium amber, 6-1/4", flask, smooth base, applied double collar mouth, American 1875-1885 (very rare) **$350-450**

Simmond's – Nabob – Trade (picture of nabob) Mark – Pure – KY Bourbon – Whiskey, red amber, 10-3/4", smooth base, glob top, American 1878-1890 . . . . **$1,100-2,000**

Smokine – Imported And Bottled – By – Alfred Andersen & Co – The Western Importers – Minneapolis Minn – And – Winnipeg, Man, reddish amber, 5-1/4", cabin shape, smooth base, tooled lip, American 1880-1895 . . . .**$285-375**

Spruance Stanley & Co – Wholesale – Liquor Dealers – San Francisco – Cal – 1869 (inside horseshoe), medium amber, 11-5/8", smooth base, applied sloping glob top, American 1885-1900 . . . .**$180-275**

Applied Handle Whiskey, Fine Old - Bourbon - Whiskey - The Travellers - Sol. Age, American, 1860-1875, **$250-350.**

Redington & Co - R&CO. - San Francisco, American, 1880-1890, **$500-700.**

Star Whiskey – New York – W.B. Crowell Jr – Handled Whiskey, medium yellow amber, 8-1/8", pontil-scarred base, applied handle, double collar mouth, tooled mouth spout, American 1855-1870 . . . .**$550-700**

S.S. Smith Jr. & Co – Cincinnati, O, medium cobalt blue, 9-3/4", smooth base, applied sloping collar mouth, American 1865-1875 (very rare). **$1,600-2,500**

Stoneware Canteen – Pat. Aug 11 1891 – The Old Dexter Jug Whiskey (reverse) Old Dexter Distilling Co, Butler Kentucky Distillers, gray pottery, 7-1/4", smooth base, handled, American 1891-1900 . . . .**$85-120**

The Campus – Gossler Bros. Prop's – N.W. Cor. 104 Ste. & Columbus Av. – N.Y. – Handled Whiskey, reddish amber, 9-5/8", smooth base (The Campus – Gossler – Bros. Prop's – N.W. Cor. 104 Ste. & Columbus Av. – N.Y.), applied handle and mouth, American 1885-1895 . . . . **$160-200**

Thoms Jacobs & Co (on seal), teal blue, 11-3/4", half-gallon, iron pontil, applied seal and mouth, American 1850-1860 . . **$160-250**

Thos Taylor & Co – Importers – Virginia, NV, medium amber, 11-3/4", smooth base, glob top, American 1870-1880 . . . . **$3,100-4,000**

Udolpho Wolf's – Schiedam – Aromatic – Schnapps (sample size), light green, 3-5/8", smooth base, applied mouth, American 1870-1880 . . . .**$160-250**

United We Stand – Old Bourbon – Whiskey – Wilmerding & Co – Sole Agent's – S.F. CA. – W. & CO, yellow amber, 12", smooth base, applied sloping double collar mouth, American 1878-1883. . . . . **$3,100-4,000**

Van Dunck's – Genever – Trade Mark – Ware & Schmitz, deep amber, 8-3/4", smooth base, applied mouth, American 1880-1890 . . . . **$160-200**

Walther's – Peptonized Port – Pittsburgh, PA – Miniature, medium amber, 4-3/8", smooth base, tooled mouth, American 1890-1900 . . . . **$85-120**

Weeks & Gilson So. Stoddard N.H., medium golden amber, 11-1/2", three-piece mold, smooth base, applied sloping double collar mouth, American 1855-1870 . . . . **$425-600**

Wharton's – Whiskey – 1850 – Chestnut Grove, medium cobalt blue, pumpkinseed flask, 5-1/4", smooth base, applied mouth, American 1860-1870 . . . . **$430-600**

Wm. H. Spears & Co – Pioneer Whiskey – (picture of a walking bear) – Fenkhausen & – Braunschweiger – Sole Agents, S.F., light amber, 11-3/4", smooth base, applied top, American 1878-1882 . . . . **$2,600-5,000**

Willmington Glass Works (on base), deep amber, 11-5/8", smooth base, blown-in three-part mold, applied sloping double collar mouth, American 1855-1875 . . . . **$110-150**

Whiskey Flask – Plain & Unembossed, light to medium pink, pint, smooth base, applied double collared mouth, American 1860-1880 (rare due to unique color) **$450-800**

Wormser Bros – San Francisco, golden yellow amber, 9-1/2", barrel shape, smooth base, applied sloping collar mouth, American 1870-1872 . . . . **$1,600-2,000**

H F & B. - N.Y., American, 1865-1875, **$700-900.**

Back Bar Bottles & Decanters

Angelo Myers Philadelphia Rye Whiskey, clear, 11-1/8", polished pontil, tooled mouth, American 1885-1910 . . . . **$260-300**

Brandy (label-under-glass bottle), clear, 10-7/8", multicolored label showing a pretty woman, smooth base, tooled mouth, original metal and cork stopper on chain, American 1890-1910 **$550-700**

Chicken Cock (standing rooster) Bourbon, clear with amethyst tint, 7", smooth base, tooled lip, American 1890-1915 (rare) **$1,500-2,000**

Established In 1844 – Robert Johnston Distiller of Copper Double Distilled – Rye – Wheat and Malt – Whiskies – Warranted Without the Use of Steam – The Only Whiskey Fit for Medicinal Use & C. – Greencastle, Franklin Co. PA (label-under-glass bottle), clear, 11-3/8", smooth base, tooled mouth, American 1880-1910 . . . . **$550-700**

Hawthorne, clear, 11-1/4", rib-pattern swirled to right and white enameled lettering, smooth base, tooled mouth, original 30 cent pour stopper, American 1880-1910 . . . . **$190-250**

Iroquois Club (torso of an Indian) Rye, clear, 8-7/8", polished pontil, tooled lip, American 1890-1915 . . . . **$1,400-1,600**

Kellerstrass Belle of Missouri Rye, clear, 9-1/8", multicolored enamel floral decoration, smooth base, tooled mouth, original ground glass stopper, American 1880-1910 . . . . **$650-800**

Phoenix Club (bird coming out of the fire), clear, 8-1/2", vertical rib pattern, polished pontil, American 1890-1910 . . . . . **$250-350**

Back bar bottle, American, 1870-1880, **$375-475.**

Back bar bottle, American, 1890-1910, **$700-900.**

Prentice, Hand Made Sour Mash J.T.S. Brown & Sons, Spring 1871 (label-under-glass bottle), clear, 9-3/4", smooth base, tooled liop with original ground glass stopper, American 1875-1910 (rare) **$385-500**

Maryland Club, clear, 8-1/4", white enamel and green shamrock decoration, polished pontil, tooled mouth, ground glass stopper, American 1885-1910 . . . . **$325-400**

Old Rosebud Whiskey, clear, 9", multicolored enamel decoration showing a jockey on a horse, smooth base, tooled mouth, mother-of-pearl whiskey stopper, American 1885-1910 . . . . . . **$650-800**

Old Underwood Baltimore Pure Rye, clear, 11-1/4", white enamel lettering, smooth base, tooled mouth, American 1890-1915 . . . . **$150-180**

Rye and Scotch – Set of Two, medium amber, 8-1/2", applied metal cages and stoppers, smooth base, tooled mouth, American 1880-1890 . . . . **$110-150**

Scotch Decanter, straw yellow, 11", rib-pattern with silver overlay lettering, smooth base, polished lip, original sterling collar and shot glass lid, American 1880-1910 . . . . **$260-350**

Sunny Brook Whiskey, clear, 10-7/8", multicolored enamel decoration showing an inspector 'The Inspector is Back of Every Bottle" holding a bottle of Sunny Brook Whiskey, smooth base, tooled mouth, ground glass stopper, American 1890-1910 . . . . **$550-700**

West Point, medium amber, 11-1/8", white enamel lettering on shoulder, smooth base, tooled mouth, copper stopper, American 1890-1910 . . . .**$225-300**

Yellowstone 100 Proof Kentucky Straight Bourbon Whiskey, Yellowstone, Inc. Louisville, KY, clear, 11-3/4", multicolored enamel decoration showing waterfall scene, smooth base, tooled mouth and rim, metal cage stopper, American 1890-1910 (very rare) **$1,600-2,500**

Pottery Whiskey Jugs

Chapin & Gore's Bourbon – 1867 – Sour Mash Whiskey – Chapin & Gore Chicago, tan with brown glaze, 8-5/8", smooth base, American 1890-1915 . . . .**$85-120**

Gilmour Thomson's Royal Stag Whisky, Gilmour Whomson & Co. Ltd Glasgow, white with brown glaze, 8-1/4", smooth base (Kennedy Bakersfield Potteries Glasgow), applied handle, Scottish 1890-1915 . . . .**$85-120**

Grannie – Taylor's – Liqueur Whisky – Taylor Brothers Co. Glasgow & London, cream with brown glaze, 8-1/4", smooth base (Govancroft Co. Glasgow), applied handle, English 1890-1915 . . . .**$90-120**

Happy Day – Famous – Old Rye Whiskey, cream with brown glaze, 7-3/4", smooth base, applied handle, American 1890-1915 . . . .**$90-140**

Kentucky Belle – Eight Year Old Hand Made Sour Mash – Bourbon-Bottled at the Distillery – Anderson Co. KY, cream with brown glaze, 8-3/8", smooth base, applied handle, American 1890-1915 (rare) **$260-350**

O'Donnel's Old Irish Whisky Belfast, cream with brown glaze, 7-5/8", smooth base, applied handle, Irish 1890-1915 .**$110-150**

Pennsylvania Club Pure Rye Whiskey, white china with dark green transfer, 7-5/8", smooth base, American 1890-1915 . . . .**$275-375**

Pointer – The Gottschalk Co – Baltimore, MD – Maryland Rye, cream with brown glaze, black transfer, 7-3/8" smooth base, American 1890-1910 . . . .**$185-275**

Roche Brand – Irish Whiskey – Type – Compounded with Pure Grain Distillates, cream with brown glaze, 7-3/8", smooth base, American 1890-1915 (rare). **$210-300**

The Cream of Irish Whiskey Shamrock, cream with brown glaze, 8-3/4", smooth base, applied handle, Irish 1890-1915 .**$110-150**

The Cream of Old Scotch Whiskey Bonnie Castle, tan with brown glaze, 9", smooth base, Scottish 1890-1915 . . . .**$120-150**

Watson's Dundee Whisky, cream with dark brown glaze, 8-5/8", smooth base (Port – Dundas Pottery Co. Glasgow), applied handle, Scottish 1890-1915 . . . .**$150-180**

New Bottles (Post-1900)

The bottles listed in this section have been divided by individual categories and/or type, since the contents hold little interest for the collector. New bottles covered in this section are valued for their decorative, appealing, and unique designs.

The objective of most new-bottle collectors is to collect a complete set of items designed and produced by a favorite manufacturer. As with the reproduction of bottles such as Coca-Cola, or new items such as Avon, the right time to purchase is when the first issue comes out on the retail market, or prior to retail release if possible. As with the old bottles, there is an excellent cross section of new bottles in various price ranges and categories rather than listings of just the rarest or most collectible pieces.

The pricing shown reflects the value of particular item listed. Newer bottles are usually manufactured in limited quantities without any reissues. Since retail prices are affected by factors such as source, type of bottle, desirability, condition, and the possibility the bottle was produced exclusively as a collector's item, the pricing can fluctuate radically at any time.

Avon Bottles

The cosmetic empire known today as Avon began as the California Perfume Company. It was the creation of D.H. McConnell, a door-to-door book salesman who gave away perfume samples to stop doors from being slammed in his face. As time went on, McConnell gave up on books and concentrated on selling perfumes. Although based in New York, the name Avon was used in 1929 along with the name California Perfume Company or C.P.C. After 1939, the name Avon was used exclusively. Bottles embossed with C.P.C. are very rare and collectible due to the small quantities issued and the even smaller quantity that have been well preserved.

Today, Avon offers the collector a wide range of products in bottles shaped as cars, people, chess pieces, trains, animals, sporting items (footballs, baseballs, etc.) and numerous other objects. The scarcest pieces and most sought after are the Pre-World War II figurals, since very few of these items were well preserved.

For the Avon collector, anything Avon is considered collectible, including boxes, brochures, magazine ads, and anything else labeled with the Avon name. Since many people who sell Avon items are unaware of the value of individual pieces, collectors can find great prices at swap meets, flea markets, and garage sales. While this book offers an excellent detailed cross section of Avon collectibles, I recommend that serious collectors obtain *Bud Hastin's Avon Collector's Encyclopedia*, 17th Edition, which offers pricing and pictures for thousands of Avon & California Perfume Co. (CPC) products from 1886 to the present.

A Man's World, globe on stand, 1969 . . . . $7-10

A Winner, boxing gloves, 1960 . . . . $20-25

Abraham Lincoln, Wild Country After Shave, 1970-1972 . . . $3-5

After Shave On Tap, Wild Country After Shave $3-5

Aladdin's Lamp, 1971 . . . . $11-13

Alaskan Moose, 1974 . . . . $5-8

Alpine Flask, 1966-1967 . . . . $35-45

American Belle, Sonnet Cologne, 1976-1978 . . . . $5-7

American Buffalo, 1975 . . . . $6-8

American Eagle Pipe, 1974-1975 . . . . $6-8

American Eagle, Windjammer After Shave, 1971-1972 . . . . . $3-4

American Ideal Perfume, California Perfume Comp., 1911 . . . . $125-140

American Schooner, Oland After Shave, 1972-1973 . . . . $4-5

Andy Capp Figural (England), 1970 . . . . $95-105

Angler, Windjammer After Shave, 1970 . . . . $5-7

Apple Blossom Toilet Water, 1941-1942 . . . . $50-60

Aladdin's Lamp, 6 oz., green glass bottle with gold cap, 1971-1973, **$11-13.**

Alpine Flask, 8 oz., brown glass with gold cap and neck chain, 1966-1967, **$35-45.**

Apothecary, Lemon Velvet Moist Lotion, 1973-1976 . . . . . . **$4-6**

Apothecary, Spicy After Shave, 1973-1974 . . . . **$4-5**

Aristocrat Kittens Soap (Walt Disney) **$5-7**

Armoire Decanter, Charisma Bath Oil, 1973-1974 . . . . **$4-5**

Armoire Decanter, Elusive Bath Oil, 1972-1975 . . . . **$4-5**

Auto Lantern, 1973 . . . . **$6-8**

Auto, Big Mack Truck, Windjammer After Shave, 1973-1975 **$5-6**

Auto, Cord, 1937 Model, Wild Country After Shave, 1974-1978
. . . . **$7-8**

Auto, Country Vendor, Wild Country After Shave, 1973 . . . **$7-8**

Auto, Dusenberg, Silver, Wild Country After Shave, 1970-1972
. . . . **$8-9**

Auto, Dune Buggy, Sports Rally Bracing Lotion, 1971-1973 . **$4-5**

Auto, Electric Charger, Avon Leather Cologne, 1970-1972 . **$6-7**

Auto, Hayes Apperson, 1902 Model, Avon Blend 7 After Shave,
1973-1974 . . . . **$5-7**

*Maxwell '23
Decanter, 6 oz.,
green glass with
beige plastic top
and trunk over
cap, 1972-1974,*
$12-14.

Auto, Maxwell 23, Deep Woods After Shave, 1972-1974 . **$12-14**

Auto, MG, 1936, Wild Country After Shave, 1974-1975.... **$4-5**

Auto, Model A, Wild Country After Shave, 1972-1974 ..... **$4-5**

Auto, Red Depot Wagon, Oland After Shave, 1972-1973... **$6-7**

Auto, Rolls Royce, Deep Woods After Shave, 1972-1975 .. **$6-8**

Auto, Stanley Steamer, Windjammer After Shave, 1971-1972 .... **$6-7**

Auto, Station Wagon, Tai Winds After Shave, 1971-1973... **$7-8**

Auto, Sterling 6, Spicy After Shave, 1968-1970........... **$6-7**

Auto, Sterling Six II, Wild Country After Shave, 1973-1974 **$4-5**

Auto, Stutz Bearcat, 1914 Model, Avon Blend 7 After Shave, 1974-1977 .... **$5-6**

Auto, Touring T, Tribute After Shave, 1969-1970 .... **$6-7**

Auto, Volkswagen, Red, Oland After Shave, 1972......... **$5-6**

Avon Calling, Phone, Wild Country After Shave, 1969-1970 .... **$15-20**

Avon Dueling Pistol II, black glass, 1972 .... **$10-15**

Avonshire Blue Cologne, 1971-1974 .... **$4-5**

Baby Grand Piano, Perfume Glace, 1971-1972 .... **$8-10**

Baby Hippo, 1977-1980 .... **$4-5**

Ballad Perfume, 3 drams, 3/8 ounce, 1939 .... **$100-125**

Bath Urn, Lemon Velvet Bath Oil, 1971-1973 .... **$4-5**

Beauty Bound Black Purse, 1964................... **$45-55**

Bell Jar Cologne, 1973................................ **$5-10**

Benjamin Franklin, Wild Country After Shave, 1974-1976.. **$4-5**

Avon Calling for Men, 6 oz., gold paint over clear glass, gold cap, black mouthpiece, black plastic earpiece, 1969-1970, **$15-20.**

Big Game Rhino, Tai Winds After Shave, 1972-1973 . . . . . . $7-8

Big Whistle, 1972 . . . . $4-5

Bird House Power Bubble Bath, 1969 . . . . $7-8

Bird Of Paradise Cologne Decanter, 1972-1974 . . . . $4-5

Blacksmith's Anvil, Deep Woods After Shave, 1972-1973 . . . $4-5

Bloodhound Pipe, Deep Woods After Shave, 1976 . . . . $5-6

Blue Blazer After Shave Lotion, 1964 . . . . $25-30

Blue Blazer Deluxe, 1965 . . . . $55-65

Blue Moo Soap On A Rope, 1972 . . . . $5-6

Blunderbuss Pistol, 1976. . . . . $7-10

Bon Bon Black, Field & Flowers Cologne, 1973 . . . $5-6

Bon Bon White, Occur Cologne, 1972-1973 . . . . $5-6

Bon Bon White, Topaz Cologne, 1972-1973 . . . . $5-6

Boot Gold Top, Avon Leather After Shave, 1966-1971. . . . . $3-4

Boot Western, 1973 . . . . $4-5

Boots & Saddle, 1968. . . . . $20-22

Brocade Deluxe, 1967 . . . . $30-35

Buffalo Nickel, liquid hair lotion, 1971-1972. . . . . $4-5

Bulldog Pipe, Oland After Shave, 1972-1973. . . . . $4-5

Bunny Puff & Talc, 1969-1972 . . . . $3-4

Bureau Organizer, 1966-1967 . . . . $35-55

Butter Candlestick, Sonnet Cologne, 1974 . . . . $7-8

Butterfly Fantasy Egg, first issue, 1974. . . . . $20-30

Butterfly, Unforgettable Cologne, 1972-1973 . . . . $4-5

Butterfly, Unforgettable Cologne, 1974-1976 . . . . $1-2

Cable Car After Shave, 1974-1975 . . . . $8-10

Camper, Deep Woods After Shave, 1972-1974 . . . . $6-7

Canada Goose, Deep Woods Cologne, 1973-1974. . . . . $4-5

Candlestick Cologne, Elusive, 1970-1971. . . . . $5-6

Car, army jeep, 1974-1975 . . . . $4-5

Caseys Lantern, Island Lime After Shave, 1966-1967 . . . . $30-40

Catch A Fish, Field & Flowers Cologne, 1976-1978 . . . . **$6-7**

Centennial Express 1876, locomotive, 1978 . . . . **$11-12**

Chevy '55, 1974-1975 . . . . **$6-8**

Christmas Ornament, green or red, 1970-1971 . . . . **$1-2**

Christmas Ornament, orange, bubble bath, 1970-1971 . . . . **$2-3**

Christmas Tree Bubble Bath, 1968 . . . . **$8-12**

Classic Lion, Deep Woods After Shave, 1973-1975 . . . . **$4-5**

Club Bottle, 1906 Avon Lady, 1977 . . . . **$25-30**

Club Bottle, 1st Annual, 1972 . . . . **$150-200**

Club Bottle, 2nd Annual, 1973 . . . . **$45-60**

Club Bottle, 5th Annual, 1976 . . . . **$25-30**

Club Bottle, Bud Hastin, 1974 . . . . **$70-95**

Club Bottle, CPC Factory, 1974 . . . . **$30-40**

Collector's Pipe, Windjammer After Shave, 1973-1974 . . . . . **$3-4**

Colt Revolver 1851, 1975-1976 . . . . **$10-12**

Corncob Pipe After Shave, 1974-1975 . . . . **$4-6**

Corvette Stingray '65, 1975 . . . . **$5-7**

Covered Wagon, Wild Country After Shave, 1970-1971 . . . . **$4-5**

Daylight Shaving Time, 1968-1970 . . . . **$5-7**

Defender Cannon, 1966 . . . . **$20-24**

Dollars 'n' Scents, 1966-1967 . . . . **$20-24**

Dutch Girl Figurine, Somewhere, 1973-1974 . . . . **$8-10**

Duck After Shave, 1971 . . . . **$4-6**

Dueling Pistol 1760, 1973-1974 . . . . **$9-12**

Chess Piece Decanter, 3 oz., silver over glass with amber plastic top, 1975-1976, $7-9.

Charlie Brown, 4 oz., red, white, and black plastic, 1968-1972, $3-5.

Christmas Tree, 4 oz., red paint over silver glass, 1968-1970, $8-12.

Christmas Ornament, 4 oz., green with silver cap, 1967, $9-14.

Dueling Pistol II, 1975 . . . . $9-12

Eight Ball Decanter, Spicy After Shave, 1973 . . . . $3-4

Electric Guitar, Wild Country After Shave, 1974-1975 . . . . . $4-5

Enchanted Frog Cream Sachet, Sonnet Cologne, 1973-1976
. . . . $3-4

Fashion Boot, Moonwind Cologne, 1972-1976 . . . . $5-7

Fashion Boot, Sonnet Cologne, 1972-1976 . . . . $5-7

Fielder's Choice, 1971-1972 . . . . $4-6

Fire Alarm Box, 1975-1976 . . . . $4-6

First Class Male, Wild Country After Shave, 1970-1971 . . . . $3-4

First Down, soap on a rope, 1970-1971 . . . . $7-8

First Down, Wild Country After Shave $3-4

First Volunteer, Tai Winds Cologne, 1971-1972 . . . . $6-7

Fox Hunt, 1966 . . . . $25-30

French Telephone, Moonwind Foaming Bath Oil, 1971 . . $20-24

Garnet Bud Vase, To A Wild Rose Cologne, 1973-1976 . . . . $3-5

Gavel, Island Lime After Shave, 1967-1968 . . . . $4-5

George Washington, Spicy After Shave, 1970-1972 . . . . . . $2-3

George Washington, Tribute After Shave, 1970-1972 . . . . . . $2-3

Gold Cadillac, 1969-1973 . . . . $7-10

Gone Fishing, 1973-1974 . . . . $5-7

Grade Avon Hostess Soap, 1971-1972 . . . . $6-8

Hearth Lamp, Roses, Roses, 1973-1976 . . . . $6-8

Hobnail Decanter, Moonwind Bath Oil, 1972-1974 . . . . . . $5-6

Hunter's Stein, 1972 . . . . $10-14

Indian Chieftan, protein hair lotion, 1972-1975 . . . . $2-3

Indian Head Penny, Bravo After Shave, 1970-1972 . . . . $4-5

Inkwell, Windjammer After Shave, 1969-1970 . . . . $6-7

Iron Horse Shaving Mug, Avon Blend 7 After Shave, 1974-1976
. . . . $3-4

Jack-in-the-Box, baby cream, 1974 . . . . $4-6

Jaguar Car, 1973-1976 . . . . $6-8

Jolly Santa, 1978 . . . . $6-7

Joyous Bell, 1978 . . . . $5-6

King Pin, 1969-1970 . . . . $4-6

Kodiak Bear, 1977 . . . . $5-10

Koffee Klatch, Honeysuckle Foam Bath Oil, 1971-1974 . . . . $5-6

Liberty Bell, Tribute After Shave, 1971-1972 . . . . $4-6

*Liberty Bell, 5 oz.,
bronze with bronze
cap, 1976,* **$10-12.**

Liberty Dollar, after shave, 1970-1972. . . . . **$4-6**

Lincoln Bottle, 1971-1972 . . . . **$3-5**

Lip Pop Colas, cherry, 1973-1974 . . . . **$1-2**

Lip Pop Colas, cola, 1973-1974 . . . . **$1-2**

Lip Pop Colas, strawberry, 1973-1974 . . . . **$1-2**

Longhorn Steer, 1975-1976 . . . . **$7-9**

Looking Glass, Regence Cologne, 1970-1972 . . . . **$7-8**

Mallard Duck, 1967-1968 . . . . **$8-10**

Mickey Mouse, bubble bath, 1969. . . . . **$10-12**

Mighty Mitt Soap on a Rope, 1969-1972 . . . . **$7-8**

Ming Cat, Bird of Paradise Cologne, 1971 . . . . **$5-7**

Mini Bike, Sure Winner Bracing Lotion, 1972-1973 . . . . . . **$3-5**

Mallard Duck, 5 oz., amber glass with green plastic head, 1974-1975, **$8-10.**

Nile Blue Bath Urn, Skin So Soft, 1972-1974 . . . . **$4-6**

No Parking, 1975-1976 . . . . **$5-7**

Old Faithful, Wild Country After Shave, 1972-1973 . . . . **$4-6**

One Good Turn, screwdriver, 1976 . . . . **$5-6**

Opening Play, dull golden, Spicy After Shave, 1968-1969 . . **$8-10**

Opening Play, shiny golden, Spicy After Shave, 1968-1969
. . . . **$14-17**

Owl Fancy, Roses, Roses, 1974-1976 . . . . **$3-4**

Owl Soap Dish and Soaps, 1970-1971 . . . . **$8-10**

Packard Roadster, 1970-1972 . . . . **$4-7**

Pass Play Decanter, 1973-1975 . . . . **$6-8**

Peanuts Gang Soaps, 1970-1972 . . . . **$8-9**

Pepperbox Pistol, 1976 . . . . **$5-10**

Perfect Drive Decanter, 1975-1976 . . . . **$7-9**

Pheasant, 1972-1974 . . . . **$7-9**

Piano Decanter, Tai Winds After Shave, 1972 . . . . **$3-4**

Pipe, Full, Decanter, Brown, Spicy After Shave, 1971-1972
. . . . **$3-4**

Pony Express, Avon Leather After Shave, 1971-1972 . . . . **$3-4**

Pony Post "Tall," 1966-1967 . . . . **$7-9**

Pot Belly Stove, 1970-1971 . . . . **$5-7**

President Lincoln, Tai Winds After Shave, 1973 . . . . **$6-8**

President Washington, Deep Woods After Shave, 1974-1976
. . . . **$4-5**

Quail, 1973-1974 . . . . **$7-9**

Rainbow Trout, Deep Woods After Shave, 1973-1974 . . . . . . $3-4

Road Runner, motorcycle $4-5

Rook, Spicy After Shave, 1973-1974 . . . . $4-5

Royal Coach, Bird of Paradise Bath Oil, 1972-1973 . . . . $4-6

Scent with Love, Elusive Perfume, 1971-1972 . . . . $9-10

Scent with Love, Field & Flowers Perfume, 1971-1972 . . . $9-10

Scent with Love, Moonwind Perfume, 1971-1972 . . . . $9-10

Side-Wheeler, Tribute After Shave, 1970-1971 . . . . $4-5

Side-Wheeler, Wild Country After Shave, 1971-1972 . . . . . . $3-4

Small World Perfume Glace, Small World, 1971-1972 . . . . $3-4

Snoopy Soap Dish Refills, 1968-1976 . . . . $3-4

Snoopys Bubble Tub, 1971-1972 . . . . $3-4

Spark Plug Decanter, 1975-1976 . . . . $2-5

Spirit of St Louis, Excalibur After Shave, 1970-1972 . . . . . . $3-5

Stage Coach, Wild Country After Shave, 1970-1977 . . . . . . $5-6

Tee Off, electric pre-shave, 1973-1975 . . . . $2-3

Ten Point Buck, Wild Country After Shave, 1969-1974 . . . . . $5-7

Twenty-Dollar Gold Piece, Windjammer After Shave, 1971-1972
. . . . $4-6

Uncle Sam Pipe, Deep Woods After Shave, 1975-1976 . . . . . $4-5

Viking Horn, 1966 . . . . $12-16

Western Boot, Wild Country After Shave, 1973-1975 . . . . . . $2-3

Western Saddle, 1971-1972 . . . . $7-9

Wild Turkey, 1974-1976 . . . . $6-8

World's Greatest Dad Decanter, 1971 . . . . $4-6

Jim Beam Bottles

The James B. Beam distilling company was founded in Kentucky in 1778 by Jacob Beam and now bears the name of Col. James B. Beam, Jacob Beam's grandson. Beam whiskey was very popular in the South during the 19th and 20th centuries but was not produced on a large scale. Because of low production, the early Beam bottles are very rare, collectible, and valuable.

In 1953, the Beam company packaged bourbon in a special Christmas/New Year ceramic decanter, which was a rarity for any distiller. When the decanters sold, Beam decided to redevelop their method of packaging, which led to production of a wide variety of series in the 1950s. The first of these was the Ceramics Series in 1953. In 1955, the Executive Series was issued to commemorate the 160th anniversary of the corporation.

In 1955, Beam introduced the Regal China Series to honor significant people, places, and events with a focus on America and contemporary situations. In 1956, political figures were introduced with the elephant and the donkey as well as special productions for customer specialties made on commission. In 1957, the Trophy Series came along to signify various achievements within the liquor industry, and in 1958, the State Series was introduced to commemorate the admission of Alaska and Hawaii into the Union. The practice has continued with Beam still producing decanters to commemorative all 50 States.

In total, over 500 types of Beam bottles have been issued since 1953. For further information, contact the International Association of Jim Beam Bottle and Specialties Clubs, PO Box 486, Kewanee, IL 61443, 309-853-3370, www.beam-wade.org.

Angelo's Delivery Truck, 1984, **$180-200.**

AC Spark Plug, 1977, replica of a spark plug in white, green, and gold **$25-30**

AHEPA 50th Anniversary, 1972, Regal China bottle designed in honor of AHEPA'S (American Hellenic Education Progressive Association) 50th Anniversary **$4-6**

Aida, 1978, figurine of character from the opera Aida . . . **$150-160**

Akron Rubber Capital, 1973, Regal China bottle honoring Akron, Ohio. **$15-20**

American Veterans **$4-8**

Antique Clock. **$35-45**

Antioch, 1967, Regal China, 10", commemorates Diamond Jubilee of Regal **$5-9**

Antique Coffee Grinder, 1979, replica of a box coffee mill used in mid-19th century **$10-15**

Antique Telephone (1897), 1978, replica of an 1897 desk phone, second in a series. **$50-60**

Antique Trader, 1968, Regal China, 10-1/2", represents *Antique Trader* newspaper **$4-6**

Armadillo. **$8-12**

Barry Berish, 1985, Executive Series **$110-140**

Barry Berish, 1986, Executive Series, bowl **$110-140**

Baseball, 1969, isssued to commemorate the 100th anniversary of baseball **$18-20**

Bell Scotch, 1970, Regal China, 10-1/2", in honor of Arthur Bell & Sons **$4-9**

The Big Apple, 1979, apple-shaped bottle with "The Big Apple" over the top **$8-12**

Bing's 31st Clam Bake Bottle, 1972, commemorates 31st Bing Crosby National Pro-Am Golf Tournament in January 1972 ....**$25-30**

Bing Crosby National Pro-Am, 1970 ....**$4-9**

Bing Crosby National Pro-Am, 1975 ....**$45-65**

Bing Crosby National Pro-Am, 1978 ....**$12-18**

Black Katz, 1968, Regal China, 14-1/2" **$7-12**

Blue Cherub Executive, 1960, Regal China, 12-1/2" **$75-90**

Blue Daisy, 1967, also known as Zimmerman Blue Daisy .**$10-15**

Blue Gill Fish **$12-16**

Bobby Unser Olsonite Eagle, 1975, replica of the racing car used by Bobby Unser **$40-50**

Bob Devaney **$8-13**

Bob Hope Desert Classic, 1974 ....**$8-12**

Bohemian Girl, 1974, issued for the Bohemian Cafe in Omaha, Nebraska, to honor the Czech and Slovak immigrants in the United States, 14-1/4" **$10-15**

Boris Godinov, with base, 1978, second in Opera Series**$355-450**

Boys Town of Italy, 1973, created in honor of the Boys Town of Italy **$10-12**

Bowl, 1986, Executive Series **$25-30**

Bull Dog, 1979, honors the 204th anniversary of the United States Marine Corps. **$15-20**

Caboose, 1980 ....**$50-60**

California Mission, 1970, issued for the Jim Beam Bottle Club of Southern California in honor of the 20th anniversary of the California Missions, 14" **$10-15**

Camellia City Club, 1979, replica of the cupola of the state capitol building in Sacramento **$18-25**

Canteen, 1979, replica of the canteen used by the armed forces **$8-12**

Cardinal (Kentucky Cardinal), 1968 . . . . **$40-50**

Carmen, 1978, third in the Opera Series. **$145-180**

Cathedral Radio, 1979, replica of one of the earlier dome-shaped radios **$12-15**

Chicago Cubs, Sports Series. **$30-40**

Christmas Tree **$150-200**

Circus Wagon, 1979, replica of a circus wagon from the late 19th century **$25-30**

Civil War North, 1961, Regal China, 10-1/4" **$10-15**

Civil War South, 1961, Regal China, 10-1/4" **$25-35**

Coffee Grinder **$8-13**

Colin Mead **$180-210**

Cobalt, 1981, Executive Series **$18-23**

Collector's Edition, 1966, set of six glass famous paintings: *The Blue Boy, On the Terrace, Mardi Gras, Austide Bruant, The Artist Before His Easel,* and *Laughing Cavalier* (each) **$2-5**

Collector's Edition Volume II, 1967, set of six flask-type bottles with famous pictures: *George Gisze, Soldier and Girl, Night Watch, The Jester, Nurse and Child,* and *Man on Horse* (each) **$2-5**

Collector's Edition Volume III, 1968, set of eight bottles with famous paintings: *On the Trail, Indian Maiden, Buffalo, Whistler's Mother, American Gothic, The Kentuckian, The Scout,* and *Hauling in the Gill Net* (each). **$2-5**

Collector's Edition Volume IV, 1969, set of eight bottles with famous paintings: *Balcony, The Judge, Fruit Basket, Boy with Cherries, Emile Zola, The Guitarist Zouave,* and *Sunflowers* (each) **$2-5**

Collector's Edition Volume V, 1970, set of six bottles with famous paintings: *Au Cafe, Old Peasant, Boating Party, Gare Saint Lazare, The Jewish Bride,* and *Titus at Writing Desk* (each) **$2-5**

Collector's Edition Volume VI, 1971, set of three bottles with famous paintings: *Charles I, The Merry Lute Player,* and *Boy Holding Flute* (each) **$2-5**

Collector's Edition Volume VII, 1972, set of three bottles with famous paintings: *The Bag Piper, Prince Baltasor,* and *Maidservant Pouring Milk* (each) **$2-5**

Collector's Edition Volume VIII, 1973, set of three bottles with famous portraits: Ludwig Van Beethoven, Wolfgang Mozart, and Frederic Francis Chopin (each) **$2-5**

Collector's Edition Volume IX, 1974, set of three bottles with famous paintings: *Cardinal, Ring-Neck Pheasant,* and *the Woodcock* (each) **$3-6**

Collector's Edition Volume X, 1975, set of three bottles with famous pictures: *Sailfish, Rainbow Trout,* and *Largemouth Bass* (each) **$3-6**

Collector's Edition Volume XI, 1976, set of three bottles with famous paintings: *Chipmunk, Bighorn Sheep,* and *Pronghorn Antelope* (each) **$3-6**

Collector's Edition Volume XII, 1977, set of four bottles with a different James Lockhart reproduction on the front (each) .. **$3-6**

Collector's Edition Volume XIV, 1978, set of four bottles with James Lockhart paintings: *Raccoon, Mule Deer, Red Fox,* and *Cottontail Rabbit* (each) **$3-6**

Collector's Edition Volume XV, 1979, set of three flasks with Frederic Remington's paintings: *The Cowboy 1902, The Indian Trapper 1902,* and *Lieutenant S.C.Robertson 1890* (each)... **$2-5**

Collector's Edition Volume XVI, 1980, set of three flasks depicting duck scenes: *The Mallard, The Redhead,* and *The Canvasback* (each)...................................... **$3-6**

Collector's Edition Volume XVII, 1981, set of three flasks bottles with James Lockhart paintings: *Great Elk, Pintail Duck,* and *The Horned Owl* (each)............................... **$3-6**

Convention Bottle, 1971, commemorates the first national convention of the National Association of Jim Beam Bottle and Specialty Clubs hosted by the Rocky Mountain Club, Denver, Colorado **$5-7**

Convention Number 2, 1972, honors the second annual convention of the National Association of Jim Beam Bottle and Specialty Clubs in Anaheim, Calif............................... **$20-30**

Convention Number 3 – Detroit, 1973, commemorates the third annual convention of Beam Bottle Collectors in Detroit.. **$10-15**

Convention Number 4 – Pennsylvania, 1974, commemorates the annual convention of the Jim Beam Bottle Club in Lancaster, Pennsylvania...................................... **$80-100**

Convention Number 5 – Sacramento, 1975, commemorates the annual convention of the Camellia City Jim Beam Bottle Club in Sacramento, Calif **$5-8**

Convention Number 12 – New Orleans, 1982, commemorates the annual convention of the Jim Beam Bottle Club in New Orleans, LA **$30-35**

Buccaneer, gold **$35-45**

Buccaneer, in color **$35-45**

Convention Number 16 – Pilgrim Woman Boston, 1986, commemorates the annual convention of the Jim Beam Bottle Club in Boston **$35-45**

Minuteman, color **$85-105**

Minuteman, pewter **$85-105**

Convention Number 17 – Louisville, 1987, commemorates the annual convention of the Jim Beam Bottle Club in Louisville, KY **$55-75**

Kentucky Colonel, blue **$85-105**

Kentucky Colonel, gray **$85-105**

Convention Number 18 – Bucky Beaver, 1988 . . . . **$30-40**

Portland rose, red **$30-40**

Portland rose, yellow **$30-40**

Cowboy, 1979, awarded to collectors who attended the 1979 convention of the International Association of Beam Clubs **$35-50**

Crappie, 1979, commemorates the National Fresh Water Fishing Hall of Fame **$10-15**

D-Day **$15-20**

Metal stopper **$10-12**

China stopper **$50-60**

Devil Dog **$15-25**

Dial Telephone, 1980, fourth in a series of Beam telephone designs **$40-50**

Don Giovanni, 1980, The fifth in the Opera Series **$140-180**

Donkey And Elephant Ashtrays, 1956, Regal China, 12" (pair) **$12-16**

Convention Series
Number 18

Top: Bucky Beaver,
1988, **$30-40.**

Bottom Left: Bottle
& Red Rose, **$30-40.**

Bottom Right:
Bottle & Yellow
Rose, **$30-40.**

Donkey and Elephant Boxers, 1964 (pair) $15-20

Donkey and Elephant Clowns, 1968, Regal China, 12" (pair) $4-7

Donkey and Elephant Football Election Bottles, 1972, Regal China, 9-1/2" (pair) $6-9

Donkey New York City, 1976, commemorates the National Democratic Convention in New York City. $10-15

Duck, 1957, Regal China, 14-1/4" $15-20

Ducks and Geese, 1955 . . . . $5-9

Ducks Unlimited Mallard, 1974. . . . . $40-50

Duck Stamp Series: Pintails, 1983-1984, **$30-40;** *Canvasbacks, 1982-1983,* **$30-40;** *Ruddy Ducks, 1981-1982,* **$30-40.**

Eagle, 1966 Regal China, 12-1/2" **$10-15**

Election, Democrat, 1988 . . . . **$30-40**

Election, Republican, 1988 . . . . **$30-40**

Elephant and Donkey Supermen, 1980 (set of two) **$10-15**

Elephant Kansas City, 1976, commemorates the National Democratic Convention in New York City **$8-10**

Emmett Kelly, Native Son. **$50-60**

Ernie's Flower Cart, 1976, honors Ernie's Wines and Liquors of Northern Calif **$25-30**

Expo 1974, issued in honor of the World's Fair held at Spokane, Wash **$5-7**

Falstaff, 1979, second in Australian Opera series, limited edition of 1,000 bottles **$150-160**

Fleet Reserve Association, 1974, issued by the Fleet Reserve Association to honor the Career Sea Service on its 50th Anniversary **$5-7**

Foremost – Black and Gold, 1956, first Beam bottle issued for a liquor retailer, Foremost Liquor Store of Chicago **$225-250**

Foremost – Speckled Beauty, 1956, the most valuable of the Foremost bottles. **$500-600**

Fox, Red Distillery. **$1,100-1,300**

French Cradle Telephone, 1979, third in the Telephone Pioneers of America series **$20-22**

George Washington Commemorative Plate, 1976, commemorates the U.S. Bicentennial, 9-1/2" **$12-15**

German Stein **$20-30**

Germany, 1970, issued to honor American armed forces in Germany **$4-9**

Golden Chalice, 1961 . . . . **$40-50**

Golden Jubilee, 1977, Executive Series **$35-40**

Golden Nugget, 1969, Regal China, 12-1/2" **$35-45**

Grant Locomotive, 1979 . . . . **$55-65**

Gray Cherub, 1958, Regal China, 12" **$240-260**

Great Chicago Fire Bottle, 1971, commemorates the great Chicago fire of 1871 and to salute Mercy Hospital, which helped the victims **$20-25**

Hank Williams Jr **$40-50**

Hansel and Gretel Bottle, 1971 . . . . **$44-50**

Harley Davidson 85th Anniversary Decanter **$175-200**

Harley Davidson 85th Anniversary Stein **$180-220**

Harolds Club – Man-in-a-Barrel, 1957, first in a series made for Harolds Club in Reno, Nevada **$380-410**

Harolds Club – Silver Opal, 1957, commemorates the 25th anniversary of Harolds Club **$20-22**

Harolds Club – Man-in-a-Barrel, 1958 . . . . **$140-160**

Harolds Club – Nevada (Gray), 1963, created for the "Nevada Centennial – 1864-1964" as a state bottle. This is a rare and valuable bottle **$90-110**

Harolds Club – Nevada (Silver), 1964 . . . . **$90-110**

Harolds Club – Pinwheel, 1965 . . . . **$40-45**

Harolds Club – VIP Executive, 1967, limited quantity issued **$55-60**

Top Left: Harley-Davidson Stein, **$175-200**.

Top Right: Harley-Davidson Decanter, **$180-220**.

Bottom: Seoul Korea, 1988 Olympics, **$60-75**.

Harolds Club – VIP Executive, 1968 . . . . **$55-65**

Harolds Club - VIP Executive, 1969, this bottle was used as a Christmas gift to the casino's executives **$260-285**

Harolds Club, 1970 . . . . **$40-60**

Harolds Club, 1982 . . . . **$110-145**

Harrahs Club Nevada – Gray, 1963, this is the same bottle used for the Nevada Centennial and Harolds Club **$500-550**

Hatfield, 1973, the Hatfield character from the story of the Hatfield and McCoy feud **$15-20**

Hawaii, 1959, tribute to the 50th state **$35-40**

Hawaii, Reissued 1967. . . . . **$40-45**

Hawaiian Paradise, 1978, commemorates the 200th anniversary of Captain Cook's landing **$15-20**

Hemisfair, 1968, commemorates the "Hemisfair 68 - San Antonio" **$8-10**

Herre Brothers **$25-35**

Holiday – Carolers. **$40-50**

Holiday – Nutcrackers **$40-50**

Home Builders, 1978, commemorates the 1979 convention of the Home Builders. **$25-30**

Hone Heke **$200-250**

Honga Hika, 1980, first in a series of Maori warrior bottles. Honga Hika was a war-chief of the Ngapuke tribe **$220-240**

Horse (Appaloosa) **$10-12**

Horse (Mare and Foal) **$35-45**

Horse (Oh Kentucky). **$70-85**

Hollywood, Florida, Glass Convention Bottles, 1984
*Left: Bourbon, **$25-30**; Right: Canadian Whiskey, **$25-30**.*

Indianapolis 500 . . . . $9-12

Indian Chief, 1979 . . . . $9-12

Jewel T Man – 50th Anniversary $35-45

John Henry, 1972, commemorates the legendary Steel Drivin' Man
. . . . $18-22

Kansas, 1960, commemorates the "Kansas 1861-1961 Centennial"
. . . . $35-45

Kentucky Derby 95th, Pink, Red Roses, 1969 . . . . $4-7

Kentucky Derby 96th, Double Rose, 1970 . . . . $15-25

Kentucky Derby 97th, 1971 . . . . **$4-7**

Kentucky Derby 98th, 1972 . . . . **$4-6**

Kentucky Derby 100th, 1974 . . . . **$7-10**

Madame Butterfly, 1977, figurine of Madame Butterfly, music box plays *One Fine Day* from the opera **$340-370**

Marbled Fantasy, 1965 . . . . **$38-45**

Marine Corps **$25-35**

Martha Washington, 1976 . . . . **$5-6**

McShane – Mother-of-Pearl, 1979, Executive Series . . **$85-105**

McShane – Titans, 1980 . . . . **$85-105**

McShane – Cobalt, 1981, Executive Series **$115-135**

McShane – Green Pitcher, 1982, Executive Series **$85-105**

McShane – Green Bell, 1983, Executive Series **$85-110**

Mephistopheles, 1979, figurine depicts Mephistopheles from the opera *Faust*, music box plays *Soldier's Chorus* **$160-190**

Milwaukee Stein **$30-40**

Mississippi Fire Engine, 1978 . . . . **$120-130**

Montana, 1963, tribute to "Montana, 1864 Golden Years Centennial 1964" **$50-60**

Mortimer Snerd, 1976 . . . . **$25-30**

Mount St. Helens, 1980, depicts the eruption of Mount St. Helens **$20-25**

Mr. Goodwrench, 1978 . . . . **$25-30**

Muskie, 1971, honors the National Fresh Water Fishing Hall of Fame **$14-18**

Nevada, 1963 . . . . **$35-40**

New Hampshire Eagle Bottle, 1971 . . . . **$18-23**

New Jersey, 1963 . . . . **$40-5O**

New Jersey Yellow, 1963 . . . . **$40-50**

New York World's Fair, 1964 . . . . **$5-6**

North Dakota, 1965 . . . . **$45-55**

Northern Pike, 1977, the sixth in a series designed for the National Fresh Water Fishing Hall of Fame **$14-18**

Nutcracker Toy Soldier, 1978 . . . . **$95-120**

One Hundred First Airborne Division, 1977, honors the division known as the Screaming Eagles **$8-10**

Oregon, 1959, honors the centennial of the state **$20-25**

Panda, 1980 . . . . **$20-22**

Pearl Harbor Memorial, 1972, honoring the Pearl Harbor Survivors Association **$15-20**

Pearl Harbor Survivors Association, 1976 . . . . **$5-7**

Poulan Chain Saw, 1979 . . . . **$25-30**

Pretty Perch, 1980, 8th in a series, this fish is used as the official seal of the National Fresh Water Fishing Hall of Fame . . . **$13-16**

Professional Golf Association **$4-7**

Queensland, 1978 . . . . **$20-22**

Rainbow Trout, 1975, produced for the National Fresh Water Fishing Hall of Fame **$12-15**

Ram, 1958 . . . . **$40-55**

Republic of Texas, 1980 . . . . **$12-20**

Republican Convention, 1972. . . . .$500-700

Republican Football, 1972. . . . .$350-450

Richard Hadlee. $110-135

Rocky Marciano, 1973 . . . . $14-16

Royal Di Monte, 1957 . . . . $45-55

Royal Gold Diamond, 1964. . . . . $30-35

Royal Gold Round, 1956 . . . . $80-90

Royal Porcelain, 1955 . . . .$380-420

Royal Rose, 1963. . . . . $30-35

Ruidoso Downs, 1968

    Pointed ears. $25-30

    Flat ears $4-6

San Bear – Donkey 1973, Political Series $1,500-2,000

San Diego, 1968, issued by the Beam Co. for the 200th anniversary
of its founding in 1769. . . . . $4-6

San Diego – Elephant, 1972. . . . . $15-25

Santa Fe, 1960. . . . .$120-140

Screech Owl, 1979 . . . . $18-22

Seoul – Korea, 1988. . . . . $60-75

Short Dancing Scot, 1963. $50-65

Short-Timer, 1975. . . . . $15-20

Snowman. $125-175

South Carolina, 1970, in honor of celebrating its tricentennial
1670-1970 . . . . $4-8

South Dakota – Mount Rushmore, 1969 . . . . **$4-9**

South Florida – Fox on Dolphin, 1980, bottle sponsored by the South Florida Beam Bottle and Specialties Club. **$15-20**

Spengers Fish Grotto, 1977. . . . . **$18-22**

Statue of Liberty, 1975 . . . . **$8-12**

Statue of Liberty, 1985 . . . . **$18-20**

St. Bernard, 1979 . . . . **$30-35**

Sturgeon, 1980, exclusive issue for a group that advocates the preservation of sturgeons **$15-20**

Stutz Bearcat, 1914 1977 . . . . **$45-55**

Submarine – Diamond Jubilee **$35-45**

Submarine Redfin, 1970, issued for Manitowoc Submarine Memorial Association. **$5-7**

Superdome, 1975, replica of the Louisiana Superdome **$5-8**

Tavern Scene, 1959. . . . . **$45-55**

Telephone No. 1, 1975, replica of a 1907 phone of the magneto wall type **$25-30**

Telephone No. 2, 1976, replica of an 1897 desk set **$30-40**

Telephone No. 3, 1977, replica of a 1920 cradle phone. . . **$15-20**

Telephone No. 4, 1978, replica of a 1919 dial phone . . . **$40-50**

Telephone No. 5, 1979, replica of a pay phone **$25-35**

Telephone No. 6, 1980, replica of a battery phone **$20-30**

Telephone No. 7, 1981, replica of a digital dial phone. . . . **$35-45**

Texas Rose, 1978, Executive Series. **$14-18**

Thailand, 1969. . . . . **$4-6**

Thomas Flyer, 1907 1976B **$60-70**

Tiffiny Poodle, 1973, created in honor of Tiffiny, the poodle mascot of the National Association of the Jim Beam Bottle and Specialties Clubs **$20-25**

Tiger – Australian **$14-18**

The Tigers, 1977, issued in honor of an Australian football team **$20-25**

Trout Unlimited, 1977, honors the Trout Unlimited Conservation Organization **$14-18**

Truth or Consequences Fiesta, 1974, issued in honor of Ralph Edwards' radio and televison show **$14-20**

Twin Bridges Bottle, 1971, commemorates the largest twin bridge between Delaware and New Jersey **$40-42**

US Open, 1972, honors the U.S. Open Golf Tourney at Pebble Beach, Calif. **$9-12**

Vendome Drummers Wagon, 1975, honors the Vendomes of Beverly Hills, Calif. **$60-70**

VFW Bottle, 1971, commemorates the 50th anniversary of the Department of Indana VFW **$5-9**

Volkswagen Commemorative Bottle – Two Colors, 1977, commemorates the Volkswagen Beetle **$40-50**

Walleye Pike, 1977, designed for the National Fresh Water Fishing Hall of Fame **$12-15**

Walleye Pike, 1987 . . . . **$17-25**

Washington, 1975, State Series bottle to commemorate the Evergreen State **$5-6**

Washington – The Evergreen State, 1974, the club bottle for the Evergreen State Beam Bottle and Specialties Club **$10-15**

*Right: Trophy Series:
Duck Decoy,* **$40-50**.

*Left: Regal China Series:
Fathers Day Card,* **$15-25**.

*Bottom: Organization Series:
Ducks Unlimited,* **$40-50**.

Washington State Bicentennial, 1976 . . . . $10-15

Waterman, 1980 . . . . $100-130

Western Shrine Association, 1980, commemorates the Shriners convention in Phoenix, Arizona $20-25

West Virginia, 1963. . . . . $130-140

White Fox, 1969, issued for the second anniversary of the Jim Beam Bottle and Specialties Club in Berkley, Calif. $25-35

Wisconsin Muskie Bottle, 1971 . . . . $15-20

Woodpecker, 1969 . . . . $6-8

Wyoming, 1965 . . . . $40-50

Yellow Katz, 1967, commemorates the 50th anniversay of the Katz Department Stores. $15-20

Yellow Rose, 1978, Executive Series $7-10

Yellowstone Park Centennial $4-7

Yuma Rifle Club $18-25

Zimmerman Oatmeal Jug $40-50

Automobile and Transportation Series

Chevrolet

1957 Convertible, black, new $85-95

1957, yellow hot rod. $65-75

Camaro 1969, blue. $55-65

Camaro 1969, burgundy. $120-140

Corvette 1984, black $70-80

Corvette 1984, gold $100-120

*Left: Red Corvette, 1984, **$55-65**.*
*Right: White Corvette, 1984, **$55-65**.*

*Left: Democratic Convention, 1988, **$30-40**.*
*Right: Republican Convention, 1988, **$30-40**.*

Corvette 1984, red $55-65
Corvette 1978, black $140-170
Corvette 1963, blue, NY. $90-100
Corvette 1955, black, new $110-140
Corvette 1955, copper, new $90-100
Corvette 1955, red, new $110-140
Corvette 1954, blue, new $90-100
Corvette 1953, white, new $100-120

Duesenburg
Convertible, cream $130-140
Convertible, dark blue. $120-130
Convertible, light blue $80-100
Convertible Coupe, gray. $160-180

Ford
International Delivery Wagon, black $80-90
International Delivery Wagon, green $80-90
Fire Chief 1928 . . . . $120-130
Fire Chief 1934 . . . . $60-70
Fire Pumper Truck 1935 . . . . $45-60
Model A, Angelos Liquor $180-200
Model A, Parkwood Supply $140-170
Model A 1903, red $35-45
Model A 1928 . . . . $60-80

Model A Fire Truck 1930 . . . . $130-170

Model T 1913, black $30-40

Model T 1913, green $30-40

Mustang 1964, black $100-125

Mustang 1964, white $25-35

Paddy Wagon 1930 . . . . $100-120

Phaeton 1929 . . . . $40-50

Police Car 1929, blue $75-85

Police Car 1929, yellow $350-450

Police Patrol Car 1934 . . . . $60-70

Roadster 1934, cream, PA, new $80-90

Thunderbird 1956, black $60-70

Thunderbird 1956, blue, PA $70-80

Thunderbird 1956, green $60-70

Woodie Wagon 1929 . . . . $50-60

Mercedes

1974, blue $30-40

1974, gold $60-80

1974, silver, Australia $140-160

1974, white $35-45

Trains

Baggage Car $40-60

Box Car, brown $50-60

Train Series:
Left: Gray Caboose, **$45-55.**
Center: Flat Car, **$20-30.**
Right: Wood Tender, **$40-45.**

Left: Train Series, Combination Car, **$55-65.**
Center: Holiday Series, Carolers, **$40-50.**
Right: Presidential Series, Carolers, 1988, **$40-50.**

Bumper $5-9

Caboose, gray $45-55

Caboose, red $50-60

Casey Jones with Tender $65-80

Casey Jones Caboose $40-55

Coal Tender, no bottle $20-30

Combination Car $55-65

Dining Car $75-90

General Locomotive $60-70

Grant Locomotive $50-65

Log Car $40-55

Lumber Car $12-18

Observation Car $15-25

Passenger Car $45-53

Track $4-6

Turner Locomotive $80-100

Watertower $20-30

Wood Tender $40-45

Wood Tender, no bottle $20-25

Other

Army Jeep $18-20

Cable Car $25-35

Circus Wagon $20-30

Golf Cart $20-30

HC Covered Wagon 1929 . . . . $10-20

Jewel Tea $70-80

Mack Fire Truck 1917 . . . . $120-135

Mississippi Pumper Firetruck 1867 . . . . $115-140

Police Patrol Car 1934, yellow $110-140

Space Shuttle $20-30

Stutz 1914, gray $40-50

Stutz 1914, yellow $40-50

Thomas Flyer 1909, blue $60-70

Thomas Flyer 1909, ivory $60-70

Vendome Wagon $40-50

Volkswagon, blue $40-50

Volkswagon, red $40-50

Miniature Bottles

Most collectors focus on larger bottles such as beer, whiskey, and bitters. But there is a distinct group of collectors who set their sights on small bottles. Their quest for that special find leads them into the world of miniatures. Until I started bottle collecting, the only miniature bottles that I knew of were the ones passengers bought on airline trips. Today, there is tremendous enthusiasm for miniature bottle collecting. Not only are there specialty clubs and dealers across the United States but throughout the world in the Middle East, Japan, England, Scotland, Australia, and Italy to name just a few. The new collector will soon discover that all miniatures are unique and extremely fascinating in their own way. Because of the low average cost of $1 to $5 per bottle, and the relatively small amount of space required for storing them, it's easy to start a collection. As is the case with the larger bottles, there are some rare and expensive miniatures.

While a number of miniatures were manufactured in the 1800s, the majority were made from the late 1920s to the 1950s, with peak production in the 1930s. While miniatures are still produced today, some of the most interesting and sought after are those produced before 1950.

Nevada legalized the sale of miniatures in 1935, Florida in 1935, and Louisiana in 1934.

If you are looking for 19th century miniatures, miniature beer bottles are a good choice. They are an example of a bottle produced for uses other than containing beer. Most of the major breweries produced them as advertisements, novelties, and promotional items. In fact, most of the bottles did not contain beer. A number had perforated caps so they could be used as salt and pepper shakers. The Pabst Blue Ribbon Beer Company was the first brewery to manufacture a beer bottle miniature commemorating the Milwaukee Convention of Spanish American War Veterans in 1889. Pabst's last miniature was manufactured around 1942. Most of the miniature beers found today date from before World War II. In 1899, there were as many as 1,507 breweries and all produced miniatures.

Miniature liquor bottles have become a special interest for other collectors as well. A number of state liquor stamps from the early 1930s and 1940s have specific series numbers that are valued by stamp collectors.

Note: As a reference for pricing, I have consulted Robert E. Kay's book *Miniature Beer Bottles & Go-Withs* and used corresponding pricing codes (CA-1, California, MN-1, Minnesota, etc).

Beer Bottles

Pre-Prohibition – Circa 1890-1933

Bohemian Beer, Pabst Brewing Co. (WI-5), paper label, 5-1/2", Milwaukee, WI, 1890 . . . . **$110-150**

George Brehn (trade mark) Baltimore County, Md – This Bottle Not To Be Sold (MD-1), embossed, 5-1/8", Baltimore, MD, 1895 . . . . **$35-50**

Indianapolis Brewing Co. (IN-2), paper label, 4-1/2", Indianapolis, IN, 1900 . . . . **$110-150**

L. Hoster Brewing Co. (OH-1), paper label, 5-1/2", Columbus, OH, 1900. . . . . **$110-150**

Oakland Bottling Co (CA-4), embossed, 5-1/4", Oakland, CA, 1905 . . . . **$35-50**

Seipp's (IL-4), embossed, 5-1/2", Chicago, IL, 1900 . . . . . **$35-50**

Silver Foam, Grand Rapids Brewing Co. (M1-3), paper label, 5-1/8", mercury glass bottle, Grand Rapids, MI **$120-150**

Post Prohibtion – Circa 1933-Present

Acme Beer, Acme Brewing Co. (CA-8), decal paper label, 3", Los Angeles, CA, 1940. . . . . **$120-150**

Atlantic Beer, Atlantic Co. (NC-2), foil paper label, 4", Charlotte, NC, 1950. . . . . **$80-100**

Ballantine's Export Beer, P. Ballantine & Sons (NJ-8), paper label, 4-1/4", Newark, NJ, 1950 . . . . **$5-15**

Barbarossa Beer, Red Top Brewing Co. (OH-10), paper label, 4", Cincinnati, OH, 1950 . . . . **$15-20**

Anderson Club, 1960; Barclay's Bourbon, 1967; Barclay's Gold Label, 1936; Barclay's Niagara, 1937; Bass River Skipper's Choice, 1960; Value Range, $10-55.

Blatz Old Heidelberg Beer, Blatz Brewing Co. (WI-6), decal paper label, 4-1/4", Milwaukee, WI, 1936. . . . . **$15-20**

Coors Beer, Adolph Coors Co. (CO-4), paper label, 4", Golden, CO, 1950. . . . .**$110-150**

Champagne Velvet Brand Beer (IN-14), foil paper label, 4", Terre Haute, IN, 1950 . . . . **$15-20**

Country Club Pilsener Beer, M.K. Goetz Brewing Co. (MO-3), decal foil label, 4-1/4", St. Joseph, MO, 1934. . . . . . . **$35-50**

E & O Pilsener Beer, Pittsburgh Brewing Co. (PA-4), decal paper label, 4-1/4", Pittsburgh, PA, 1936 . . . . **$35-50**

Eastside Beer, Los Angeles Brewing Co (CA-13), foil paper label, 4-1/4", Los Angeles, CA, 1950. . . . .**$110-150**

Falls City Beer, Falls City Brewing Co., Inc. (KY-4), paper label, 4-1/4", Louisville, KY, 1950 . . . . **$5-15**

Felsenbrau Beer, The Clyffside Brewing Co. (OH-6), decal paper label, 4-1/4", Cincinnati, OH, 1936 . . . . **$15-20**

Fisher Beer, Fisher Brewing Co (UT-1), decal paper label, 3-1/4", Salt Lake City, UT, 1936 . . . . **$25-35**

Frederick's 4 Crown Lager Beer (IL-9), decal paper label, 4-1/4", Chicago, IL, 1940 . . . . **$110-150**

Gettleman $100 Beer, Gettleman Brewing Co. (WI-34), foil paper label, 4-1/4", Milwaukee, WI, 1945-1950 . . . . **$5-15**

Grain Belt Beer, Minneapolis Brewing Co. (MN-13), decal paper label, 4", Minneapolis, MN, 1950 . . . . **$15-25**

Harry Mitchell's Beer, Harry Mitchell Brewing Co. (TX-1), decal paper label, 4-1/4", El Paso, TX, 1936 . . . .**$110-150**

Echo Spring, 1950; Echo Spring, 1968; Echo Spring, 1972; Ezra Brooks, 1960; Ezra Brooks, 1960; Value Range, $10-25.

*8-Ball Whiskey, 1940;
Family Club, 1940;
Fleischmann's Preferred,
1953; Fleischmann's
Preferred, 1960;
Fleischmann's Preferred,
1967; Value Range,
$10-30.*

E.M. Fleischmann's Reserve, 1940; E.M. Fleischmann's Special, 1940; Fort McHenry, 1939; Four Decades Brand, 1941; Samuels Four Decades Brand, 1940; Value Range, **$20-40.**

Jax Beer, Jackson Brewing Co. (LA-2), foil paper label, 4-1/4", New Orleans, LA, 1952 . . . . **$10-15**

Lang's Bohemian Beer, Gerhard Lang Brewery (NY-25), decal paper label, 3", Buffalo, NY, 1940 . . . . **$120-150**

Meister Brau, Peter Hand Brewery Co. (IL-15), foil paper label, 4-1/4", Chicago , IL, 1952 . . . . **$10-20**

Million's Wisconsin Select Beer, Million Brewery, Inc. (WI-97), decal paper label, 3", New Lisbon, WI, 1940 . . . . . **$55-75**

Old Craft Brew, Menominee-Marinette Brewing Co. (MI-4), decal paper label, 4-1/4", Menominee, MI, 1936 . . . . . **$110-150**

Old Export Beer, The Cumberland Brewing Co. (MD-6), decal paper label, 4", Cumberland, MD, 1948 . . . . **$25-35**

Old Milwaukee Beer, Bottled By G. Ferlita & Sons (FL-3), decal paper label, 3", Tampa, FL, 1940 . . . . **$110-150**

Old Tap Brand Bohemian Beer, Enterprise Brewing Co. (MA-2), decal paper label, 3", Fall River, MA, 1940 . . . . **$15-25**

Nectar Beer, Ambrosia Brewing Co. (IL-8), decal paper label, 4-1/4", Chicago, IL, 1941 . . . . **$120-150**

Royal Pilsen Beer, Abne Drury Brewery, Inc. (DC-2), decal paper label, 4-1/4", Washington, D.C., 1934 . . . . **$110-150**

Senate Beer, Diamond State Brewery, Inc. (DC-3), decal paper label, 4", Washington, D.C., 1950 . . . . **$120-150**

Southern Beer, Southern Breweries, Inc. (VA-2), decal paper label, 3-1/4", Norfolk, VA, 1936 . . . . **$105-150**

Southern Select Beer, Galveston-Houston Breweries, Inc (TX-6), decal paper label, 3-1/4", Galveston, TX, 1936 . . . . . **$80-100**

Spearman Beer, The Spearman Brewing Co. (FL-2), decal
paper label, 4-1/4", Pensacola, FL, 1936 . . . . **$110-150**

Stein's Beer, George F. Stein Brewery, Inc. (NY-11), decal paper
label, 3", Buffalo, NY, 1940 . . . . **$15-25**

Topper Beer (IL-11), decal paper label, 3", Chicago, IL, 1940
. . . . **$110-150**

Valley Forge Beer, Adam Scheidt Brewing Co. (PA-27), decal
paper label, 4", Norristown, PA, 1952 . . . . **$15-25**

**West Virginia Special Export Beer, Fesenmeier Brewing Co.
(WV-1)**, decal paper label, 4-1/4", Huntington, WV, 1936 **$35-45**

Foreign Beer Bottles

Guinness Extra Stout, Arthur Guinness (IRL-30), foil paper
label, 4-1/4", Dublin, Ireland, 1960 . . . . **$5-10**

O'Keefe Ale, O'Keefe Ale Brewery Limited, (CAN-1), decal
paper label, 4-3/4", Toronto, Ottawa, Winnipeg, Saskatoon, Canada
(CA-1) **$5-10**

Castle Ale, Type 1, Rhodesian Breweries Ltd. (RHOD-1),
paper label, 4-1/4", Rhodesia, 1960 . . . . **$15-25**

Sol (MEX-2), enamel label, 4-1/4", Mexico, 1965 . . . . . . **$10-20**

Stjerne Export Beer, Brewery Stjerne (DEN-4), foil paper label,
4", Copenhagen, Denmark, 1955 . . . . **$10-20**

Whiskey Flasks (Circa 1928-1935)

Boss of The Road $180

Clipper's Special $210

Hello World $160

Kentucky Prince $160

Lord Cedric $120

Murlee $190

99 . . . . $85

Old Armitage $85

Old Colonel Dan $185

Old Forman – Distilled Spring $160

Old Guide $185

Old Honesty $185

Old Kentucky Home $55

Old Reliable $185

Old Royalty $210

Old 73 . . . . $210

Pride of Nelson $65

R.A. Baker $110

Special Select $160

Stone Haven $80

Belle of Anderson,
1927-1930, **$25-45.**

Belle of Kentucky, 1927, **$50-75.**

Broad Ripple, 1934,
$40-55.

Early Times Brand, 1936, **$35-50.**

Stagg's Elkhorn, 1919, **$45-55.**

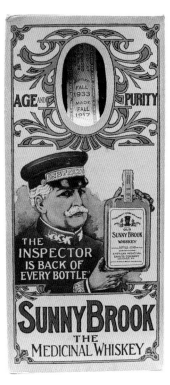

Sunny Brook, 1933, **$50-75.**

Scotch Whisky

Ambassador $140-175

Ancient Memories $140-175

Auld Glen Ross $185-255

B. Grant's $255-350

Bentley Royal $95-175

Bonnie Charlie $50-90

Cardhu Highland Malt Whisky (French) $140-175

Dalmore 8 . . . . $260-350

Eddie Cairns $100-175

Gannochy Brig $260-350

Glenfiddich $460-550

John Adair $50-90

Heather Bell $260-350

Highland Shepherd $180-255

House of Commons $460-550

Invercauld $100-175

King Edward $90-175

MacKinlay's Old Benvorlich $180-255

O B Saunders $50-90

Old Bar $140-175

Old Keg $140-175

Pageant $140-175

Queen Elizabeth $130-175

*Whiskey Nipper - Here's to Both of You,
1930s,* **$45-55.**

Whiskey nipper, A Wee Scotch - Old Whiskey, 1930s, **$40-50.**

Whiskey nipper, Old Scotch, 1930s, **$50-60.**

Real MacKay $260-350

Royal Highlander $100-175

Royal MacKenzie $90-175

Royal Toby $46-550

Scots Piper $90-175

Stag's Head $185-255

Sterlini $50-90

Talisker $180-255

Teachers $260-350

Tiny Tot $460-550

Trocadero $185-255

Weston's 8 Years Old $50-90

Soda Bottles - Applied Color Label

Anyone who has ever had a cold soda on a hot summer day from a bottle with a painted label probably didn't realize that the bottle would become rare and collectible. Today, collecting Applied Color Label (ACL) soda bottles has become one of the fastest growing and most affordable areas of bottle collecting. This rapid growth has resulted in the Painted Soda Bottle Collectors Association, which is the national collector's group dedicated to the promotion and preservation of ACL Soda Bottles.

So, what is an Applied Color Label soda bottle? The best description is this excerpt from an article written by Dr. J.H. Toulouse, a noted expert on bottle collecting and glass manufacturing in the late 1930s:

"One of the developments of the last few years has been that of permanent fused on labels on glass bottles. The glass in a glass furnace is homogenous in character, all of one color and composition. When the bottles are ready for decoration, the color design is printed on them in the process that superficially resembles many printing or engraving processes. The color is applied in the form of a paste-like material, through a screen of silk, in which the design has been formed. The bottles, which contain the impression of that design, must then be dried and then fired by conducting it through a lehr, which is long, tunnel-like enclosure through which the bottles pass at a carefully controlled rate of speed and in which definite zones of temperature are maintained. The maximum temperature chosen is such that the glass body will not melt, but the softer glass involved in the color will melt and rigidly fuse on the glass beneath it."

The first commercially sold soda was Imperial Inca Cola. Promoted by promising medical benefits, its name was inspired by the Native American Indian. The first truly successful cola drink, Coca-Cola, was developed in 1886 by Dr. John Styth Pemberton of Atlanta, Georgia. Carbonated water was added in 1887, and by 1894, bottled Coca-Cola was in full production. The familiar configuration of the Coke bottle was designed in 1915 by Alex Samuelson. Numerous inventors attempted to ride on the coattails of Coke's success. The most successful of these inventors was Caleb Bradham, who created Brad's drink in 1890 and in 1896 changed its name to Pep-Kola. In 1898, it was changed to Pipi-Cola and by 1906 to Pepsi-Cola.

The ACL Soda Bottle was conceived in the 1930s when Prohibition forced numerous brewing companies to experiment with soda. What started out as a temporary venture saved many brewing companies from bankruptcy; some companies never looked back. From the mid-1930s to the early 1960s, with peak production in the 1940s and 1950s, many small, local bottlers throughout the United States created bottle labels that will forever preserve unique moments in American history. The labels featured Western scenes, cowboys, Native Americans, various aircraft from biplanes to jets, clowns, famous people, birds, bears, boats, Donald Duck, and even Las Vegas (Vegas Vic). Since Native Americans and cowboys were popular American figures, these bottles are among the most popular and most collectible. In fact, the Big Chief ACL sodas are the most popular bottles, even more than the embossed types. These small bottlers actually produced the majority of the better-looking labels, in contrast to the largely uniform bottles made by major bottlers like Coca-Cola and Pepsi-Cola. Because these bottles were produced in smaller quantities, they are rarer and, thus, more valuable. While rarity affects value, a bottle with a larger label is even more desirable for collectors. The most sought-after bottles are those with a two-color label, each color adding more value to the bottle.

Note: Unless otherwise noted, all soda bottles listed have a smooth base and a crown top.

Applied Color Label Bottles

A Good, Anderson, IN, orange, 8 oz., 1948 . . . . $50

Ace High, Albert Lea, MN, light green, 7 oz., 1945 . . . . $25

Artic, Conroe, TX, dark green, 10 oz., 1948 . . . . $20

Bali, Los Angeles, CA, amber, 7 oz., 1941 . . . . $25

Barr's Soda, Hardwick, VT, orange, 8 oz., 1967 . . . . $15

Bells Of Kentucky, Paris, KY, dark green, 7 oz., 1946 . . . . . $11

Bingo, Waukesha, WI, dark green, 10 oz., 1966 . . . . $20

Blue Bird, Chicago, IL, clear, 7 oz., 1947 . . . . $7

Bubble Up, St. Louis, MO, dark green, 7 oz., 1946 . . . . $7

Chey Rock, **$31;** *Wyoming,* **$150;** *Old Faithful* **$70;** *Oregon Trail,* **$75;** *Alamo,* **$300;** *Santa Fe Trail,* **$130,** *Circa 1925-1960.*

Cannon, Dodge City, KS, orange, 10 oz., 1958 . . . . $25

Castle Beverages, Ansonia, CT, dark green, 7 oz., 1957 . . . . $10

Circle A, Booneville, MO, clear, 10 oz., 1954 . . . . $7

Clear Water, Pittsburgh, PA, dark green, 32 oz., 1961 . . . . . . $12

College Club, Windsor, PA, dark green, 30 oz., 1969 . . . . . . $15

Dart, Emporia, KS, clear, 8 oz., 1952 . . . . $75

Dash, Verona, PA, light green, 7 oz., 1945 . . . . $9

Desert Cooler, Tucson, AZ, dark green, 10 oz., 1954 . . . . . . $20

Dixie Dew, Waynesboro, GA, medium green, 10 oz., 1952 . . $25

Eight Ball, Altoona, PA, green, 16 oz., 1955 . . . . $50

Elk's Beverages, Leavenworth, KS, light brown, 12 oz., 1941 $9

Flathead, Kalispell, MT, clear, 12 oz., 1953 . . . . $175

Frostie, Camden, NJ, clear, 10 oz., 1965 . . . . $8

Fudgy, Ludlow, MA, amber, 6 oz., 1943 . . . . $400

Fuller's Spring, Jamestown, ND, amber, 7 oz., 1952 . . . . . . $20

Golden Age, Youngstown & Akron, OH, clear, 12 oz., 1938. $55

Golden Harvest, Freeport, IL, clear, 10 oz., 1959 . . . . $17

Golden Slipper, Philadelphia, PA, clear, 7 oz., 1951 . . . . . $85

Hall Of Waters, Excelsior Springs, MO, clear, 10 oz., 1959 $25

Hava Drink, Monett, MO, clear, 12 oz., 1948 . . . . $8

Hazel Club, Ellwood City, PA, dark green, 32 oz., 1962 . . . . . $9

Herby Cola, Leavenworth, KS, clear, 10 oz., 1959 . . . . $7

Hornet Brand, Tulia, TX, clear, 10 oz., 1962 . . . . $45

I C Cola, Denver, CO, clear, 16 oz., 1959. . . . . $25

*Coca-Cola - Jackson, Tenn
- Coca-Cola - Registered
- Coca-Cola Bottling Wks,
1900-1910,* **$150-200.**

Dad's Root Beer, $7; Dad's Root Beer, $5; Duffy's, $8; Duffy's, $8; Elwing, $5; Elks, $12; Elks, $11; Elks, $15, Circa 1950s.

Drink Mor, $13; Dr. Enuf, $18; Dr. Nut, $5; Dr. Pepper 10-2-4, $5; Dr. Pepper, $10; Dr. Pepper, $5; Dr. Pepper, $12; Dr. Swells Root Beer, $11, Circa 1950s-Early 1960s.

Idaho, Caldwell & Buhl, ID, clear, 10 oz., 1950 . . . . **$25**

Indian Club, Santa, Ana, CA, clear, 9 oz., 1950 . . . . **$65**

Jet, Waco, TX, clear, 8 oz., 1958. . . . . **$35**

Jo-Jo, Milwaukee, WI, clear, 7 oz., 1956. . . . . **$38**

Ju-See, Brookfield, MO, clear, 10 oz., 1949 . . . . **$9**

Kanner's 7-11, Los Angeles, CA, green, 7 oz., 1946 . . . . **$7**

Kik, Canada, clear, 12 oz., 1940 . . . . **$38**

Kist, Chicago, IL, clear, 10 oz., 1959. . . . . **$9**

Kleer Kool, Topeka, KS, clear, 10 oz., 1954 . . . . **$25**

Lemmy, Tecumseh, NB, clear, 10 oz., 1950 . . . . **$35**

Log Cabin, Niagara Falls, NY, clear, 10 oz., 1956 . . . . **$105**

Los Banos, Los Banos, CA, clear, 7 oz., 1948 . . . . **$15**

Mason's Root Beer, Chicago, IL, amber, 10 oz., 1954 . . . . . . **$8**

Mountain Maid, Nevada City, CA, clear, 10 oz., 1964 . . . . **$25**

Mountaineer, Clarskburg, VA, clear, 9 oz., 1957 . . . . **$18**

Nesbitt's, Los Angeles, CA, clear, 7 oz., 1954 . . . . **$5**

Norton Big Chief, Norton, KS, clear, 9 oz., 1956 . . . . **$23**

Nugget, Providence, RI, clear, 12 oz., 1956 . . . . **$20**

Old Time Root Beer, Reading, PA, clear, 12 oz., 1950 . . . . **$45**

Old Mill, Brookville, IN, green, 7 oz., 1957. . . . . **$40**

Orange Crush, Evanston, IL, amber, 7 oz., 1966. . . . . **$7**

Pep-up, Wilkes-Barre, PA, dark green, 32 oz., 1973. . . . . . . **$15**

Polar Club, Salem, MA, clear, 12 oz., 1938 . . . . **$13**

Polly's Soda, Independence, MO, clear, 12 oz., 1961 . . . . . . **$12**

Legge's Quality, **$5***; Legge's Quality,* **$5***; Laynes,* **$5***; LC Cola,* **$5***; Mountain Dew,* **$21***; Mason's Root Beer,* **$5***; Mason's Root Beer,* **$5***; Mug Root Beer,* **$12***, Circa 1950s-Early 1960s.*

Mission, **$5***; Mission,* **$5***; NuGrape,* **$5***; Nesbitt's,* **$5***; NC,* **$8***; Orange Crush,* **$6***; Orange Crush,* **$5***; Orange Crush,* **$5***, Circa 1950s.*

Pop Kola, Marceline, MO, clear, 10 oz., 1952 . . . . $7

Quality Beverages, Manitowoc, WI, green, 7 oz., 1953 . . . . . $9

Rancho, Ontario, CA, clear, 10 oz., 1948 . . . . $43

Royal Flush, Portland, OR, clear, 7 oz., 1947 . . . . $33

Sal-u-taris, St. Clair, MN, amber, 7 oz., 1950 . . . . $14

Spring Grove, Spring Grove, MN, clear, 10 oz., 1960. . . . . $17

Stone Fort, Nacogdoches, TX, clear, 9 oz., 1950 . . . . $100

Swallow's Root Beer, Lima, OH, clear, 10 oz., 1952. . . . . . $35

Tally Ho, Los Angeles, CA, clear, 10 oz., 1947. . . . . $28

Terry's, Scottsdale, NE, clear, 12 oz., 1949. . . . . $140

Twang Root Beer, Chicago, IL, clear, 12 oz., 1956 . . . . . . $78

Uncle Dan's Root Beer, Detroit, MI, clear, 16 oz., 1961 . . . $30

Valley Spring, Phoenix, AZ, clear, 32 oz., 1949 . . . . $13

Viking, St. Paul, MN, clear, 12 oz., 1972 . . . . $24

West Bend, West Bend, WI, clear, 7 oz., 1950 . . . . $7

Whistle, St. Louis, MO, clear, 10 oz., 1950 . . . . $8

Wolf's, Harrisburg, IL, clear, 10 oz., 1974 . . . . $9

X-Tra, Wolcott, CT, clear, 12 oz., 1966 . . . . $7

Yakima Chief, Yakima, WA, clear, 10 oz., 1955 . . . . $35

Yorkshire Ginger Beer, Los Angeles, CA, clear, 12 oz., 1941 $35

Yucca, Clovis, NM, clear, 12 oz., 1941 . . . . $17

Zee Beverages, Erie, PA, clear, 7 oz., 1958. . . . . $13

Zeisler, St. Charles, MO, clear, 10 oz., 1951 . . . . $12

Treasure Isle, **$4***; My Pic,* **$35***; Lindy,* **$41***; Lift,* **$22***, Circa 1940s-1950s.*

Sun Glo, **$6**; *Sunset*, **$5**; *Sun-Shine*, **$5**; *Sun-Rich*, **$33**; *Sun-Rich*, **$25**; *SunTex*, **$5**; *SunTex*, **$5**, *Sunny Isles Pineapple Soda*, **$20**, *Circa 1950s*.

Embossed

Big Chief, Clinton, MO, light green, 9 oz., 1948 . . . . **$28**

Crystal, Osceola, MO, light green, 7 oz., 1930 . . . . **$9**

Dr. Pepper, Dennison, IA, clear, 6-1/2 oz., 1947 . . . . **$12**

Kramer's, Mt. Carmel, PA, clear, 7 oz., 1965 . . . . **$7**

Pepsi-Cola, Durham, NC, light green, 6-1/2 oz., 1929 . . . . . **$105**

Violin and Banjo Bottles

While roaming the aisles of bottle and antique shows, I often see a violin- or banjo-shaped bottle on a table, admire its shape and color, then set it back down and move on to the whiskeys and medicine bottles. I didn't gain a full appreciation of these unique bottles, however, until I attended the June 1999 National Bottle Museum Antique Bottle Show in Saratoga, New York, to participate in a book signing. Before the show, there was a silent auction that included a spectacular display of violin and banjo bottles. At that time, I had the pleasure of meeting several knowledgeable collectors and members of the Violin Bottle

Collectors Association and received a short lesson and history of violin bottles. With the special help of many dedicated members of the Violin Bottle Collectors Association, we've written a chapter that will assist both the veteran and the novice collector with understanding the fun and collecting of violin and banjo bottles.

While gathering the information for this chapter, it became clear that the majority of bottle and antique collectors and dealers (including this collector) had very little knowledge about violin and banjo bottles and their beginnings. Are they considered antiques? How old are violin bottles? Why and where were they manufactured? Most of these bottles were manufactured in the 20th century with heavy production not taking place until the 1930s. Interestingly, violin and banjo bottles are original designs not copied from earlier bottles such as historic flasks and bitters. This makes these bottles antique in the sense that they are the first of their design and style and not preceded by any other types. As with other specialty groups, violin and banjo bottles have specific categories, and classes and codes with each category. For the serious collector, I recommend Robert A. Linden's *The Classification of Violin Shaped Bottles*, 2nd Edition (1999) and 3rd Edition (2004), and Don and Doris Christensen's *Violin Bottles, Banjos, Guitars, and Other Novelty Glass*, 1st Edition (1995). Information on the association can be obtained by writing to the Violin Bottle Collector's Association, 1210 Hiller Road, McKinleyville, CA 95519 or by contacting Frank Bartlett, Membership Chairman, at fbviobot@hotmail.com.

Violin Bottles

Category 1: American Styles

LV – Large Violin-Shaped Bottle (**FIGURE 1**)
Eight molds have been identified:
- **Molds 1, 4, and 6** – Produced at Clevenger Brothers Glass Works
- **Molds 2, 3, and 7** – Produced at Dell Glass Company
- **Mold 5** – Maker Unidentified
- **Mold 8** – Produced in Japan

Additional Information:
- Bottles had no contents and were made only for decorative purposes.
- Production began in the 1930s; first identified in the marketplace in the 1940s.
- Height range of 9" to 10-1/4"; body width 4-1/4" to 4-3/8"; 1-1/2" thick near base.
- Colors (various shades) – amber, amberina, amethyst, blue, cobalt, green, yellowish, and vaseline.

FIGURE 1

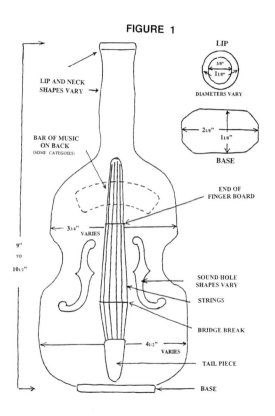

LIP AND NECK
SHAPES VARY →

LIP
3/8"
1 1/8"
DIAMETERS VARY

2 1/8"
1 1/8"
BASE

BAR OF MUSIC
ON BACK
(SOME CATEGOIES)

END OF
FINGER BOARD

← 3 3/4" →
VARIES

9"
TO
10 1/2"

SOUND HOLE
SHAPES VARY

STRINGS

BRIDGE BREAK

← 4 1/2" →
VARIES

TAIL PIECE

BASE

SV – Small Violin-Shaped Bottle (FIGURE 2)

Three molds have been identified:

- **Mold 1** – Produced at Clevenger Brothers Glass Works and Old Jersey Glass Co. (a Dell Glass Company)
- **Mold 2** – Produced at Dell Glass Company
- **Mold 3** - Produced at Clevenger Brothers Glass Works

Additional Information:

- Less common than large violin bottles.
- Bottles had no contents and were made only for decorative purposes.
- First identified in the marketplace in the 1940s.
- Height range of 7-1/4"; body width 3"; 1-1/4" thick near base.
- Colors (various shades) – cobalt, clear, blue, green, amber, and amethyst.

FIGURE 2

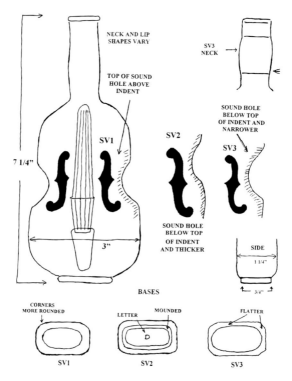

NECK AND LIP
SHAPES VARY

TOP OF SOUND
HOLE ABOVE
INDENT

SV3
NECK

SOUND HOLE
BELOW TOP
OF INDENT AND
NARROWER

SV1

SV2

SV3

7 1/4"

SOUND HOLE
BELOW TOP
OF INDENT
AND THICKER

3"

SIDE
1 1/4"

3/4"

BASES

CORNERS
MORE ROUNDED

LETTER   MOUNDED

FLATTER

D

SV1

SV2

SV3

EV - Violin-Shaped Bottle with tuning pegs or "ears" on the neck (**FIGURE 3**)

Four molds (A, B, C, and D) have been identified (FIGURE 4)

- **EVA1 to EVA7** – Each has an "A" neck shape with 1 of 7.
- **EVB1 to EVB7** - Each has a "B" neck shape with 1 of 7.
- **EVC1 to EVC7**- Each has a "C" neck shape with 1 of 7.
- **EVD1 to EVD7** - Each has a "D" neck shape with 1 of 7.

Additional Information:
- Produced at Maryland Glass Company
- ABM product (mold line goes up through neck, ears, and lip)
- Bottles had contents such as cosmetic lotion.
- Labeled as flasks, figurals, vases, and cosmetic bottles.
- Production began in the mid-1930s through the mid-1950s.
- Height 8"; body width 4"
- Colors (various shades) – blue, amber, and clear.

FIGURE 3

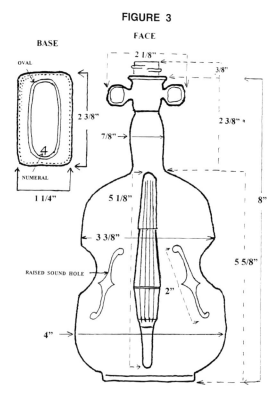

BASE

FACE

OVAL

2 1/8"

3/8"

2 3/8"

2 3/8"

7/8" →

NUMERAL

1 1/4"

5 1/8"

8"

3 3/8"

RAISED SOUND HOLE

5 5/8"

2"

4" →

FIGURE 4

NECK SHAPES

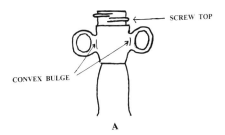

SCREW TOP

CONVEX BULGE

A

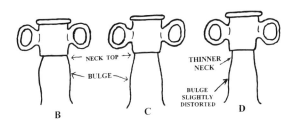

NECK TOP

BULGE

THINNER NECK

BULGE SLIGHTLY DISTORTED

B   C   D

Violin bottles (EV) with "ears" or "tuning pegs," cobalt blue, amber, **$10-20** *(each).*

BV - Bardstown Violin-Shaped Whiskey Bottle
(FIGURE 5 and FIGURE 6)

During the late 1930s, bourbon whiskey was distilled in Bardstown, Kentucky, and distributed throughout the Eastern United States and Canada. Bardstown used violin-shaped bottles in several sizes and featured many attractive labels, which became a common identifier until production ceased in 1940. Interestingly, while the violin bottle molds spanned 16 years, the molds were only used for four years. Due to the limited production, Bardstown bottles with full labels are very difficult to find.

Two molds have been identified (Owens-Illinois and Anchor-Hocking)

Mold 1 – Cork Top
- BVC1: 11"; quart
- BVC2: 11"; 4/5 quart
- BVC3: 10-1/8"; pint
- BVC4: 9-5/8"; pint
- BVC5: 8-1/8"; 1/2 pint

Mold 2 – Screw Top
- BVS1: 14"; half gallon
- BVS2: 9-1/2" to 10"; pint
- BVS3: 7-3/4" to 8-1/8"; half pint
- BVS4: 4-3/4" to 4-7/8"; nip

Additional Information:
- Only American violin figural designed and patented specifically with alcoholic content.
- Production from the 1930s until 1940, when production ceased.
- Color – amber.

FIGURE 5

Dec. 7, 1937.

H. D. HENSHEL

Des. 107,353

BOTTLE

Filed Oct. 19, 1937

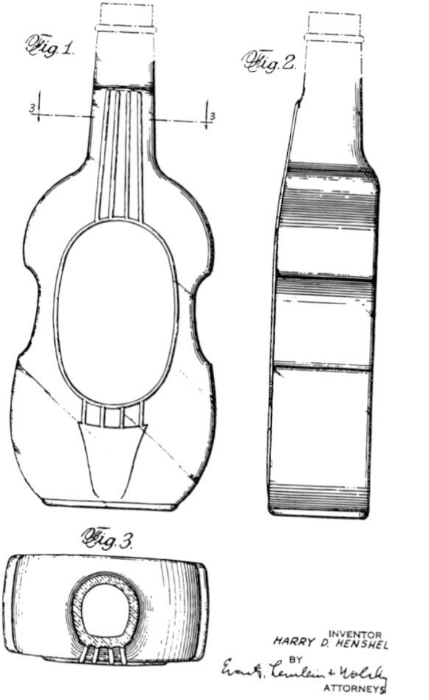

Fig 1.

Fig.2.

Fig.3.

INVENTOR
HARRY D. HENSHEL
BY

ATTORNEYS

FIGURE 6

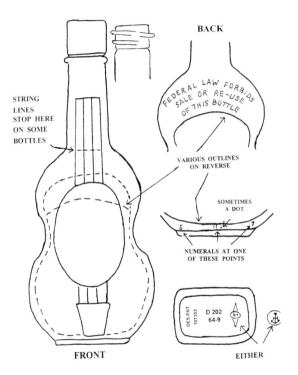

BACK

STRING
LINES
STOP HERE
ON SOME
BOTTLES

FEDERAL LAW FORBIDS
SALE OR RE-USE
OF THIS BOTTLE

VARIOUS OUTLINES
ON REVERSE

SOMETIMES
A DOT

NUMERALS AT ONE
OF THESE POINTS

FRONT

DES. PAT.
107353

D 202
64-9

EITHER

255

Category 2 – European Styles

DV – Definitive Violin-shaped bottles

FV – Violin-shaped bottle embossed "Bottles Made in France" on base.

CV - Violin-shaped bottle etched "Czecho" and "Slovakia" on base.

Category 3 – Special Styles

OV – Other violin-shaped bottles, including miniatures

Category 4 – Banjo-Shaped Bottles (FIGURE 7)

LB – Large Banjo-Shaped Bottles
Six molds have been identified:

- **LB1** – Does not have a base (mold line goes all around the body) and no embossing.
- **LB2** – Plain oval base and no embossing. Possible prototype for future models.
- **LB 3** – Only type produced to contain alcohol. LB 3 bottles have the following embossed legend "Federal Law Forbids Sale or Reuse of this Bottle," which was required from 1933 (repeal of prohibition) to 1966.
- **LB 4** – Minor changes with a "new" face and a clean reverse side.
- **LB 5** – Same as LB 4, with a pontil mark and the famous base embossing removed.

FIGURE 7

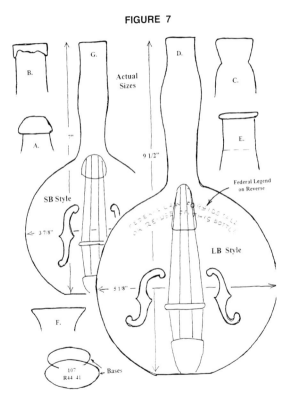

B.

G.

D.

C.

Actual
Sizes

A.

E.

7"

9 1/2"

Federal Legend
on Reverse

SB Style

FEDERAL LAW FORBIDS SALE
OR REUSE OF THIS BOTTLE

LB Style

← 3 7/8" →

← 5 1/8" →

F.

107
R44 41 ← Bases

- **LB 6** – No pontil marks since snap case tools were used. Finer and more delicate string and sound hole embossing.

Additional Information:

- All large banjos have the same discus body shape, approximate height, width, and neck measurements. (Height 9-1/2"; diameter 5-1/4"; 1-5/8" thick; oval base 1-1/2" long by 3/4" wide).
- Production began in 1942 and continued until 1975.
- Produced at Clevenger Brothers Glass Works, Dell Glass Company, and the Maryland Glass Company.
- Colors (various shades) – amber, green, blue, and amethyst.

SB – Small Banjo-Shaped Bottles

Two molds have been identified:

- **SB 1** – Smaller version of LB; height 7"; discus diameter 3-7/8"; lady's neck 3-1/8"; oval base 1-1/8" by 3/4".
- **SB 2** – Squared sides with height 7-7/8"; discus diameter 4-1/2"; straight neck 3-1/2"; oval base 2" by 1-1/8" with a 1" kick-up in center of bottle (scarce).

Additional Information:

- Produced at Clevenger Brothers Glass Works, Dell Glass Company, and the Maryland Glass Company.
- Colors (various shades) – amber, green, blue, amethyst.

OB – Other Banjo-Shaped Bottles

Three molds have been identified:

- **OB1** – Corked-stopped whiskey measuring 10-3/4" tall; 5-5/8" wide; and 2-1/2" thick. Embossed on back is "Medley Distilling Company Owensboro, Kentucky 4/5 Quart." Color - clear.
- **OB2** – Produced in Italy for 8" to 12" liquor bottles. Base embossing with "Patent Nello Gori." Color - clear.
- **OB3** – Possible miniature, 4-1/2" tall, cobalt salt and pepper shakers in the image of a banjo. Produced by Maryland Glass Company in the 1930s.

Violin Bottle Pricing:

LV1a1 (United Church Bandstand)

   amethyst. $160-250

LV1a2 (Auburn Die Company)

   amethyst. $250-375

LV1a3 (VBCA, 1997)

   cobalt $50-100

LV1a4 (VBCA, 1999)

   amethyst. $50-150

*Large violin bottle
(LV1a3), cobalt blue,
$50-100.*

*Large violin bottle (LV1),
amber, $40-50.*

LV1 (Clevenger)

blue $25-35

green $25-35

amethyst. $35-45

Jersey green $35-45

amber. $45-55

cobalt $60-100

amberina $400-550

LV2 (Dell)

blue $20-25

green $20-25

amethyst. $35-45

LV3 (Dell)

blue $20-25

green $20-25

amethyst. $35-45

LV4 (Clevenger)

green $55-65

amethyst. $55-65

amber. $55-65

cobalt $80-100

Large violin bottle (LV3), amethyst, $30-45.

Large violin bottle (LV5), yellow, $100-120.

LV5 (Dell Glass)

royal blue $55-75

clear $55-75

deep green $90-110

golden amber $100-120

yellow $100-120

fluorescing green $250-350

LV6 (Clevenger)

blue $25-35

green $25-35

Jersey green $30-40

amethyst $35-45

amber $45-55

clear $45-55

cobalt $50-100

vaseline $250-350

Large violin bottle (LV6), blue, **$20-30**; *green,* **$20-30**; *amber,* **$40-50**.

LV7 (Dell Glass)

light blue $25-35

light green $30-35

light amethyst $35-45

milk glass . . . . $400+

LV8 (Japan)

light blue $65-80

dark blue $65-80

dark green $65-80

dark amethyst $65-80

SV1 (Clevenger)

blue $25-35

green $25-35

amethyst. $35-45

Jersey green $35-45

amber $45-65

clear $45-65

cobalt $45-65

Large violin bottle (LV7), light amethyst, **$30-45**.

Large violin bottle (LV8), light blue, **$60-80.**

*Small violin bottle (SV1), green, **$25-35**; clear, **$45-60**; cobalt blue, **$45-60**; blue, **$25-35**; amber, **$45-60**.*

SV2 (Dell)

blue $20-25

green $20-25

amethyst. $25-35

SV3 (Clevenger)

blue $25-35

green $25-35

amethyst. $35-45

amber. $45-65

cobalt $45-65

SV3 app (Pairpoint Glass)

ruby red $65-75

EV'S (Maryland Glass Company)

light cobalt. $15-20

dark cobalt. $15-20

amber. $15-20

clear $15-20

Small violin bottle (SV2), amethyst, **$20-30.**

Violin bottle (EV) with "ears" or "tuning pegs," cobalt blue, **$10-20.**

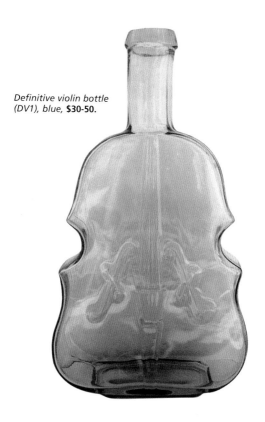

Definitive violin bottle (DV1), blue, **$30-50.**

DV1 (unknown)

blues $35-50

greens. $35-50

clear $35-50

ambers $45-60

red $80-100

DV2 (unknown)

clear $20-25

blues $20-30

greens. $20-30

ambers $25-40

red $60-100

DV3 (unknown)

clear $20-25

blues $20-30

greens. $20-30

ambers $25-40

red $60-100

FV1-3 (French)

clear **$20-30**

blue tint **$40-60**

green tint **$40-60**

light peach **$55-75**

OV2 (Wheaton)

clear **$5-10**

blue **$5-10**

green **$5-10**

OV12 (George West)

amber **$150-250**

cobalt **$500-600**

OV14 (Stumpy)

light blue **$45-60**

green **$60-80**

amethyst **$60-80**

Definitive violin bottles (DV 2 & 3), ruby red, **$60-100** *(each).*

French violin bottle (FV1-3), blue tint, **$40-60**; *green tint,* **$40-60**; *light peach,* **$50-75**.

Special style violin bottle, amber, **$150-250.**

OV16 (Decanter)

light blue $150-300

green $150-300

amethyst. $150-300

clear $150-300

Banjo Bottle Pricing:

LB1 9" – No base or embossing, mottled glass, small applied tooled lip. Unknown origin.

Green . . . . $75-$125

Large banjo bottle (LB1: 9"), green, **$75-125.**

LB2 9-1/2" – Oval base, no embossing. Unknown origin.

blue . . . .**$45-$70**

amethyst. . . . .**$45-$70**

green . . . .**$75-$100**

LB3 9-1/2" – 107 R44 41 embossed on base. "Federal Law Forbids Sale Or Reuse Of This Bottle" embossed on reverse. Maryland Glass pre-1966.

blue . . . .**$70-$100**

LB4 9-1/2" – 107 R44 41 embossed on base, strings and soundholes. Dell Glass 1940s.

blue . . . .**$30-$40**

amethyst. . . . .**$30-$40**

green . . . .**$30-$40**

LB5 9-1/2" – No embossing on base, strings and soundholes. Dell Glass 1940s.

blue . . . .**$30-$40**

amethyst. . . . .**$30-$40**

green . . . .**$30-$40**

*Large banjo bottles (LB4 & 5: 9-1/2"),
blue, amethyst, green,* **$25-40.**

LB6 9-1/2" – No embossing on base, strings and soundholes. Clevenger 1940s.

Type E Neck

blue . . . . **$35-$50**

amethyst. . . . . **$35-$50**

green . . . . **$35-$50**

cobalt . . . . **$75-$100**

Flared Lip

blue . . . . **$75-$100**

amethyst. . . . . **$55-$75**

green . . . . **$55-$75**

amber. . . . . **$150-$200**

LB6 9-1/2" – Embossed Slug Plate Commemoratives. No embossing on base, strings and sound holes. Clevenger 1970s.

LB6a Depiction of East Bridgewater Church.

amber. . . . . **$150-$250**

LB6b Just the words "American Handmade, Clevenger Brothers Glass Works, Clayton, NJ."

amber. . . . . **$100-$150**

LB6c Depiction of two glassblowers, words "Clevenger Brothers Glass Works, American Made Mouth Blown."

blue . . . . **$75-$100**

amethyst. . . . . **$75-$100**

green . . . . **$75-$100**

amber. . . . . **$75-$100**

LB6d Bicentennial "Celebrating 200 Years of Freedom 1776-1976."

green . . . . **$50-$100**

LB6 9-1/2" – Embossed Slug Plate Commemoratives. No embossing on base, strings and sound holes. Pairpoint Glass 2001.

LB6e VBCA 2000 Commemorative.

cobalt . . . . **$50-$65**

LB6f VBCA blank slug plate

cobalt . . . . **$50-$65**

LB6g Chelmsford Historical Society/Ezekial Byam Commemorative.

teal . . . . **$40-$50**

SB1 7" – Embossed strings and sound holes. Old Jersey Glass/Dell 1940s.

blue . . . . **$30-$50**

amethyst. . . . . **$30-$50**

green . . . . **$75-$100**

SB2 7-7/8" with 4-1/2" diameter disc body, embossed strings, no sound holes. Origin unknown.

blue . . . . **$40-$60**

amethyst. . . . . **$40-$60**

green . . . . **$75-$100**

Small banjo bottle (SB1: 7"), blue, $25-50; amethyst, $25-50; green, $75-100.

*Large banjo bottle
(LB6b), green,* **$100-150.**

Trademarks

Trademarks are very helpful for determining the identification, age, and value of a bottle. In addition, researching trademarks will give the bottle collector a deeper knowledge and the companies that made the bottles and their contents.

What is a trademark? It's a word, name, letter, number, symbol, design, phrase, or a combination of all of these items that identifies and distinguishes a product from its competitors. Usually, the markings appear on the bottom of the bottle. A trademark only protects the symbol that represents the product, not the product itself.

Trademarks have been around for a long time. The first glass makers to use identification marks was Ennion of Sidon who lived in the first century, along with two of his students, Jason and Aristeas, who imprinted their identification into the sides of the molds.

In the 1840s, English glass manufacturers continued this practice by identifying their flasks by side lettering inside the molds in a similar fashion. Identifying marks have been found on antique Chinese porcelain, on pottery from ancient Greece and Rome, and on items from India dating back to 1300 BC.

In Medieval times, the craft and merchant owners also relied upon the marks to distinguish their products from makers of inferior goods to gain buyers' loyalties. Trademarks then were applied to just about everything; watermarks on paper, bread, leather goods, and weapons. Goldsmiths and silversmiths also began to rely on trademarks. In the late 1600s, bottle manufacturers began to mark their products with a glass seal that was applied to the bottle while still hot. Because the concept of trademarks had their roots in Europe, they were widely adopted in North America as immigrants flooded the new land.

For many early trademark owners, protection for the trademark owner was almost non-existent. While the United States Constitution provided rights of ownership in copyrights and patents, Congress didn't enact the first federal trademark law until 1870.

If you're able to determine the owner of the mark, and when it might have been used, you will usually be able to determine the date of a bottle. If the mark was not used for long, it will be easy to pinpoint the age of the bottle. If the mark was used for a long time, however, you'll have to rely on other references to help with the dating process.

Very few companies used identical marks, which is amazing, considering the vast number of manufacturers. Unfortunately, most numbers appearing with trademarks are not part of the trademark and are not useful for dating bottles.

While more than 1,200 trademarks have been created for bottles and fruit jars, only a sampling are included in this chapter.

The words and letters in bold are the company's trademarks as they appear on the bottle. Each trademark is followed by the complete name and location of the company and the approximate period of time during which the trademark was used.

United States Trademarks

A

A: Adams & Co., Pittsburgh, PA, 1861-1891

A: John Agnew & Son, Pittsburgh, PA, 1854-1866

A: Arkansas Glass Container Corp., Jonesboro, AR, 1958 to date (if machine made)

A (in a circle): American Glass Works, Richmond, VA and Paden City, WV, 1908-1935.

A & B together (AB): Adolphus Busch Glass Manufacturing Co., Belleville, IL, and St. Louis, MO, 1904-1907

ABC: Atlantic Bottle Co., New York City, NY, and Brackenridge, PA, 1918-1930

ABCo.: American Bottle Co., Chicago, IL, 1905-1916; Toledo, OH, 1916-1929

ABCO (in script): Ahrens Bottling Company, Oakland, CA, 1903-1908

A B G M Co.: Adolphus Busch Glass Manufacturing Co., Belleville, IL, 1886-1907; St. Louis, MO, 1886-1928

A & Co.: John Agnew and Co., Pittsburgh, PA, 1854-1892

A C M E: Acme Glass Co., Olean, NY, 1920-1930

A & D H C - A. & D.H.: Chambers, Pittsburgh, PA, Union Flasks, 1843-1886

AGCo: Arsenal Glass Co. (or Works), Pittsburgh, PA, 1865-1868

AGEE and Agee (in script): Hazel Atlas Glass Co., Wheeling, WV, 1919-1925

AGNEW & CO.: Agnew & Co., Pittsburgh, PA, 1876-1886

AGWL, PITTS PA: American Glass Works, Pittsburgh, PA 1865-1880, American Glass Works Limited, 1880-1905

AGW: American Glass Works, Richmond, VA, & Paden City, WV, 1908-1935

AMF & Co.: Adelbert M. Foster & Co., Chicago, IL, Millgrove, Upland, and Marion, IN, 1895-1911

Anchor figure (with H in center): Anchor Hocking Glass Corp., Lancaster, OH, 1955

A. R. S.: A. R. Samuels Glass Co., Philadelphia, PA, 1855-1872

A S F W W Va.: A.S. Frank Glass Co., Wellsburg, WV, 1859

ATLAS: Atlas Glass Co., Washington, PA, and later Hazel Atlas Glass Co., 1896-1965

B

B: Buck Glass Co., Baltimore, MD, 1909-1961

B (in circle): Brockway Machine Bottle Co., Brockway, PA, 1907-1933

Ball and Ball (in script): Ball Bros. Glass Manufacturing Co., Muncie, IN, and later Ball Corp., 1887-1973

Baker Bros. Balto. MD: Baker Brothers, Baltimore, MD, 1853-1905

BAKEWELL: Benjamin P. Bakewell Jr. Glass Co., 1876-1880

BANNER: Fisher-Bruce Co., Philadelphia, PA, 1910-1930

BB Co: Berney-Bond Glass Co., Bradford, Clarion, Hazelhurst, and Smethport, PA, 1900

BB & Co: Berney-Bond Glass Co., Bradford, Clarion, Hazelhurst, and Smethport, PA, 1900

BB48: Berney-Bond Glass Co., Bradford, Clarion, Hazelhurst, and Smethport, PA, 1920-1930

BBCo: Bell Bottle Co., Fairmount, IN, 1910-1914

Bennett's: Gillinder & Bennett (Franklin Flint Glass Co.) Philadelphia, PA, 1863-1867

Bernardin (in script): W. J. Latchford Glass Co., Los Angeles, CA, 1932-1938

The Best: Gillender & Sons, Philadelphia, PA, 1867-1870

B F B Co.: Bell Fruit Bottle Co., Fairmount, IN, 1910

B. G. Co.: Belleville Glass Co., IL, 1882

Bishop's: Bishop & Co., San Diego and Los Angeles, CA, 1890-1920

BK: Benedict Kimber, Bridgeport and Brownsville, PA, 1825-1840

BLUE RIBBON: Standard Glass Co., Marion, IN, 1908

BOLDT: Charles Boldt Glass Manufacturing Co., Cincinnati, OH, and Huntington, WV, 1900-1929

Boyds (in script): Illinois Glass Co., Alton, IL, 1900-1930

BP & B: Bakewell, Page & Bakewell, Pittsburgh, PA, 1824-1836

Brelle (in script) Jar: Brelle Fruit Jar Manufacturing Co., San Jose, CA, 1912-1916

Brilliante: Jefferis Glass Co., Fairton, NJ and Rochester, PA, 1900-1905

C

C (in a circle): Chattanooga Bottle & Glass Co. and later Chattanooga Glass Co., 1927-Present

C (in a square): Crystal Glass Co., Los Angeles, CA, 1921-1929

C (in a star): Star City Glass Co., Star City, WV, 1949-Present

C (in upside-down triangle): Canada Dry Ginger Ale Co., N.Y.C., 1930-1950

Canton Domestic Fruit Jar: Canton Glass Co., Canton, OH, 1890-1904

C & Co. or C Co: Cunninghams & Co., Pittsburgh, PA, 1880, 1907

CCCo: Carl Conrad & Co., St. Louis, MO, (beer), 1860-1883

C.V.Co. No. 1 & No 2: Milwaukee, WI, 1880-1881

C C Co.: Carl Conrad & Co., St. Louis, MO, 1876-1883

C C G Co.: Cream City Glass Co., Milwaukee, WI, 1888-1894

C.F.C.A.: California Fruit Canners Association, Sacramento, CA, 1899-1916

CFJCo: Consolidated Fruit Jar Co., New Brunswick, NJ, 1867-1882

C G I: California Glass Insulator Co., Long Beach, CA, 1912-1919

C G M Co: Campbell Glass Manufacturing Co., West Berkeley, CA, 1885

C G W: Campbell Glass Works, West Berkeley, CA, 1884-1885

C & H: Coffin & Hay, Hammonton, NJ, 1836-1838, or Winslow, NJ, 1838-1842

C L G Co.: Carr-Lowrey Glass Co., Baltimore, MD, 1889-1920

CLARKE: Clarke Fruit Jar Co., Cleveland, OH, 1886-1889

CLOVER LEAF (in arch with picture of a clover leaf), marked on ink and mucilage bottles, 1890.

Clyde, N.Y.: Clyde Glass Works, Clyde, NY, 1870-1882

The Clyde (in script): Clyde Glass Works, Clyde, NY, 1895

C Milw: Chase Valley Glass Co., Milwaukee, WI, 1880-1881

Cohansey: Cohansey Glass Manufacturing Co., Philadelphia, PA, 1870-1900

CO-SHOE: Coshocton Glass Corp., Coshocton, OH, 1923-1928

C R: Curling, Robertson & Co., Pittsburgh, PA, 1834-1857 or Curling, Ringwalt & Co., Pittsburgh, PA, 1857-1863

CRYSTO: McPike Drug Co., Kansas City, MO, 1904

D

D 446: Consolidated Fruit Jar Co., New Brunswick, NJ, 1871-1882

DB: Du Bois Brewing Co., Pittsburgh, PA, 1918

Dexter: Franklin Flint Glass Works, Philadelphia, PA, 1861-1880

Diamond (plain): Diamond Glass Co., 1924-Present

The Dictator: William McCully & Co., Pittsburgh, PA, 1855-1869

Dictator: William McCully & Co., Pittsburgh, PA, 1869-1885

D & O: Cumberland Glass Mfg. Co., Bridgeton, NJ, 1890-1900

D O C: D. O. Cunningham Glass Co., Pittsburgh, PA, 1883-1937

DOME: Standard Glass Co., Wellsburg, WV, 1891-1893

D S G Co.: De Steiger Glass Co., LaSalle, IL, 1879-1896

Duffield: Dr. Samuel Duffield, Detroit, MI, 1862-1866 and Duffield, Parke & Co, Detroit, MI, 1866-1875

Dyottsville: Dyottsville Glass Works, Philadelphia, PA, 1833-1923

E

E4: Essex Glass Co., Mt. Vernon, OH, 1906-1920

Economy (in script) TRADE MARK: Kerr Glass Manufacturing Co., Portland, OR, 1903-1912

Electric Trade Mark (in script): Gayner Glass Works, Salem, NJ, 1910

Electric Trade Mark: Gayner Glass Works, Salem, NJ, 1900-1910

Erd & Co., E R Durkee: E. R. Durkee & Co., New York, NY, post-1874

The EMPIRE: Empire Glass Co., Cleveland, NY, 1852-1877

E R Durkee & Co: E. R. Durkee & Co., New York, NY, 1850-1860

Eureka 17: Eurkee Jar Co., Dunbar, WV, 1864

Eureka (in script): Eurkee Jar Co., Dunbar, WV, 1900-1910

Everett and EHE: Edward H. Everett Glass Co., (Star Glass Works) Newark, OH, 1893-1904

Everlasting (in script) JAR: Illinois Pacific Glass Co., San Francisco, CA, 1904

E W & Co: E. Wormser & Co., Pittsburgh, PA, 1857-1875

Excelsior: Excelsior Glass Co., St. John, Quebec, Canada, 1878-1883

F

F (inside a jar outline or keystone): C. L. Flaccus Glass Co., Pittsburgh, PA, 1900-1928

F WM. Frank & Sons: WM. Frank & Co., Pittsburgh, PA, 1846-1966, WM. Frank & Sons, Pittsburgh, PA, 1866-1876

F & A: Fahnstock & Albree, Pittsburgh, PA, 1860-1862

FERG Co: F.E. Reed Glass Co., Rochester, NY, 1898-1947

FF & Co: Fahnstock, Fortune & Co., Pittsburgh, PA, 1866-1873

F G: Florida Glass Manufacturing Co., Jacksonville, FL, 1926-1947

FL or FL & Co.: Frederick Lorenz & Co., Pittsburgh, PA, 1819-1841

FLINT – GREEN: Whitney Glass Works, Glassborough, NJ, 1888

FOLGER, JAF&Co., Pioneer, Golden Gate: J. A. Folger & Co., San Francisco, CA, 1850-Present

G

G (in circle with bold lines): Gulfport Glass Co., Gulfport, MS, 1955-1970

G E M: Hero Glass Works, Philadelphia, PA, 1884-1909

G & H: Gray & Hemingray, Cincinnati, OH, 1848-1851; Covington, KY, 1851-1864

G & S: Gillinder & Sons, Philadelphia, PA, 1867-1871 and 1912-1930

Gillinder: Gillinder Bros., Philadelphia, PA, 1871-1930

Gilberds: Gilberds Butter Tub Co., Jamestown, NY, 1883-1890

GLENSHAW (G in a box underneath name): Glenshaw Glass Co., Glenshaw, PA, 1904

GLOBE: Hemingray Glass Co., Covington, KY (The symbol "Parquet-Lac" was used beginning in 1895), 1886

Greenfield: Greenfield Fruit Jar & Bottle Co., Greenfield, IN, 1888-1912

G W K & Co.: George W. Kearns & Co., Zanesville, OH, 1848-1911

H

H and H (in heart): Hart Glass Manufacturing Co., Dunkirk, IN, 1918-1938

H (with varying numerals): Holt Glass Works, West Berkeley, CA, 1893-1906

H (in a diamond): A.H. Heisey Glass Co., Oakwood Ave., Newark, OH, 1893-1958

H (in a triangle): J. T. & A. Hamilton Co., Pittsburgh, PA, 1900

Hazel: Hazel Glass Co., Wellsburg, WV, 1886-1902

H.B.Co: Hagerty Bros. & Co., Brooklyn, NY, 1880-1900

Helme: Geo. W. Helme Co., Jersey City, NJ, 1870-1895

Hemingray: Hemingray Brothers & Co. and later Hemingray Glass Co., Covington, KY, 1864-1933

H. J. Heinz: H.J. Heinz Co., Pittsburgh, PA, 1860-1869

Heinz & Noble: H. J. Heinz Co., Pittsburgh, PA, 1869-1872

F. J. Heinz: H.J. Heinz Co., Pittsburgh, PA, 1876-1888

H. J. Heinz Co.: H. J. Heinz Co., Pittsburgh, PA, 1888-Present

HELME: Geo. W. Helme Co., N.J., 1870-1890

HERO: Hero Glass Works, Philadelphia, PA, 1856-1884 and Hero Fruit Jar Co., Philadelphia, PA, 1884-1909

HS (in a circle): Twitchell & Schoolcraft, Keene, NH, 1815-1816

I

IDEAL: Hod C. Dunfee, Charleston, WV, 1910

I G Co.: Ihmsen Glass Co., Pittsburgh, PA, 1855-1896

I. G. Co: Ihmsen Glass Co., 1895

I. G. Co.: Monogram, Ill. Glass Co. on fruit jar, 1914

IPGCO: Ill. Pacific Glass Company, San Francisco, 1902-1926

IPGCO (in diamond): Ill. Pacific Glass Company, San Francisco, CA, 1902-1926

IG: Illinois Glass, F inside of a jar outline, C. L. Flaccus 1/2 glass 1/2 co., Pittsburgh, PA, 1900-1928

Ill. Glass Co.: 1916-1929

I G: Illinois Glass Co., Alton, IL, before 1890

I G Co. (in a diamond): Illinois Glass Co., Alton, IL, 1900-1916

Improved G E M: Hero Glass Works, Philadelphia, PA, 1868

I P G: Illinois Pacific Glass Co., San Francisco, CA, 1902-1932

I X L: I X L Glass Bottle Co., Inglewood, CA, 1921-1923

J

J (in keystone): Knox Glass Bottle Co., of Mississippi, Jackson, MS, 1932-1953

J (in a square): Jeannette Glass Co., Jeannette, PA, 1901-1922

JAF & Co., Pioneer and Folger: J.A. Folger & Co., San Francisco CA, 1850-Present

J D 26 S: Jogn Ducan & Sons, New York, NY, 1880-1900

J. P. F.: Pitkin Glass Works, Manchester, CT, 1783-1830

J R: Stourbridge Flint Glass Works, Pittsburgh, PA, 1823-1828

JBS monogram: Joseph Schlitz Brewing Co., Milwaukee, WI, 1900

JT: Mantua Glass Works and later Mantua Glass Co., Mantua, OH, 1824

JT & Co: Brownsville Glass Works, Brownsville, PA, 1824-1828

J. SHEPARD: J. Shepard & Co., Zanesville, OH, 1823-1838

K

K (in a keystone): Knox Glass Bottle Co., Knox, PA, 1924-1968

Kensington Glass Works: Kensington Glass Works, Philadelphia, PA, 1822-1932

Kerr (in script): Kerr Glass Manufacturing Co. and later Alexander H. Kerr Glass Co., Portland, OR; Sand Spring, OK; Chicago, IL; Los Angeles, CA, 1912-Present

K H & G: Kearns, Herdman & Gorsuch, Zanesville, OH, 1876-1884

K & M: Knox & McKee, Wheeling, WV, 1824-1829

K & O: Kivlan & Onthank, Boston, MA, 1919-1925

KO – HI: Koehler & Hinrichs, St. Paul, MN, 1911

K Y G W and KYGW Co: Kentucky Glass Works Co., Louisville, KY, 1849-1855

L

L (in a keystone): Lincoln Glass Bottle Co., Lincoln, IL, 1942-1952

L: W. J. Latchford Glass Co., Los Angeles, CA, 1925-1938

Lamb: Lamb Glass Co., Mt. Vernon, OH, 1855-1964

LB (B inside L): Long Beach Glass Co., Long Beach, CA 1920-1933

L & W: Lorenz & Wightman, PA, 1862-1871

LGW: Laurens Glass Works, Laurens, SC, 1911- 1970

L G Co: Louisville Glass Works, Louisville, KY, 1880

Lightning: Henry W. Putnam, Bennington, VT, 1875-1890

LP (in a keystone): Pennsylvania Bottle Co., Wilcox, PA, 1940-1952

L K Y G W: Louisville Kentucky Glass Works, Louisville, KY, 1873-1890

M

Mascot, Mason and M F G Co.: Mason Fruit Jar Co., Philadelphia, PA, 1885-1890

Mastadon: Thomas A. Evans Mastadon Works, and later Wm. McCully & Co. Pittsburgh, PA, 1855-1887

MB Co: Muncie Glass Co., Muncie, IN, 1895-1910

M B & G Co: Massillon Bottle & Glass Co., Massillon, OH, 1900-1904

M B W: Millville Bottle Works, Millville, NJ, 1903-1930

McL (in circle): McLaughlin Glass Co., Vernon, CA, 1920-1936, Gardena, CA, 1951-1956

MEDALLION: M.S. Burr & Co., Boston, MA (manufacturer of nursing bottles), 1874

M (in keystone): Metro Glass Bottle Co., Jersey City, NJ, 1935-1949

MG: straight letters 1930-1940; slant letters 1940-1958; Maywood Glass, Maywood, CA

M.G. CO.: Modes Glass Co., Cicero, IN, 1895-1904

M.G.W.: Middletown Glass Co., NY, 1889

Moore Bros.: Moore Bros., Clayton, NJ, 1864-1880

MOUNT VERNON: Cook & Bernheimer Co., New York, NY, 1890

N

N (in a keystone): Newborn Glass Co., Royersford, PA, 1920-1925

<u>N</u>**:** H. Northwood Glass Co., Wheeling, WV, 1902-1925

N (bold N in bold square): Obear-Nester Glass Co., St. Louis, MO, and East St. Louis, IL, 1895

N B B G Co: North Baltimore Bottle Glass Co., North Baltimore, OH, 1885-1930

N G Co: Northern Glass Co., Milwaukee, WI, 1894-1896

N - W: Nivison-Weiskopf Glass Co., Reading, OH, 1900-1931

O

O (in a square): Owen Bottle Co., 1911-1929

O B C: Ohio Bottle Co., Newark, OH, 1904-1905

O-D-1-O & Diamond & I: Owens Ill. Pacific Coast Co., CA, 1932-1943. Mark of Owen-Ill. Glass Co. merger in 1930

O G W: Olean Glass Co. (Works), Olean, NY, 1887-1915

Oil City Glass Co.: Oil City, PA, 1920-1925

OSOTITE (in elongated diamond): Warren Fruit Jar Co., Fairfield, IA, 1910

O-U-K I D: Robert A Vancleave, Philadelphia, PA, 1909

P

P (in keystone): Wightman Bottle & Glass Co., Parker Landing, PA, 1930-1951

PCGW: Pacific Coast Glass Works, San Francisco, CA, 1902-1924

PEERLESS: Peerless Glass Co., Long Island City, NY, 1920-1935 (was Bottler's & Manufacturer's Supply Co.), 1900-1920

P G W: Pacific Glass Works, San Francisco, CA, 1862-1876

Picture of young child in circle: M. S. Burr & Co., Boston, MA (manufacturer of nursing bottles), 1874

Premium: Premium Glass Co., Coffeyville, KS, 1908-1914

P (in square) or Pine (in box): Pine Glass Corp., Okmulgee, OK, 1927-1929

P S: Puget Sound Glass Co., Anacortes, WA, 1924-1929

Putnam Glass Works (in a circle): Putnam Flint Glass Works, Putnam, OH, 1852-1871

P & W: Perry & Wood and later Perry & Wheeler, Keene, NH, 1822-1830

Q

Queen (in script) Trade Mark (all in a shield): Smalley, Kivian & Onthank, Boston, MA, 1906-1919

R

Rau's: Fairmount Glass Works, Fairmount, IN, 1898-1908

R & C Co: Roth & Co., San Francisco, CA, 1879-1888

Red (with a key through it): Safe Glass Co., Upland, IN, 1892-1898

R G Co.: Renton Glass Co., Renton, WA, 1911

Root: Root Glass Co., Terre Haute, IN, 1901-1932

S

S (inside a star): Southern Glass Co., LA, 1920-1929

S (in a triangle): Schloss Crockery Co., San Francisco, CA, 1910

SB & GCo: Stretor Bottle & Glass Co., Streator, IL, 1881-1905

SF & PGW: San Francisco & Pacific Glass Works, 1876-1900

S & C: Stebbins & Chamberlain or Coventry Glass Works, Coventry, CT, 1825-1830

S F G W : San Francisco Glass Works, San Francisco, CA, 1869-1876

SIGNET (blown-in bottom): Chicago Heights Bottle Co., Chicago, Heights, IL, 1913

Squibb: E.R. Squibb, M.D., Brooklyn, NY, 1858-1895

Standard (in script, Mason): Standard Coop. Glass Co. and later

Standard Glass Co., Marion, IN, 1894-1932

Star Glass Co: Star Glass Co., New Albany, IN, 1867-1900

Swayzee: Swayzee Glass Co. Swayzee, IN, 1894-1906

T

T C W: T.C. Wheaton Co. Millville, NJ, 1888-Present

THE BEST (in an arch): Gotham Co., New York, NY, 1891

TIP TOP: Charles Boldt Glass Co., Cincinnati, OH, 1904

T W & Co.: Thomas Wightman & Co., Pittsburgh, PA, 1871-1895

T S: Coventry Glass Works, Coventry, CT, 1820-1824

U

U: Upland Flint Bottle Co., Upland, Inc., 1890-1909

U (in a keystone): Pennsylvania Bottle Co., Sheffield, PA, 1929-1951

U S: United States Glass Co., Pittsburgh, PA, 1891-1938, Tiffin, OH, 1938-1964

W

WARRANTED (in an arch) FLASK: Albert G. Smalley, Boston, MA, 1892

W & CO: Thomas Wightman & Co., Pittsburgh, PA, 1880-1889

W C G Co: West Coast Glass Co., Los Angeles, CA, 1908-1930

WF & S MILW: William Franzen & Son, Milwaukee, WI, 1900-1929

W G W: Woodbury Glass Works, Woodbury, NJ, 1882-1900

WYETH: a drug manufacturer, 1880-1910

W T & Co: Whitall-Tatum & Co., Millville, NJ, 1857-1935

W T R Co.: W. T. Rawleigh Manufacturing Co., Freeport, IL, 1925-1936

Foreign Trademarks

A (in a circle): Alembic Glass, Industries Bangalore, India

Big A in center GM: Australian Glass Mfg. Co., Kilkenny, So. Australia

A.B.C.: Albion Bottle Co., LTD., Oldbury, Worcs., England, 1928-1969

A.G.W.: Alloa Glass Limited, Alloa, Scotland

A G B Co.: Albion Glass Bottle Co., England, trademark is found under Lea & Perrins, 1880-1900

AVH: A. Van Hoboken & Co., Rotterdam, the Netherlands, 1800-1898

B & C Co. L: Bagley & Co. Ltd., England, established 1832 and still operating

Beaver: Beaver Flint Glass Co., Toronto, Ontario, Canada, 1897-1920

Bottle (in frame): Veb Glasvoerk Drebkau Drebkau, N.L. Germany

Crown (with three dots): Crown Glass, Waterloo, N.S.. Wales

Crown (with figure of a crown): Excelsior Glass Co., St. Johns, Quebec and later Diamond Glass Co., Montreal, Quebec, Canada, 1879-1913

CS & Co.: Cannington, Shaw & Co., St. Helens, England, 1872-1916

CSTS (in center of hot air balloon): C. Stolzles Sohne Actiengeselischaft fur Glasfabrikation, Vienna, Austria, Hungary, 1905

D (in center of a diamond): Dominion Glass Co., Montreal, Quebec, Canada

D.B. (in a book frame): Dale Brown & Co., Ltd., Mesborough, Yorks, England

Fish: Veb Glasvoerk Stralau, Berlin

Excelsior: Excelsior Glass Co., St. John, Quebec, Canada, 1878-1883

HH: Werk Hermannshutte, Czechoslovakia

Hamilton: Hamilton Glass Works, Hamilton, Ontario, Canada, 1865-1872

Hat: Brougba, Bulgaria

Hunyadi Janos: Andreas Saxlehner, Buda-Pesth, Austria-Hungary, 1863-1900

IYGE (all in a circle): The Irish Glass Bottle, Ltd. Dublin, Ireland

KH: Kastrupog Holmeqaads, Copenhagen

L (on a bell): Lanbert S.A., Belgium

LIP: Lea & Perrins, London, England, 1880-1900

LS: In a circle, Lax & Shaw, Ltd., Leeds, York, England

M (in a circle): Cristales Mexicanos, Monterey, Mexico

N (in a diamond): Tippon Glass Co., Ltd., Tokyo, Japan

NAGC: North American Glass Co., Montreal, Quebec, Canada, 1883-1890

NP: Imperial Trust for the Encouragement of Scientific and Industrial Research, London, England, 1907

NS (in middle of bottle shape): Edward Kavalier of Neu Sazawa, Austria-Hungary, 1910

P & J A: P. & J. Arnold, LTD., London, England, 1890-1914

PRANA: Aerators Limited, London, England, 1905

PG: Verreries De Puy De Dome, S. A. Paris, France

R: Louit Freres & Co., France, 1870-1890

S (in a circle): Vetreria Savonese, A. Voglienzone, S.A. Milano, Italy

S.A.V.A. (all in a circle): Asmara, Ethiopia

S & M: Sykes & Macvey, Castleford, England, 1860-1888.

T (in a circle): Tokyo Seibin, Ltd., Tokyo, Japan

vFo: Vidreria Ind., Figuerras Oliveiras, Brazil

VT: Ve.Tri S.p.a., Vetrerie Trivemta Vicenza, Italy

VX: Usine de Vauxrot, France

WECK (in a frame): Weck Glaswerk G. mb.H, ofigen, in Bonn, Germany

Y (in a circle): Etaria Lipasmaton, Athens, Greece

Glossary

ABM (Automatic Bottle Machine): The innovation of Michael Owens in 1903 to allow an entire bottle to be made in one step.

ACL: Applied Color Label created by pyroglaze or enameled lettering, usually used with soda pop bottles from 1920 to 1960.

Agate Glass: A glass made from mix incorporating blasting furnace slag. Known in tints of chocolate brown, caramel brown, natural agate, tanned leather, showing striations of milk glass in off-white tints. Made from 1850 to 1900s.

Amethyst-Colored Glass: A clear glass that, when exposed to the sun or bright light for a long period of time, will turn various shades of purple. Only glass containing manganese turns purple.

Amber-Colored Glass: Nickel was added in glass production to obtain this common bottle color. The dark color was believed to prevent the sun from ruining the contents of the bottle.

Annealing: The gradual cooling of hot glass in a cooling chamber or an annealing oven.

Applied Color Labeling: Method of decorating a bottle by applying glass with a low melting point to a bottle through a metal screen and then baking it.

Applied Lip/Top: On pre-1880s bottles, the neck was applied after removal from the blow-pipe. This type of top may be consist of only a ring of glass trailed around the neck.

Aqua-Colored Glass: A natural color of glass. Its shade depends on the amount of ion oxide contained in the raw materials. Produced until the 1930s.

Bail: Wire clamp consisting of a wire that goes over the top of the lid or lip, and a "locking" wire that is pushed down to cause pressure on the bail and the lid, resulting in an airtight closure.

Barber Bottle: In the 1880s, these colorful bottles decorated the shelves of barbershops and usually were filled with bay rum.

Batch: A mixture of the ingredients necessary in the manufacturing of glass.

Battledore: A wooden paddle used to flatten the bottom or sides of a bottle.

Bitters: An herbal medicine, medicinal and flavoring, which contains a great quantity of alcohol, usually corn whiskey.

Black Glass: This type of glass produced between 1700 and 1875 is actually a dark olive green caused by the carbon in the glass production.

Bottle made from "black glass," which is actually a dark olive green formed by carbon.

Blob Seal: A coin-shaped blob of glass applied to the shoulder of a bottle, into which a seal with the logo or name of the distiller, date, or product name was impressed. The information contained on the blob seal provides a way of identifying an unembossed bottle.

Blob Top: A large thick blob of glass placed around the lip of soda or mineral water bottles. A wire held the stopper, which was seated below the blob and anchored the wire when the stopper was closed, to prevent the carbonation from escaping.

Blown in Mold, Applied Lip (Bimal): The process by which a gather of glass is blown into a mold to take the shape of the mold. The lip on these types were added later and the bases often have open pontil scars.

Blowpipe: A hollow iron tube wider and thicker at the gathering end than at the blowing end. It is used by the blower to pick up the molten glass, which is then blown-in mold or free-blown outside the mold. The pipe can vary from 2-1/2 ft. to 6 ft. long.

Blow-Over: A bubble-like extension of glass above a jar or bottle lip blown so the blowpipe could be broken free from the jar after blowing. The blow-over was then chipped off and the lip was ground.

Borosilicate: A type of glass originally formulated for making scientific glassware.

Calabash: A type of flask with a rounded bottom. This type of bottle is known as a "Jenny Lind" flask and was common in the 19th century.

Camphor Glass: A white cloudy glass that resembles refined gum camphor. Bottles made with this glass are known in blown, blown-mold, and pressed forms.

Carboys: Cylindrical bottles with short necks.

Clapper: A glassmaker's tool used in shaping and forming the footing of an object.

Cobalt Colored Glass: This color was used with patented medicines and poisons to distinguish them from regular bottles. Excessive amounts resulted in the familiar "cobalt blue" color.

Codd: A bottle enclosure patented in 1873 by Hiram Codd of England. A small ball is blown inside of the bottle. The ball is forced to the top of the neck by pressure, creating a method of sealing the contents from the outside air.

Crown Cap: A metal cap formed from a tin plate to slip tightly over the rolled lip of a bottle. The inside of the cap was filled with a cork disk to create an airtight seal.

Cullet: Clean, broken glass added to a batch to bring about rapid fusion to produce new glass.

Date Line: The mold seam or mold line on a bottle. The line helps estimate the approximate date in which the bottle was manufactured.

De-Colorizer: A compound added to natural aquamarine-colored bottle glass to render the glass clear.

Dip Mold: A one-piece mold open at the top.

Embossed Lettering: Raised or embossed letter on a bottle denoting the name of the product.

Fire Polishing: The reheating of glass to eliminate unwanted blemishes.

Flared Lip: Bottles produced prior to 1900 have lips that were worked out or flared out to reinforce the strength of the opening.

Flashing: A method of coloring glass by dipping a bottle into a batch of colored glass.

Flint Glass: Glass composed of a silicate of potash and lead. Commonly referred to as "lead crystal" in present terminology.

Free Blown Glass: Glass produced with a blowpipe rather than a mold.

Frosted Glass: A textured surface produced when a bottle's surfaced is sandblasted.

Gaffer: A master blower in early glass houses.

Gather: A gob of molten glass adhering to the blowpipe.

Glass Pontil: The earliest type of pontil, in which a sharp glass ring remains.

Glory Hole: The small furnace used for the frequent re-heating necessary during the making of a bottle. The glory hole was also used in fire polishing.

Green Glass: Refers to a composition of glass and not a color. The green color was caused by the iron impurities in the sand which could not be controlled by the glass makers.

Ground Pontil: When a rough pontil scar has been ground off, the remaining smooth circle is a ground pontil.

Hobbleskirt: The paneled shape used to describe Coca-Cola bottles.

Hobnail: A pattern of pressed glass characterized by an all-over pattern of bumps that resemble hobnail heads.

Hutchinson: A spring-type internal closure that seals soda bottles patented by Charles Hutchinson in 1879.

Imperfections: Bubbles (tears) of all sizes and shapes, bent shapes and necks, imperfect seams, and errors in spelling and embossing.

Improved Pontil: Bottles having an improved pontil have reddish or blackish tinges on their base.

ISP (Inserted Slug Plate): Special or unique company names or names of people were sometimes embossed on ale, whiskey, and wine bottles with a plate inserted into the mold.

Iron Pontil: The solid iron rod heated and affixed to the bottle's base creates a scar as a black circular depression often turning red upon oxidation.

Kick-Up: A deep indentation in the bottom of many bottles. This is formed by placing a projected piece of wood or metal in the base of the mold while the glass is still hot. The kickup is common on wine bottles and calabash flasks.

Laid-On Ring: A bead of glass trailed around the neck opening to reinforce the opening.

Lady's Leg: Bottles shaped like long curving necks.

Lightning Closure: A closure that used an intertwined wire bale configuration to hold the lid on fruit jars. This closure was also common with soda bottles.

Bottle with kick-up in bottom.

Lipper: A wood tool used to widen lips and form rims and spouts of pitchers, carafes, and wide-mouthed jars.

Manganese: Used as a decolorizer between 1850 and 1910, manganese will cause glass to turn purple under extreme heat.

Melting Pot: A clay pot used to melt silicate in the process of making glass.

Metal: Molten glass.

Milk Glass: A white-colored glass created by adding tin to the glass batch during glass production. Milk glass was used primarily for cosmetic bottles.

Mold, Full-Height, Three-Piece: A mold that formed an entire bottle. The two seams run the height of the bottle to below the lip on both sides.

Mold, Three-Piece Dip: In this mold, the bottom part of the bottle mold was one piece and the top, from the shoulder up, was two separate pieces. Mold seams appear circling the bottle at the shoulder and on each side of the neck.

Opalescence: This is seen on the frosty bottle or variated color bottle that has been buried in the earth in mud or silt. The minerals in these substances have interacted with the glass to created these effects.

Open Pontil: The blowpipe was affixed to the base instead of a separate rod with a scar that is a depressed or raised circle called a moile.

Painted Label: Another name for Applied Color Label (ACL), which is baked on the outside of the bottle. ACLs were commonly used on soda pop bottles and milk bottles.

Panelled: A bottle that isn't circular or oval, but rather is formed from four to twelve panels.

Paste Mold: A mold made from two or more pieces of iron that were coated with a paste to prevent scratches on the glass. The mold eliminated seams, as the glass was turned in the mold.

Pattern Mold: A designation for a type of glass "patterned" before completed blowing.

Plate Glass: Pure glass comprised of lime and soda silicate.

Pontil, Puntee, or Punty Rod: The iron rod attached to the base of a bottle by a gob or glass to hold the bottle during the finishing.

Pontil Marks: To remove the bottle from the blowpipe, an iron rod with a small amount of molten glass was applied to the bottom of the bottle after the neck and lip were finished. A sharp tap removed the bottle from the pontil leaving a jagged glass scar called a pontil mark.

Bottle with panelled sides.

Potstone: Impurities in the glass batch that, when blown into a piece of finished glass, resemble a white stone.

Pressed Glass: Glass that has been pressed into a mold to take the shape of the mold or the pattern within the mold.

Pucellas: A tool that is essential in shaping both the body and opening in blown bottles.

Pumpkinseed: A small round flat flask, often found in areas of the American West. Generally made of clear glass, the shape resembles the seed of the grown pumpkin. These bottles are also known as "Mickies," "Saddle Flasks," and "Two-Bit Ponies."

Ribbed: A bottle with vertical or horizontal lines embossed into the bottle.

Round Bottom: A soda bottle made of heavy glass in the shape of a torpedo. The bottle is designed to lie on its side, keeping the liquid in contact with the cork to prevent the cork from drying and popping out of the bottle.

Satin Glass: Smooth glass manufactured by exposing the surface of the glass to hydrofluoric acid vapors.

Seal: A circular or oval slug of glass applied to the shoulder of a bottle with an imprint of the manufacturer's name, initials, or mark.

Seam: The mark on a bottle caused by glass assuming the shape of the mold where the two halves meet.

Sheared Lip: After a bottle was blown, a pair of scissor-like shears clipped the hot glass from the blowpipe. No top was applied and sometimes a slight flange was created.

Sick Glass: Glass bearing a superficial decay or deterioration that takes on a grayish tinge caused by erratic firing.

Slug Plate: A metal plate about 2 inches by 4 inches with a firm's name on it was inserted into a mold so the glass house could use the same mold for many companies.

Smooth Base: Bottles that do not have a pontil.

Snap Case: A tool that replaced the pontil rod. The snap case's vertical arms curved out from a central stem to grip a bottle firmly during finishing of the neck and lip, thus eliminating pontil scars or marks on the bottom of the bottle. The snap case may leave grip marks on the side however.

Squat: A form of bottle used to contain beer, porter, and soda.

Tooled Top: A top formed in a bottle mold, rather than added separately. These molded tops were made after 1885.

Torpedo: A beer or soda bottle with a rounded base meant to lie on its side to keep the cork wet.

Turn-Mold Bottles: Bottles that were turned while forming in a mold using special solvents. The continuous turning with the solvent eventually erased all of the seams and mold marks. This also resulted in a distinct luster to the bottle.

Wetting Off: Marking the neck of a hot bottle with water so that it can easily be broken from the blow pipe.

Whittle Marks: Bottles with small irregularities created by forming them in wood-carved molds. These flaws were also caused by forming glass in cold early morning molds, creating "goose pimples" on the surface of these bottles. As the molds warmed, later bottles became smoother.

Bibliography

Books

Barnett, R.E. *Western Whiskey Bottles*, 4th Edition. Bend, OR: Maverick Publishing, 1997.

Ham, Bill. *Bitters Bottles*. Self Published, 1999, Supplement 2004, P.O. Box 427, Downieville, CA 95936.

Hastin, Bud. *Avon Products & California Perfume Co. Collector's Encyclopedia*, 17th Edition, Kansas City, MO: Bud Hastin Publications, 2003.

Kovill, William E. Jr. *Ink Bottles and Ink Wells*. Taunton, MA: William L. Sullwold, 1971.

Leybourne, Doug. *Red Book #9, Fruit Jar Price Guide*, Privately Published, North Muskegon, MI, 2001.

Linden, Robert A. *The Classification of Violin Shaped Bottles*, 2nd Edition, Privately Published, 1999.

———. *Collecting Violin & Banjo Bottles, A Practical Guide*, 3rd Edition, Privately Published, 2004.

McCann, Jerry. *2007 Fruit Jar Annual*. Chicago, IL: J. McCann Publisher, 2007.

McKearin, Helen and George S. *American Glass*. New York, NY: Crown Publishers, 1956.

———. *Two Hundred Years of American Blown Glass*. New York, NY: Crown Publishers, 1950.

McKearin, Helen and Kenneth M. Wilson. *American Bottles and Flasks and Their Ancestry*. New York, NY: Crown Publishers, 1978.

Polak, Michael. *Antique Trader-Bottles: Identification and Price Guide*, 5th Edition. Krause Publications, Iola, WI, 2006.

———. *Official Price Guide to American Patriotic Memorabilia*, 1st Edition. House of Collectibles, New York, NY, 2002.

Rensselaer, Stephen Van, *Early American Bottles and Flasks*. Stratford, CT: J. Edmund Edwards Publisher, 1969.

Sweeney, Rick. *Collecting Applied Color Label Soda Bottes, 3rd Edition*. La Mesa, CA: Painted Soda Bottles Collectors Assoc., 2002.

Toulouse, Julian Harrison. *Bottle Makers and Their Marks*. Camden, NJ: Thomas Nelson Incorporated, 1971.

Zumwalt, Betty. *Ketchup, Pickles, Sauces*. Sandpoint, ID: Mark West Publishers, 1980.

Periodicals

Ale Street News, P.O. Box 1125, Maywood, NJ 07607, E-Mail: JamsOD@aol.com, Web Site: www.AleStreetNews.com

Antique Bottle & Glass Collector, Jim Hagenbuch, 102 Jefferson Street, P.O. Box 187, East Greenville, PA 18041

Antique Bottle Collector UK Limited, Llanerch, Carno, Caersws, Powys SY17 5JY, Wales

Australian Antique Bottles and Collectibles, AABS, Box 235, Golden Square, 3555, Australia

BAM (Bottles and More) Magazine, P.O. Box #6, Lehighton, PA 18235

Bottles & Bygones, 30 Brabant Rd, Cheadle Hulme, Cheadlek, Cheshire, SKA 7AU, England

Bottles & Extra Magazine, 1966 King Springs Road, Johnson City, TN 37601

British Bottle Review (BBR), Elsecar Heritage Centre, Barnsley, S. York, S74, 8HJ England

Canadian Bottle & Stoneware Collector Magazine, 102 Abbeyhill Drive, Kanata, ON K2L 1H2, Canada, Web site: www.cbandsc.com

Crown Jewels of the Wire, P.O. Box 1003, St. Charles, IL 60174-1003

Fruit Jar Newletter, FJN Publishers, 364 Gregory Avenue, West Orange, NH 07052-3743

Root Beer Float, P.O. Box 571, Lake Geneva, WI 53147

The Miniature Bottle Collector, P.O. Box 2161, Palos Verdes Peninsula, CA 92074, Brisco Publications

The Soda Spectrum, A Publication by Soda Pop Dreams, P.O Box 23037, Krug Postal Outlet, Kitchener, Ontario, Canada N2B 3V1

Treasure Hunter's Gazette (Collector's Newsletter), 14 Vernon St., Keene, NH, 03431, George Streeter - Publisher & Editor

Web Sites

American Bottle Auctions – www.americanbottle.com

Antique Bottle Forum – www.antique-bottles.net

Antique Fruit Jars – www.antiquebottles.com

Antique Pottery/Stoneware Auctions – www.antiques-stoneware.com

The "Bottle Bible" – www.bottlebible.com

The Bottle Den – www.bottleden.com

Breweriana – www.brewerygems.com

Canadian Bottles – www.glassco.com

Digger Odell Bottle Price Guides – www.bottlebooks.com

Federation of Historical Bottle Collectors – www.fohbc.com

Glass Works Auctions – www.glswrk-auction.com

Norman C. Heckler Auctions – www.hecklerauction.com

Painted Soda Bottle Collectors Association – www.psbca.thesodafizz.
com

TIAS (The Internet Antique Shop) – www.tias.com

Photo Index

Avon Bottles

Banjo Bottles

Barber Bottles

Beer Bottles

Bitter Bottles

Blown/Pattern-Molded Bottles

Fire Grenades

Flasks